Muslim Women in Contemporary North America

Muslim Women in Contemporary North America is a provocative study of how strongly held and divergent opinions, values, and beliefs, as well as misconceptions, overgeneralizations, and political agendas pertaining to Muslim women in the region, enter the public frame of reference.

Interrogating contested topics in a series of case studies from both Canada and the United States, this book probes below the surface in pursuit of deeper understanding and more productive dialogue. Chapters analyze controversies over "clash" literature, dissident reformists, female religious leadership, veils, and the nature of emancipation in a compelling examination of the ways in which "Muslim," "American," and "Canadian" identities and values are being defined, differentiated, and projected. By pinpointing both sources of dissonance and unexpected patterns of resonance among complex, composite, and at times overlapping identity constellations, this book uncovers the impact of controversies on broader cultural negotiations in the United States and Canada.

Transforming controversy and cliché into genuine conversation, *Muslim Women in Contemporary North America* is an invaluable resource for scholars and students in the fields of Islamic and Muslim Studies, Gender Studies, International Relations, Political Science, and Sociology.

Meena Sharify-Funk is Associate Professor of Religion and Culture at Wilfrid Laurier University, Canada.

Muslim Women in Contemporary North America

Controversies, Clichés, and Conversations

Meena Sharify-Funk

Routledge
Taylor & Francis Group

LONDON AND NEW YORK

Designed cover image: HamidEbrahimi / Getty Images

First published 2023
by Routledge
4 Park Square, Milton Park, Abingdon, Oxon OX14 4RN

and by Routledge
605 Third Avenue, New York, NY 10158

Routledge is an imprint of the Taylor & Francis Group, an informa business

British Library Cataloguing-in-Publication Data
A catalogue record for this book is available from the British Library

Library of Congress Cataloging-in-Publication Data
Names: Sharify-Funk, Meena, author.
Title: Muslim women in contemporary North America : controversies,
clichés, and conversations / Meena Sharify-Funk.
Description: 1. | New York City : Routledge, 2022. | Includes
bibliographical references and index.
Identifiers: LCCN 2022028489 | ISBN 9780367356927 (hardback) | ISBN
9780367356897 (paperback) | ISBN 9780429341151 (ebook)
Subjects: LCSH: Muslim women--North America--Social conditions--21st
century. | Muslim women--United States--Social conditions--21st century.
| Muslim women--Canada--Social conditions--21st century.
Classification: LCC HQ1170 .S4625 2022 | DDC
305.48/697097--dc23/eng/20220705
LC record available at https://lccn.loc.gov/2022028489

ISBN: 978-0-367-35692-7 (hbk)
ISBN: 978-0-367-35689-7 (pbk)
ISBN: 978-0-429-34115-1 (ebk)

DOI: 10.4324/9780429341151

Typeset in Bembo
by KnowledgeWorks Global Ltd.

To my parents, Nancy Olga Sharify and
Majdeddin Sharify-Hosseini, who taught me that
differences expand our horizons, and that love
knows no boundaries. I am eternally grateful to
both of you.

دل به دل راه داره

"Between hearts there is no separation..."

Contents

Acknowledgments

Resilient is a wonderful word to describe the many women in my life who have inspired me to remember the goodness and beauty as well as wonder that are present within this precious world, even in times of difficulty. In particular, my grandmothers, Olga Borghill Moen Bragee and Mohtaram Zaman Javadi, and my mother, Nancy Olga Sharify, and my mother-in-law, Jan Kay Potter – all have been amazing role models. I offer deep reverence to their ways of wisdom, care, generosity, honesty, loyalty, and love. I am grateful for all the positive attributes they have modeled for me, qualities which provided life lessons from which I have gleaned and upon which I have leaned during these challenging, pandemic times of uncertainty and anxiety as well as throughout my life.

I also would like to acknowledge a variety of individuals to whom I am genuinely indebted for their enduring support, unending patience, and kind understanding. First, I would like to thank the incredible staff at Routledge Publishers: Ceri McLardy, Iman Hakimi, Alison Macfarlane, Rebecca Clintworth, Emma Yuan, and Amy Doffegnies. Each in their own way helped this book come to fruition and I am grateful for their unwavering assistance throughout the writing and publishing processes.

Friendship and collegiality are essential to any creative process, and I owe deep appreciation to those who have accompanied and inspired me while working on this project. To all my colleagues in the Department of Religion and Culture and the Muslim Studies Option at Wilfrid Laurier University as well as the Department of Religious Studies at the University of Waterloo, it is an honor to work with all of you and I thank you for all that you do to maintain a collaborative and intellectually dynamic space within the academy – my professional "home away from home."

Over the years, I have gleaned from the support of brilliant research assistants who have helped me to explore the nuances of specific case studies about Muslim women in North America: Deborah Birkett, Judith Ellen Brunton, Munira Haddad, and Christina Woolner. I thank each of them for stimulating conversations and collaborations. For this book, Elysia Guzik was essential, and I am beholden to her for meticulous research, editorial assistance, and, most of all, great friendship.

My unending gratitude goes out to dear sisters of the heart around the world, including Margarita, Judy, Karuna, Hamil, Shahrzad, Shobhana, Brandi, Betsy, and Ayse. Your ways of being and friendships inspire me to mind my heart and remember the greater aspects of life. I also would like to extend this spirit of gratitude to Rory for all the rich and ongoing existential and intellectual dialogues about life, the academy, and Islamic thought and identity.

My deepest gratitude goes to my soulmate and best friend, Nathan C. Funk. There are few words that can express what you mean to me. One is the Arabic word, *baraka*. It is a true blessing to be on this journey of life with you and to witness your wisdom, grace, patience, and ways of peace. Lastly, to Mikael Aziz, may this book remind you to constantly explore the depths of this beautiful world and all its diversity. May you seek for the patterns of connection and find inspiration in the unexpected. May you always be open to the wonder that is in and all around you.

Introduction

"Women and Islam." It is a subject that is surrounded by strongly held and divergent opinions, values, and beliefs, as well as by misconceptions, over-generalizations, and yes, political agendas. In the 21st century, there are many competing voices attempting to define who Muslim women are and what their identities and values should be. Many of these protagonists attempt in some way to establish or reinforce a "*single narrative*" – a singular story that cannot possibly do justice to the lived experiences and varied aspirations of real women in diverse social contexts.

Amid these contending narratives and associated political projects, Muslim women are caught in a web of contradictory "isms" – from Islamism and secularism to traditionalism, Orientalism, and liberalism, just to name a few. Ideological fragmentation within Muslim societies and even within academic analysis makes the subject of "women and Islam" intrinsically polarizing and creates a tendency toward reductive and even clichéd representations of the multiple challenges and pressures facing Muslim women. These representations colonize our intellectual landscape and fill our heads with preconceptions and images that beg for scholarly critique and engagement.

In contemporary America and Canada,[1] Muslim women are frequently in the news. Often, the focus is on divisive debates over women's head cover (*niqab* and *hijab*), Islamic *shariah*, honor crimes, and the stances taken by "liberated" Muslim women. Such media portrayals reflect not only real contestation among Muslims as they engage broader societies, but also the preoccupations and concerns of the viewing public. Particularly since September 11, 2001, rapidly growing Muslim communities in America as well as in Canada have been very much in the spotlight, and often under the magnifying glass. Controversial issues pertaining to the status of women have been regarded as a key barometer of Muslim values, and as a basic indicator of cultural integration and readiness to embrace "mainstream" values. These controversial issues provide a focus for underlying questions about Muslim minorities that are not always spoken, and have sparked recurrent social and political debates concerning cultural compatibility and acceptance as well as accommodation.

DOI: 10.4324/9780429341151-1

Although each context has its own distinctive history and dynamics, media coverage, and public discourse in both countries reveal widespread anxiety about the mores, customs, and intentions of this increasingly prominent religious minority group. For some North Americans, the reluctance of Muslims to fully assimilate or conform to majority-culture expectations is viewed with great distress and experienced as a threat not only to core values but also to safety and security. While discomfort with these widespread anxieties is nearly universal among Muslims, perceptions nonetheless differ on how to respond. Although abandoning all visible forms of Muslim distinctiveness is generally viewed as inappropriate or even impossible given the reality of intersections between religion, ethnicity, and race, opinions differ on which aspects of traditional Muslim culture and practice are non-essential and therefore negotiable. Economic and civic integration, however, are widely regarded as positive objectives, and calls for Muslims to change and become "more Western" are commonly perceived as symptoms of Islamophobia, a deeply embedded bias against Muslims that permits practices of discrimination and impedes full participation in public life.

Difficulties are compounded by the fact that public discourse about Islam, Muslim women, and citizenship in America or Canada is fraught with clichés. The entire notion of homogenous mainstream "American" or "Canadian" cultures is deeply problematic in both countries, as are common characterizations of Muslim women as victims who lack agency unless their value orientations happen to correspond with liberal individualist expectations. Neither non-Muslim nor Muslim communities are remotely monolithic and, despite representations to the contrary, their cultures overlap and intermingle far more than they clash. While controversies involving the rights and practices of Muslim communities are not entirely byproducts of media sensationalism – the worldviews and cultures of Americans and Canadians who define their identities in Judeo-Christian or secular modernist terms genuinely do differ in some respects from those of "visible Muslims" – newspaper and television coverage as well as social media conversations consistently amplify adversarial voices, and thereby shape the contours of public conversations in which zero-sum, "our way or theirs" thinking can flourish. As a result, more nuanced and civil ways of discussing cultural differences and the complex journeys of Muslim women are marginalized in relation to discourses that rush to attribute blame. Outside visible Muslim circles can manifest in calls to "tighten the screws" on people who have been labeled "ungrateful" and "inflexible," and who are generally (and often quite fallaciously) presumed to be newcomers. Within the Muslim communities themselves, heightened scrutiny and societal pressure often serves to reinforce a defensive posture vis-à-vis what is perceived as an overbearing and misinformed majority-culture.

This book is organized in a manner that engages the public frame of reference in each country (structured largely around controversies and even clichés), exploring a series of contested topics with an intent to probe below the surface in pursuit of deeper understanding and bases for more productive dialogue. Examining controversies over "clash" literature, dissident reformists, female religious leadership, veils, and even the nature of women's liberation provides a provocative means of analyzing ways in which "Muslim" and "American" as well as "Canadian" identities and values are being defined, differentiated, and projected. The book also investigates controversies for what they reveal about the current state of identity negotiations in America and Canada, as a means of pinpointing sources of dissonance as well as unexpected patterns of resonance among complex, composite, and at times overlapping identity constellations. Throughout, analysis seeks to clarify the concerns and stakes for all parties, in an attempt to enrich public dialogue and suggest ways in which controversy and cliché might give way to more genuine conversation.

To the extent that they are faced directly and probed for the questions and concerns that animate them, controversies within North American contexts present rich opportunities for dialogue and for rediscovery of both self and other – opportunities for values to be not only contested but also expanded, redefined, and applied more inclusively. Among the many different questions which animate public controversies in America and Canada, many hinge on convictions concerning the status and conduct of Muslim women: Is the Muslim veil an impediment to integration, or an indispensable basis for religiously authentic female empowerment? Does allowing a Muslim woman to "hide" behind a face veil undermine human rights, or does it give more substantive meaning to the same principles? Is the proper place for a Muslim woman at the front of a mosque, or is the popular interest in such phenomena yet another expression of cultural imperialism? Exploring diverse responses to such questions reveals non-trivial differences, but can also provide opportunities for reflection, and for destabilization of simplistic platitudes about the nature of "Muslim"—"majority-culture" relations in America and Canada. In the face of many pessimistic readings of the intercultural and interreligious encounters underway within religious communities, workplaces, legislative forums, and social media conversations, this book seeks to illuminate ways in which processes of mutual adjustment are already underway. Behind the headlines, Muslim women are actively negotiating both their own identities and spaces for themselves within the larger American and Canadian cultural mosaics, and are being met not only with suspicion and fear, but also with goodwill, genuine curiosity, and willingness to reopen discussion of what it can mean to be North American.

In adopting a "North American" frame of reference, this book identifies similarities between controversies and public discourses in the United States of America and in Canada,[2] while also attending to significant differences between and indeed within each national setting. The historical experiences and demographic compositions of Muslim communities in each country are not identical, with the African-American Muslim experience figuring prominently in the United States and with Canadian norms shaped by distinctive experiences such as public investment in multiculturalism (a norm that is itself contested, especially within the province of Quebec). The focus on controversies in the 21st century, however, highlights meaningful correspondences between issues that draw public concern in each country, and ways in which different Muslim constituencies are responding. The resultant case studies and illustrations invite readers to reflect on important similarities and differences in ways that issues surrounding Muslim women are contested.

Summary of book chapters

The book begins by establishing the context of the present study and setting the scene in contemporary America and Canada. Chapter 1, "Mapping the Terrain of Muslim Women in 21st Century North America," offers a brief overview of larger contextual frameworks for understanding experiences of contemporary Muslim women. Through a comparative discussion of major similarities and differences, the following cross-cutting themes are explored: (1) the varied ways in which women from different ethnic, cultural, sectarian, or interpretive contexts seek sacred meaning; (2) the complexity associated with manifesting a collective Muslim identity while living as a minority community within liberal democratic states; (3) the contextualized nature of Muslim women's issues within internal as well as external dynamics of identity politics; and (4) the presence of persistent suspicion and anxiety toward Muslims and Islam.

Chapter 2, "Living the Dialogical: Negotiating Identity and Meaning," presents the approach this volume takes to controversies involving Muslim women and Muslim minorities more generally. The chapter offers an overview of a "dialogical" framework for Western-Islamic scholarship and identifies as well as analyzes major features of "the dialogical" both as an outlook and as an analytical approach to topics in religious studies and the social sciences. Particular attention is given to the applicability of this approach to the politics of religion, culture, and identity within as well as across cultural contexts, and its relevance for understanding "everyday" processes of identity construction and negotiation for Muslim women. In connection to the emergence of relational thinking, this chapter explores how the term "dialogue" is experiencing a renaissance in contemporary scholarship of social and political theory. Specific cross-cutting themes of the dialogical are explored, such as the hermeneutics of openness, the relation to cosmopolitanism, and the idea of the dialogical self as a composite of "complementary contradictions."

In Chapter 3, "Pervasive Anxiety about Islam and Muslims: 'Clash Literature' in North America," helps the reader to understand the influence of North American "clash literature" – a genre of post-9/11 writings that popularize elements of Samuel Huntington's "clash of civilizations" thesis, with particular reference to putative threats posed to Western civilization by Islam and Muslims. Particular attention is given to a series of salient themes used by multiple texts and authors, in a manner that creates an overarching narrative of Western moral superiority vis-à-vis a monolithic, authoritarian, and misogynistic Islamic culture; betrayal of Western culture by "politically correct" intellectual elites wedded to ideas of multicultural accommodation; and a cascading threat posed by the rapid influx of unassimilable Muslim immigrants who are poised to mount a demographic takeover of Europe and, most likely, America and Canada as well. The content of clash texts is then analyzed and evaluated in light of its detachment from relevant scholarship, its reliance on highly essentialized identity constructs, its use of demographic extrapolations and alarming anecdotes, and its stark rejection of contemporary pluralism. The chapter concludes with reflections on how scholars might respond to the identity insecurities revealed by clash literature as they seek to advance alternative narratives based on values of dialogue and coexistence.

One of the most salient themes of discourse in "clash literature" and the Western media is the theme of Muslim women's liberation. Chapter 4, "Dissidence, Dissonance, and the Politics of Muslim Women's Emancipation," continues to probe this theme as it has been raised by controversial public spokespersons and in best-selling books about Islam, many of which have been authored by "dissident" or "dissenting" Muslim women authors upholding values of Western liberalism in opposition to traditional Islamic practices and positions. This chapter analyzes and critiques central arguments used by leading female "dissident Muslim" writers, with the intention of distinguishing recurrent patterns while also mapping a spectrum of views among specific authors in North America (i.e., Ayaan Hirsi Ali, Irshad Manji, and Raheel Raza). Attention is therefore given to both unity and diversity in style and content. Analysis begins by exploring how dissident writers portray their works as responses to terror perpetuated by Muslim extremists, and present reform within Islam as an urgent priority. The focus then turns to ways in which each dissident author develops a distinct position (and, frequently, a critical one) toward "moderate Muslims," together with an argument about how they are part of the solution or the problem when it comes to reform. This discussion of views on "moderation" is connected to a third and related topic: The manner in which dissident authors share a common emphasis on the virtues of Western liberalism and secularism, while also articulating varied positions on the prospects for Islamic reform. These positions on prospects for reform, in turn, reflect differing opinions regarding the likelihood of an ultimate reconciliation between Western values and Islamic cultures, and of a desired emancipation of Muslim women. The chapter ends with a brief discussion of diverse responses to dissident writing.

In the beginning of the 21st century, tensions arose not only in "majority-culture" – Muslim relations, but also in intra-Muslim debates over social values and roles. Chapter 5, "Muslim Woman Prayer Leadership and Gendered Sacred Space," explores the dynamics of gender justice in the Islamic feminist movement and its critics as connected to women prayer leaders and gender-inclusive mosques in North America. In particular, it attends to Islamic feminist understandings of basic textual debates and the conception of Muslim women's needs in prayer leadership and gendered sacred space. Throughout, this chapter attempts to clarify a central paradox of the Islamic feminist movement: That it is *both* a highly contingent response to specific cultural and political circumstances *and* a manifestation of long-term negotiations within the larger Muslim community that favor the opening of new spaces for women within religious and social life. The chapter concludes by exploring the development of "women-friendly," "women-only," and "gender-inclusive" mosques – relatively new varieties of gendered sacred spaces within American and Canadian Muslim communities. Norms relating to these spaces are connected to the larger debate about Muslim women prayer leaders.

In North America as well as in Europe, the Muslim veil has long been regarded as a visible manifestation of essential differences between Western and Islamic values – a position that is shared, albeit from another perspective, by Muslim revivalists and traditionalists. Chapter 6, "Veil Controversies: The Dynamics of Inclusion and Exclusion," explores a variety of controversies in America and Canada surrounding both the *hijab* and its more uncommon and conservative cousin, the face veil or *niqab*. From *hijab* sports controversies, in which women and girls were barred from athletic competitions to state-level as well as provincial legislative campaigns seeking to deny public services to veil wearers, this chapter demonstrates the extent to which anxiety about Muslim veiling practices can shape popular opinions and political agendas while reinforcing defensive reactions. Whereas for many outside the visible Muslim community all forms of veiling signify entrenched gender inequality and outdated attitudes toward relationships between men and women, the majority view within most Muslim communities regards the veil as an important symbol of religious identity and values – a symbol that does not necessarily impede (and, in the view of religious authorities, facilitates and renders acceptable) integration within the larger society. These differences in perspective on veiling are linked to further differences concerning the meaning of terms such as "liberation" and "secularism." Recent attempts to define cultural limits and boundaries with respect to veiling practices point to a persistent, mutual mistrust of "the other," and to disagreement about basic social rules and mores.

The last chapter offers some concluding thoughts about contextualizing the cases analyzed in this volume within the broader setting of a global, diversified cultural experience that is replete with new opportunities as well as vexing challenges. After noting some underlying factors behind the various cases and contradictory positions explored in the book, it concludes by underscoring the vital need for conversations that move beyond surface clichés and stereotypical representations, toward greater apprehension of the multiple realities of Muslim women in North America. The move from contradiction and cliché toward genuine conversation can only be achieved by cultivating greater capacity for dialogical engagement in modes that embrace diverse intersections of gender, religion, race, culture, and status, even while fostering new discoveries of common humanity.

Note about the author

In my first single-authored manuscript, *Encountering the Transnational: Women, Islam and the Politics of Interpretation* (2008), I wanted to understand how the transnational influenced Muslim women's activism across national borders as well as their understandings of self, other, society, and Islam. In doing so, I also learned more about the transnational and transcultural in me, and that I am not and never will be a product of a monolithic culture or possessor of a single collective identity. Rather my construction and understanding of selfhood is an assemblage of different nationalities, cultural, and religious legacies as well as political and intellectual landscapes. Naturally, throughout my scholarly career, I have felt at home in the dialogical – in relations with diverse and sometimes contradictory ways of knowing and being.

As a product of an author who has also resided in both America and Canada, this book is a continued exploration of the dialogical but also of identity construction among Muslim women negotiating social controversies and conflicts in 21st century North America. In a world of collapsing distances, "global pandemics" manifest not just through disease pathogens but also through infectious ideas and attitudes of conflict and contradiction that generate deep suspicion and polarizing controversy, and which have impacted my own life as a mother and scholar. In writing about outbreaks of the latter variety, I am hoping to gesture toward a preventive as well as reparative medicine, and thereby contribute toward the healing of divisive social wounds infected by contagions of Islamophobia, misunderstanding, and distrust. When used in creative ways, words can serve as physicians of the heart and mind, healing divisive modes of thought while acting as a sort of immunization against extreme positions. Ultimately, words have the potential to promote the practice of intellectual hygiene and become the foundation for more peaceful cultural conditions and relations of humanity as a whole.

Notes

1 When focusing on cases in the United States of America, this book will often use terminology such as "America" and "American" for the sake of brevity and simplicity, while recognizing that the term "American" might also be applied to people living in other North American and South American countries.
2 Although inclusion of Mexican Muslim cases within a North American framework for comparative analysis would also be desirable, the scope of this book is limited to the United States and Canada. In addition, some of the controversies analyzed in this text exhibit similarities to European cases which are also worthy of comparative treatment, and yet beyond the scope of the book's coverage.

Chapter 1

Mapping the Terrain of Muslim Women in 21st Century North America

The lived realities, spiritual practices, and cultural outlooks of North American Muslim women are remarkably diverse. A Persian Shia refugee in Denver, Colorado, reads Shams al-din Hafez[1] and begins her morning with *dhikr* (remembrance of the one God through evoking the names of God). A Pakistani-Canadian mother attends the evening prayer at a Sunni mosque in Toronto, Ontario, while her children play in the background. An African-American convert to Islam leads a gender-inclusive congregation in New York City. In Laval, Quebec, *hijab*-wearing permanent resident of Algerian origins fights for her right to play soccer.

Though external stereotypes and particular communities may frame one way of "being Muslim" as more authentic than another, even the most cursory effort to probe beneath the surface of preconceived notions reveals an irrepressible range of experiences among Muslim women who embrace an Islamic or culturally Muslim identity while manifesting it in ways that demonstrate the superficiality of images and discourses that assert a singular vision of what a Muslim woman is or should be. Real-life experiences of these women in North American settings involve complex negotiations – conscious as well as unconscious – within intersections of religion, nationality, ethnicity, race, class, culture, work, and education. One should not be surprised, therefore, to find Muslim women who challenge the notion that certain images of the "typical Muslim woman" can be privileged over any other way of being. Who can be the judge of who is genuinely "more Muslim" than others? And who is to define the most appropriate way of being Canadian or American – of belonging in a North American national context?

Regardless of their conclusions about how to be Muslim in North America, all Muslim women's experiences in 21st century North America share in common certain negotiations and encounters with divisive controversies and clichés that impact their lives and demand an existential response. Although these controversies and clichés take on distinctive overtones in particular North American settings, they are not unique to

DOI: 10.4324/9780429341151-2

the United States or to Canada, and are formed within the present global context of intercultural, social, and economic relations. With the rise of the Internet and of almost instantaneous global communication, national and cultural as well as religious and political experiences have become increasingly porous; accelerated movement, communication, and interaction among world regions have produced powerful social interconnectivity but have not led to homogenization. Indeed, contemporary social and political discourses – in "Islamic" and "Western" contexts alike – are marked by an emphasis on distinction and differentiation – on inescapable social and cultural heterogeneity. Even as many voices call for new forms of intergroup solidarity and cosmopolitan identity forged through an embrace of dialogical encounters with difference, others manifest a sharply conservative and at times reactionary spirit marked by a refusal to embrace those seeking equality for their expressions of racial, religious, and ethnic diversity. Women of all cultural and religious backgrounds often find themselves at the center of these controversies, in which particular images of what a woman ought to be are deployed in debates over national, cultural, and religious authenticity and belonging.

One key goal of this book is to demonstrate, through specific North American case studies, how divergent ideas about American, Canadian, and Muslim women's identities animate significant social and political debates. These debates are experienced acutely by Muslim women, who engage the accompanying issues in diverse ways and often with a heightened awareness that many popular, binary conceptions (e.g., insider/outsider, authentic/inauthentic, faithful/unfaithful) impose a difficult burden. Analyzing both the substance of the debates and the varied experiences of Muslim women provides a vehicle for reflection not just on the stakes of intercultural negotiations, but also on daily realities of multiple belonging and of ongoing dialogue within as well as across the boundaries of different communities. Although Muslim women's experiences are not unique, they underscore both the challenges and the potential of forging community and identity amid the turbulent dynamics of the 21st century.

This chapter offers a brief overview of larger contextual frameworks for understanding experiences of Muslim women in America and Canada. Through a comparative discussion of major similarities and differences, the following cross-cutting themes are explored: (1) the varied ways in which women from different ethnic, cultural, sectarian, or interpretive contexts seek sacred meaning; (2) the complexity associated with manifesting a collective Muslim identity while living as a minority community within liberal democratic states; (3) the contextualized nature of Muslim women's issues within internal as well as external dynamics of identity politics; and (4) the presence of persistent suspicion and anxiety toward Muslims and Islam.

Patterns of connection and difference across North America

Seeking sacred meaning through diverse understandings

According to reports from the Pew Research Center (a nonpartisan think tank based in Washington, D.C.), the Muslim population in the United States is projected to double, from 2.6 million in 2010 to 6.2 million in 2030 (Pew Research Center, 2011). Based on the Pew Research Center's 2017 survey of Muslims in the United States (which was conducted in English, Arabic, Farsi, and Urdu) and other demographic research, there were an estimated 3.45 million Muslims living in the United States in 2017 – approximately 1.1% of the total U.S. population (Mohamed, 2018).[2] By 2050, this population is projected to reach 8.1 million (Mohamed, 2018). Survey data from 2007 notes that 54% of adult Muslims in the United States are male, while 46% are female (Pew Research Center, 2011). Among U.S. Muslims who were born outside of the United States, 35% come from South Asia, 23% from other parts of the Asia-Pacific region, 25% from the Middle East-North Africa region, 9% from sub-Saharan Africa, 4% from Europe, and 4% from elsewhere in the Americas (Pew Research Center, 2017a). According to a demographic profile by the Pew Research Center, 41% of Muslim American adults are white (including those who describe their race as Arab, Middle Eastern, Persian/Iranian, and various other ways), 28% are Asian, 20% are Black, 8% are Hispanic, and 3% identify with another race or with multiple races (Pew Research Center, 2017a). More than half (55%) of U.S. Muslim women surveyed said they have experienced at least one type of anti-Muslim discrimination in the past year (Gecewicz, 2017).

In comparison, the Muslim population in Canada is expected to nearly triple, from 940,000 in 2010 to 2.7 million in 2030 (Pew Research Center, 2011). In the 2011 National Household Survey, just over one million individuals self-identified as Muslims, making up approximately 3% of the Canadian population (Statistics Canada, 2016).[3] While the male-to-female ratio of Canadian Muslims aged 0–24 is comparable to the ratio for Canada as a whole, the ratio of Muslim men to Muslim women is higher among those aged 25 and older when compared with the general population (Pew Research Center, 2011). A survey of Muslims in Canada found that regular mosque attendance is twice as likely to be reported by men than by women (Environics, 2016, p. 17). Additionally, 64% of Canadian Muslims self-identify as Sunni, 8% self-identify as Shia, 10% self-identify with another sectarian affiliation (including Ismaili, Ahmadiyya, nondenominational, and other), and 18% do not self-identify with any specific sectarian affiliation (Shah, 2019). Based on National Household Survey, 2011 data, 36% of Canadian Muslims self-identify as South Asian, 25% as Arab, 13% as West Asian (including Iranians, Afghans, and people from former Soviet states),

9% as Black, and a small percentage as Chinese, Japanese, Korean, Filipino, other visible minorities, multiple visible minorities, and not a visible minority (Hamdani, 2015). In 2011, more than 1,000 Muslims self-identified as First Nations or Métis (Environics, 2016). A more recent study echoed the ethnic diversity among Muslims in Canada, noting that:

> From highest to lowest percentages of the Canadian Muslim ethnic identity: West Central Asian and Middle Eastern, African, other South Asian, East Indian, Canadian, other Southern European, other East and Southeast Asian, British Isles, Latin, Central and South American, other Caribbean, French, English, Oceanic, Chinese, Russian, Filipino, other North American, other Eastern European, German, Jamaican, other European, Italian, Portuguese, Irish, Spanish, Ukrainian, North American Aboriginal, Greek, Scottish, other Western European origins, and Polish.
>
> (Shah, 2019, pp. 6–7)

One-third (35%) of respondents to the Environics Survey of Muslims in Canada reported having experienced discrimination or unfair treatment in the past five years because of their religion (22%), ethnic or cultural background (22%), language (13%), or sex (6%) (Environics, 2016, p. 38).

There is limited data and information on the sectarian backgrounds of, and interpretive differences among, Muslims in Canada.[4] However, recent academic literature has explored topics such as denominational differences and culturally relevant dimensions of religiosity among Canadian Muslims (Haji et al., 2020), the ways in which Islamic doctrines are expressed in the designs of Islamic prayer centers (Keshani, 2018), intergenerational differences (Birani, 2017), and attitudes toward queer identity (Page & Shipley, 2021).

In addition to ethnic diversity among Muslims in Canada and the United States, there are a variety of sectarian and interpretive differences. The Pew Research Center found that a majority of U.S. Muslims who responded to their 2017 survey "say there is more than one true way to interpret Islam, and about half say traditional understandings of the faith need to be reinterpreted to address current issues" (Pew Research Center, 2017b). This report goes on to state:

> Slightly more than half of Muslim Americans identify with the Sunni branch of Islam (55%), while 16% identify as Shiite, 4% identify with other groups (such as Ahmadiyya or the Nation of Islam), and 14% do not specify a tradition. An additional 10% declined to answer the question. These results are consistent with data on Muslims around the world in that Muslims are more likely to identify with Sunni Islam than any other branch.
>
> (ibid.)

Based on this survey, there appears to be a pattern between educational level and openness to or acceptance of multiple interpretations of Islam. The report notes that:

> The view that there are multiple valid ways to interpret Islam is especially common among those who have a college degree (75%) and those who say religion is *not* very important in their lives (72%). It is also much more common among Shiite Muslims (87%) than among Sunnis (59%). Muslim men and women, as well as older and younger Muslims, express similar views on this question.
>
> A separate question asked whether the traditional understandings of Islam need to be reinterpreted to address modern issues, or whether the traditional understandings of the religion are all that is needed. Fully half of U.S. Muslims (52%) say Islam's teachings need to be reinterpreted, while 38% say this is not necessary.
>
> (ibid.)

Diversification of Muslims is highlighted in most scholarship on Islam in America and in Canada, and women's experiences are shaped by all these differences and distinctions.

All this diversity exists behind the façade of monolithic constructions – both external stereotypes and traditional ways of depicting womanhood and expectations of femininity. Such stereotypes about Muslim women have been explored and interrogated in multidisciplinary scholarship over the last decade, including studies of Dutch Muslim women's representations (van Es, 2019), images of "oppressed Muslim women" (van Es, 2016), Muslim women who voluntarily practice *hijab* (Al Wazni, 2015), societal racism experienced by Canadian Muslim women who wear the *hijab* (Rahmath et al., 2016), perceptions of Muslim women since 9/11 (Allison, 2013; Hussein, 2019), and media portrayals of Muslim women (Hammer, 2012; Khalil, 2018; Terman, 2017). There is no single American or Canadian experience of being a Muslim woman in North America, which stresses the necessity for non-Muslim Americans and Canadians, and ultimately Muslims, to know more about the diversity of Muslims and the different beliefs, traditions, and practices which influence gender roles.

Even though this chapter cannot do justice to the diversity present among Muslim women, it remains important to bear in mind certain patterns and even commonalities within their varied experiences and aspirations. Despite their many differences, women who define themselves as Muslim share identification with core, symbolic reference points of Islamic history, community, faith, and spirituality. Though they differ profoundly about the significance and content of this identification, even those who define themselves as "non-practicing" or "non-religious" Muslims share at least some elements of a common story and point to values that are deemed essential to a broader community experience. And for the great many who experience their identity as a link to that which transcends social reality, being a Muslim woman also means aspiring to experience the sacred as a connection to the prophetic message of the Qur'an and to a metaphysical reality that is both unifying and transcendent to the boundaries created by human identity constructions. Even within this context, however, there is also differentiation among Muslim women, as Muslim women experience spirituality in remarkably diverse ways, even while invoking the Divine in similar ways, through Quranic principles and practices.

While it is important not to impose a homogenizing metaphysical lens on the entirety of Muslim women's negotiations of rights, place, and belonging in North American contexts, it is nonetheless crucial to recognize that a great many Muslim women are seeking space to manifest spiritual as well as cultural, ethnic, social, and political identities within North America. For many, advocacy for gender equality can be connected to upholding Quranic principles of *fitrah* (the principle of innate goodness which defines human nature) and *adab*, the height of moral human behavior. The spiritual act of *dhikr* (remembrance of the one God) can be seen as decolonial. Combatting racism in one's community may be perceived as a Muslim woman's right to shed light on the Islamic notion of human dignity. Many more examples could be given, but the main point is that Muslim women define themselves in their broader societies and sub-*Ummahs*[5] in relation to metaphysical as well as social values and convictions. Furthermore, by bringing their distinctive experiences in from the margins of social inquiry, we have the potential to perceive new patterns within American and Canadian histories – patterns which have been shaped by Muslim women through their own definitions of self and religion in relation to race, religious pluralism, and national identity (GhaneaBassiri, 2010).

Although the deeper history of Muslims in North America includes the mostly lost stories of West African slaves brought to the continent early in the colonial era, immigration and conversion are prominent in more recent dynamics. Researchers at Pew Research Center note that 20% of the Muslim population in the United States self-identify as Black. Close to half (49%) of Black Muslims are converts to Islam. In comparison, 15% of non-Black Muslims are converts to Islam.[6] The majority of Black Muslims in the United States self-identify as Sunni (52%), or with no specific Islamic denomination (27%). Furthermore, Black Muslims are more likely than non-Black Muslims to have been born in the United States (69% vs. 36%) (Mohamed & Diamant, 2019). According to a 2021 Canadian Council of Muslim Women (CCMW) report:

> Data from Statistics Canada 2013 General Social Survey on Social Identity, across different types of discrimination (including any discrimination, as well as sex-based, ethnicity or culture, race or skin colour,

physical appearance, religion, and language), Black Canadian Muslim women report the highest percentage of discriminatory experience. [...] More Black Muslim women report experiencing sex-based discrimination (32%) compared to non-Muslim Black women (26%), non-Black non-Muslim women (15%), and non-Black Muslim women (6%). Black Muslim women experience almost six times as much sex-based discrimination compared to non-Black Muslim women (32% vs 6%). Another way to understand this: one in three Black Muslim women experience sex-based discrimination, while less than one in ten non-Black Muslim women do.

(p. 8)

Whereas for African-American and Canadian converts to Islam,[7] the idea of "reversion" is a key aspect of embracing a Muslim identity,[8] many others have come to the experience of being Muslim in North America through a journey across borders, a first- or second-generation navigation of a broader social milieu, or a conscious embrace of Islam as a spiritual and social framework.

Despite the connection provided by modern communication technologies and by ongoing participation in transnational networks, migration necessarily involves experiences of rupture, transformation, and identity reconstruction. As a Muslim woman, reconstructing identity in North American contexts involves not only the conscious preservation of certain traditions connected to cultural, ideological, and political experiences in now-distant "homelands," but also a rejection or distancing of the self from traditions and realities that are no longer experienced to be essential. In this process, there is a corresponding negotiation of self-identity and communal identity in relation to the broader social and cultural reality in which one has now become immersed, and an accompanying effort to define what can and cannot be embraced without conflict or loss of authenticity. In addition, increased levels of Muslim migration to North America that began during the second half of the 20ᵗʰ century brought an influx of diverse national identities.[9]

These diverse national and cultural identities have provided bases – not just distinctive dynamics – of negotiation vis-à-vis the new home country – dynamics that may sometimes be influenced by concerns about foreign policy impacts on the original home country. Such identities have also informed new efforts to define what is "essentially Muslim" when establishing social relations with Muslims whose cultural traditions diverge in surprising ways. Ultimately, the processes of migrating and settling in a new country are processes of negotiating (and at times reconciling) multiple claims and allegiances. For the migrant, the fear of identity loss may create a profound sense of insecurity and instability, and a sharpened awareness of cultural marginality.

With knowledge of diversity also comes challenges, especially for minority communities. In both Canada and America, one finds what Aminah

McCloud (2004) characterizes as "cultural misunderstandings" in which Arab, South Asian, African, Persian, etc., Muslims are relating to one another without full understanding or appreciation. Often, due to cultural nuances and variation in traditions, Muslim women are influenced by what Sulayman Nyang calls "islandization" of Muslims, wherein specific groups develop self-sustaining community clusters in specific localities throughout North America (2004, p. xxiii). "Tehranto" in Toronto, Ontario, and "Tehrangeles" around Westwood Boulevard near Beverly Hills in Los Angeles are examples of such communities (Amirani, 2012).

Even in such clustered communities, differences abound, including cultural gaps among different generations and between "old" and "new" immigrants. These differences may include divergent notions of a "pure" Islam – for example, versions of Islamic authenticity that are connected to a specific cultural homeland versus revivalist or reformist understandings that may be consciously deterritorialized, and distanced from particular homeland cultures. On the one hand, immigrant Muslims from "authentically traditional Muslim lands" may perceive their approach to Islamic practice to have greater legitimacy than the practices of Muslims who have been influenced by "foreign" cultural traditions, including those of a prevailing non-Muslim culture. On the other hand, second-generation Muslims may claim that they have left behind the "cultural attachments" that veiled their parents from "the true Islam" (Pratt, 2005), and espouse an approach to faith that they regard either as intrinsically purer or as more suitable to life beyond the parental homeland. Given the presence of such divergent orientations toward culture and homelands, there is a great deal of contestation associated with claims to Islamic authenticity. Muslim women embody religious identity in different ways, depending on their social circumstances and choices among different Islamic schools of thought.

Additionally, contemporary Muslim minority communities manifest many forms of diversity. Cultural and ethnic traditions, for example, are by no means monolithic, and may come with their own internal sectarian and interpretive differences. The many different forms and understandings of Sunni, Shia, and Sufi Islam can be found throughout Canada and America. For example, there are more than 20 branches of traditional Sufi orders present within North America. Each with their own negotiations when it comes to questions of gender, tradition, authority, authenticity, and communal relations.

Gender roles differ greatly within and among Muslim communities, and are strongly influenced by the interpretive practices of different creedal schools of thought. As will be pointed out in Chapter 5, these schools of thought shape expectations for different female leadership roles within diverse Muslim communities. For instance, in the Ismaili Shia Muslim community in Canada, women and men can be authoritative religious leaders, and they share many responsibilities – for example, leading daily prayer for a local congregation, and consulting or advising community members on matters from marriage to professional development. In addition to these varying public roles of women, gender also plays a role in transmitting religion and in religious socialization across the many different sectarian groups in America and Canada.

In 21ˢᵗ century North America, stances on the status and roles of Muslim women have become an important marker for both "progressive" and "conservative" religious agendas. Despite ongoing concerns about being overwhelmed by Western cultural norms, issues related to gender equality have begun to receive a broader hearing in Muslim communities. In particular, new interpretive labels, like "progressive Islam," are emerging in connection with gender relations among Muslims.[10] Consequently, the creation of a progressive "Muslima theology" has started to emerge, with gender justice and equality as main aspects (Aslan, Hermansen, & Medeni, 2013). As will be discussed in Chapter 5, there are a variety of contemporary female "imamah" leaders throughout North America who are religious authoritative figures guiding their community members in the ways of life and faith.

It is also interesting to note that many progressive Muslim academics have been heavily influenced by Sufi expressions of Islam (Safi, 2003). Though they are at times contested advocates of more literalist and exoteric faith stances, Sufi understandings of Islam have experienced a renaissance in recent generations. Adherence to Sufi Islam, however, does not predetermine one's stance on social or political issues, or toward contemporary scriptural interpretation. Different interpretive tendencies among Sufis may include Muslim Traditionalists who assert a decolonial critique of modern Western values, as well as "progressive" or universalist Muslims who stress democratic pluralism and cosmopolitan identity.

Liberal democracy and the language of diversity: Opportunities and adjustments

For most North American Muslim immigrants, the experience of liberal democracy in American and Canadian contexts has brought both opportunities and adjustments. Many, for example, have celebrated the enhanced political and religious freedoms that can be experienced in a democratic setting. At the same time, the practice of liberal democracy in the United States and Canada is bundled with a set of norms and meanings that differ from prevailing cultural norms in most contemporary Muslim-majority states.

Though it is worth underscoring that Muslim immigrants have come from a very wide range of different political contexts – some of which have well-established electoral practices that advocate for and pursue principles of democracy – many have migrated to North America in no small part because governance in their original homelands exhibits more authoritarian tendencies. In the latter contexts, the idea of political pluralism is not well established, and values of collective solidarity are more strongly affirmed than individual choice. Building on insights conveyed by Moroccan feminist and sociologist Fatima Mernissi, Ali Mirsepassi and Tadd Graham Fernée observe that:

> Neither the colonial nor the nationalist governments that replaced them – based on an elitist-closed rather than plural-democratic practice and conception of power – employed the 'state and its institutions (as) the means of transmitting the ideas of tolerance and respect for the individual'.
> (Mirsepassi & Fernée, 2014, p. 189)

This experience of living under authoritarian governance traditions is a major "push" factor that – along with considerations of economic opportunity – drives migration toward countries with greater pluralism and economic dynamism.

In Canada and the United States, Muslim immigrants encounter realities that meet many of their expectations, as well as challenges they did not expect. Many of these challenges are associated with obstacles faced by immigrants from many different backgrounds (ranging from the recognition of foreign educational credentials to economic disadvantage and racial bias). However, some forms of cultural and religious adjustment required by the new context, though not unique to Muslim experiences, are worth exploring in greater detail, particularly as they relate to North American notions of freedom and democracy.

Although Canadian and American versions of democracy have distinctive features and differ in significant ways, both manifest cultural tendencies that differ from the prevailing ethos of many Muslim-majority countries. In both contexts, ideals of democracy have come to refer to competitive, pluralistic politics as well as to social and even family relations. And while Canadian democracy goes farther than American democracy in the affirmation of group rights inherent in multiculturalism, both countries have developed conceptions of toleration that embrace not just tolerance for differing political ideas but also tolerance for differences of all kinds. The conceptions of freedom that predominate are centered on the rights of the individual rather than on the collective (which, in contrast, is privileged in post-colonial polities), and are linked to the free expression of personal interests, including the pursuit of choice and opportunity by women, youth, and members of historically marginalized communities. Although freedom of religion is included in liberal democratic systems, the practice of this freedom is bounded by understandings of individual freedom by other rights ensconced within the constitutional order.

Canadian democracy is recognized internationally for its strong articulation not just of individual rights, but also for constitutional provisions accommodating bilingualism and multiculturalism as bases for national cohesion.

In addition, compared to the United States, Canada manifests a more decentralized political structure (with greater provincial autonomy and a distinct Quebec-centered Francophone experience) and yet also a stronger articulation of the collective good (as manifest, for example, in the health-care system). Within this broad framework, norms of relating to multiculturalism have evolved over time, though they are not unbounded and exist within a liberal and to a certain extent social democratic framework that places limits on the rights of the cultural groups even while affirming the right to cultural expression (Kymlicka & Walker, 2013).

As pointed out by Saeed Rahnema (2006), early understandings of multiculturalism focused primarily on cultural preservation, language, and cultural practices. However, with the arrival of more "visible minorities," policy shifted to "the removal of racially discriminatory barriers" (p. 28). In 1982, multiculturalism was integrated into Canada's *Charter of Rights and Freedoms* in order to affirm Canada as "a culturally and ethnically plural society" and "to assure the cultural freedom and equality of all Canadians" (Rahnema, 2006, p. 28). Unfortunately, despite the legal and institutional efforts, Rahnema argues that multicultural policies "reduce social cohesiveness and add to a greater fragmentation of Canadian society" (2006, p. 29).

As the cases in this book demonstrate, official multiculturalism does not preclude social controversy or politicization of religious differences. The idea of multiculturalism is itself contested in Quebec, where intercultural integration and preservation of a Francophone culture is more highly valued.[11] Many scholars point out that multiculturalism as connected to "diversity" should also explicitly include *religious* diversity and not just racial and ethnic diversity. Some critiques of the predominant practice of multiculturalism note that it reflects an experience of secularization within a Christian majority-culture, while still offering relatively comfortable (though not tension-free) accommodation for Christian subcultures. This positioning suggests that Christianity is the "normal" or "natural" religion of Canada. For example, one does hear discussions about the Mennonite diaspora in Canada but is more likely to hear about the Sikh diaspora in Canada. This prejudice emerged in two forms: Canada is a Christian country, and so non-Christian religions are new, foreign, and "a problem"; and Canada is a secular country, and so non-Christian religions as well as non-European forms of Christianity are new, foreign, and "a problem".[12]

Although in America and Canada there is a shared sense of freedom to act out one's own faith in accordance to what the individual values, the emphasis on individual freedoms is more acute in the American experience than Canadian.[13] Also, as noted above, there is a somewhat stronger assertion of religious rights. Although cultural diversity has come to define the urban American experience, and bilingualism is a deepening reality for much of the country, both principles are more contested than in Canada. With respect to religion, the official separation of church and state is more strongly asserted than in Canada (where the official head of state, the English monarch, is also the formal head of the Anglican church), yet religion remains an important part of the traditional American understandings of local communities pursuing the civic good. Some analysts go so far as to suggest that the official separation of church and state, far from being an intrinsically anti-religious principle, is actually a complex formation of the American Protestant ethos, inflected across generations in ways that involve incremental secularization and an increasingly consumerist culture.

In general, the U.S. formulation of secular political order is one that places considerable emphasis on the autonomy of religious communities. In contrast to a French or Quebec-based version of secularism, American secularism has (despite growing flashpoints over divisive social issues) traditionally framed religious engagement as a positive civic phenomenon, even while construing the construction of religious identities as an individual pursuit that ought to be free of political intervention.

To many Muslim immigrants, such ideals are extremely welcome. After all, state collusion with religious authorities has been experienced by many Muslims as a factor that limits religious freedom as well as the authenticity of religious thought and experience. The principle of freedom from religious persecution is also an attractive part of the American experience. However, conflicts in the domain of international relations have sharpened controversies over Islam in recent decades, and the emergence of strong political currents with explicitly anti-Muslim rhetoric has generated increasing discomfort.

Identity politics of being a Muslim woman in North America

For a variety of reasons – including religion, culture, and race as well as politics – being Muslim in contemporary North America often means being acutely conscious of issues related to identity. Maintaining a distinctive collective cultural and religious experience amid homogenizing and individualizing influences of the prevailing culture is not a tension-free process, and involves conscious choice and internal effort to differentiate between what is essential in a North American Muslim identity and what is not. Divergence of opinion on such questions means that identity is continually under negotiation, and the process becomes more complex and contested in the presence of broader political dynamics that stigmatize Muslim identity and represent it as intrinsically foreign or threatening. Discussions about Muslim identity necessarily involve internal as well as external audiences, reference points, and concerns.

As social psychologists and anthropologists have emphasized, identity presupposes a boundary – an inside and an outside. To have a personal or collective identity is necessarily to be conscious of boundaries between "self" and "other," and of particular values, qualities, and symbols that differentiate a particular "self" or community from actual or potential counterparts. To the extent that these differentiating factors take on heightened salience within an intergroup relationship (national, political, economic, sectarian, cultural, ethnic, interpretive, etc.), that relationship becomes infused not just with a politics of interests – the mundane negotiation of tangible, instrumental concerns – but also with a politics of identity.

Identity negotiations and identity politics suffuse contemporary North American relationships, at international as well as intercommunal and interpersonal levels. For this book, it is crucial to problematize the use of terms "Islamic" and "Western" in relation to each other. While there are numerous critiques concerning the utility and validity of "Islamic"-"Western" distinctions (there are Muslims in the "West," Westerners in "Islam," "Westernized" Muslims, "Islamicized" Westerners, and so forth), the categories of "Islam" and "West" are actively used and abused in identity construction, and have real consequences for daily relationships and events. In a globalized world, Muslims have come to know themselves in relation to (and often in contrast to) European and North American powers who have long exerted strong political, economic, and cultural influence over Muslim lands, particularly since the advent of the colonial era. "Western" consciousness of Islam has been less central to identity definition in America and Canada, but has nonetheless become significant after September 11, 2001, and the subsequent wars in Afghanistan and Iraq. As is explored in this book, Muslims and non-Muslims in North America frequently define their identities through comparisons and contrasts with each other, often in ways that are colored by dramatic political events and controversies. Contemporary North American identity politics, therefore, reflect the emotional content of relationships fraught with a high degree of fear, resentment, and insecurity.[14]

This "external" dynamic of identity politics, according to which members of one collectivity seek to define and police the boundary between their group and another communal entity, tracks closely with a corresponding "internal" dynamic. Efforts to define identity and values in relation to an "other" necessarily presuppose distinctions not only between obvious "insiders" and "outsiders," but also between contending norms for in-group behavior – that is, between "authentic" and "inauthentic" values, as well as between correct and incorrect forms of thought and action. Ways of defining a collective "self" and a collective "other" have significant consequences for insiders, and polarization between groups tends to correlate with an intensified dynamic of "internal" identity politics, according to which different voices compete to define what constitutes authentic as well as inauthentic behavior, or to claim the right to authority within the group.

The external dynamics of North American identity politics have profound consequences for Muslim women. They are confronted with a persistent set of dilemmas as they navigate the internal dynamics of their cultural, religious, and political communities while also seeking to participate within secular and/or cosmopolitan spaces. On the one hand, many "internal" voices within Muslim identity groups consistently contrast Islamic principles with changes in gender norms, and therefore describe such changes as inauthentic. Muslim women who seek to expand scope for action, voice, and public involvement must often accentuate their Islamic identity in order to avoid being "othered" within their own community, and dismissed as inauthentic. On the other hand, barriers can also arise from "external" sources – even from the same "Western" voices who claim solidarity with Muslim women. Muslim women in both America and Canada must work within a cultural environment in which some voices equate Islam with traditional or reactionary practices, and argue that excluding Islamic symbolism (e.g., traditional Muslim head coverings) from public life fosters liberation among Muslim women. Muslim women then experience a "Catch 22" situation, in which strategies conducive to advancement in the larger society result in a loss of status within their community, and choices to conform to communal expectations result in limited opportunities for public employment.[15]

A generation later: Living in and with the persistence of suspicion

A generation may have passed, yet the tragic events of September 11, 2001 – and the dynamics they unleashed – continue to exert an influence. For Muslims in North America, the most significant impacts include fear of Islamic "otherness" and a persistent need to lay claim to "loyal minority group" status. For Muslim women, however, there are distinctive aspects to the post-9/11 experience, often associated with a heightened politicization of "status of Muslim women" questions.

In Natasha Bakht's *Belonging and Banishment* (2008), Haroon Siddiqui poignantly observes the real victims of 9/11 are none other than Muslims themselves. While Siddiqui's observation obviously diverges from "commonsense" North American and especially American understandings of 9/11, it captures significant layers of meaning for Muslim communities. In addition to the international armed conflicts that ensued after 9/11, and a burden of anxiety about basic human security issues that has been borne by people of many different backgrounds, Muslims within and beyond North America have often felt the pain of an additional burden – the burden of living under heightened suspicion, and the devastating assumption that the actions of few could become symptomatic of all. A variety of scholars, including Mahmood Mamdani, Leila Ahmed, Nathan Lean, and Jasmin Zine, have commented on the constancy and persistence of suspicion toward Muslims, and on the accompanying sense of urgency imposed on Muslims in the 21ˢᵗ century to demonstrate benign intentions.[16] In a North American context, this means a need to display loyalty to American or Canadian identities, and a testing of loyalty that bifurcates the "bad" Muslims from the "good" Muslims.

Given the elevated security concerns of the post-9/11 era, many non-Muslims in American and Canadian societies tend to be more curious about the intensity of patriotism and the extent of acculturation among Muslim citizens than about Muslim efforts to formulate coherent worldviews and complex understandings of political affairs. It should come as no surprise, then, that in defining desirable characteristics for the "Western Muslim," a growing community of scholars, policymakers, and media professionals have defined labels such as "moderate Islam" and "moderate Muslims" in ways that are instrumental to the goal of winning a fight against the narrow militant, political, and/or radical Islam. As a result, many Muslims feel frustrated or ambivalent about these labels.

One concern about the "moderate Muslim" label is that it appears to mark its bearer as an "uncritical ally" of "the West," at a time when Muslim alienation and disaffection is increasing. While the connotation of being "against violence" still appeals, there is an additional undesirable implication: Being indifferent to policies that fail to address root causes of Muslim militance. As some scholars have observed, labeling Muslims as either "moderate" or "immoderate" tends to silence a majority of Muslim voices, and reinforces illusive "good Muslim" versus "bad Muslim" dichotomies (Barlas, 2005).

In this era of Islamophobia – or of what Juan Cole refers to as "Islam anxiety" (Cole, 2009) – American and Canadian Muslim women are not immune from perceptions of complicity in the 9/11 atrocities.[17] As Sheema Khan states, "guilt by religious identity" (2009, p. 30) imposes collective responsibility for the misdeeds of individuals and radicalized movements, and creates a pervasive anxiety about Islam and for Muslims. As is discussed in more detail in Chapter 3, influential forms of "clash literature" evoke and channel this anxiety, in the service of far-right movements that seek to stigmatize and exclude the entire religion of Islam.

The persistent suspicion of difference need not be a conscious or intentional phenomenon – as in the case of "clash literature" and nativist movements – to exert a problematic influence on minority community experiences. Often anxiety about Islam finds expression in preoccupation with questions of assimilation and integration into "mainstream culture," with a particular symbolic emphasis on "status of women" issues and underlying negative assumptions about Muslim women's condition. The status of Muslim women is construed both as a major defect in Muslim culture and as a potential wedge issue in the struggle between Islam and "the West." Muslim women are presented as inexcusably oppressed, in a manner that faithfully reflects fixed and inflexible Islamic beliefs. An Islamophobic worldview sees these beliefs as the primary determining factor in a number of negative cultural dynamics, particularly abusive patriarchal authority, submissive and voiceless women, and the perpetuation of dangerous Muslim countercultures characterized by resentment and rapid population growth. Those who have been influenced by such stereotypical assumptions frequently aspire to amplify the most aggrieved and confrontational voices among Muslim or ex-Muslim women, who are represented as reliable interpreters of the overall Islamic experience.[18]

Stereotypical notions about what a "Muslim woman" is or ought to be are pervasive, both in "the West" and in "the Muslim world." Muslim women's lives and realities are – and have always been – diverse. Historically, Muslim women (like women in other religious and cultural contexts) have faced many barriers to advancement in public life, particularly in the domains of religion and politics. Nonetheless, advocates of women's rights within Muslim contexts like to note that women were among the greatest followers and caretakers of the Prophet Muhammad. Moreover, Muslim women scholars and mystics developed some of the most important Islamic traditions still practiced today. While it is true that some Muslim women are plagued by a landscape of barriers that includes unfair divorces, the threat of domestic violence, and even the horror of honor killings,[19] the diversity of Muslim women's experiences – within and beyond North America – belies any simplistic notion about Muslim women who need "saving" (Abu-Lughod, 2013).

Unfortunately, public discourse about the "Muslim woman" – particularly but not exclusively in America and Canada – often relies on "single image" preconceptions. Muslim women are presented as inexcusably oppressed, and as passive, submissive victims of abusive patriarchal authority. These stereotypes are both inaccurate and potentially dangerous, particularly when the idea of "saving" Muslim women becomes linked to larger political or foreign policy agendas. The "truth" about Muslim women may not correspond with images purveyed by the most conservative Muslim governments or by defensive apologists who insist on the purity of historical practices, but the gross overgeneralizations promoted by some politicians, institutes, and popular authors fall far from the mark.

As is discussed in more detail in Chapter 4, bestselling books in America and Canada with titles, such as *Infidel*, *Surrender*, and *America Alone*, reveal more about their authors' biases and misconceptions than they do about the lives of the "typical" Muslim woman. Such literature advances hostile representations of Islam as a faith that in its immutable essence promotes gender inequality and violence toward women – through genital mutilation, honor killings, stoning of adulteresses, and holding women responsible for being raped. Such portraits generalize from the most oppressive cases and contexts, and take no note of variation in Muslim women's experiences in accordance with interpretive beliefs, geography, culture, or social class. A reasonable argument can be made that traditional forms of Muslim patriarchy pose barriers to the advancement of Muslim women and to the successful integration of Muslim communities within Western societies. The "bestselling" literature about Muslim women, however, thrives on the shock value of particular images and is marketed in ways that take advantage of negative preconceptions.

Although it would be unwise to overstate the popular appeal of literature premised on "kill the Muslim, save the woman" notions – after all, an increasing number of Western readers have daily contact with three-dimensional, "real-life" Muslim women – most writers of what I later define in Chapters 3 and 4 as Western-sourced "clash" literature regard fighting to liberate Muslim women as a critical front in the culture war between "Islam and the West." These writers use "women and Islam" themes to underscore the "otherness" of Islam, and tend to either ignore or dismiss "mainstream" voices of reform and moderation within Muslim communities. Instead, they give disproportionate attention to "ex-Muslim" individuals who have written off Islamic reform movements and denounced Islamic cultures categorically. The predominant tendency is to use the "status of women" issue as a key talking point in generalized critiques of Islam, with the goal of demonstrating the superiority of contemporary Western norms.

A tipping point: London, Ontario, in June 2021

In response and reaction to pervasive anxiety about Islam, many Muslim women in America and Canada have sought to reclaim their faith both from internal extremists and from extreme outsider groups who thrive on demonizing all things Islamic. They have raised their voices against misrepresentations, and the thought that the actions of a few can be used to malign the many. By asserting their identities and giving expression to their experiences, Muslim women in public spheres are combatting stereotypes and taking ownership of their faith and tradition (Haddad, 2011, p. 82).

Progress in this struggle is always tentative and uncertain, but sometimes dramatic and even tragic events can exert a powerful impact by defining the stakes and opening broader audiences to the message delivered by "mainstream" Muslim women. In America and Canada, there have been "tipping points" that trigger greater public awareness of Muslim experiences and action against intolerance. One such triggering and horrific event occurred in London, Ontario, on June 6, 2021, when three Muslim women – a daughter, mother, and grandmother – were intentionally struck by a motor vehicle and killed.[20] In a 2021 report, CCMW describes this shocking event and its mobilizing impact:

> On the evening of June 6, 2021, Talat Afzaal, her son Salman, her daughter-in-law Madiha, her granddaughter Yumna, and her grandson Fayez were out for a late spring walk in their London, Ontario, neighbourhood when the lives of four members of that beautiful family came to a crashing halt. Nine-year-old Fayez survived after sustaining serious injuries and is now an orphan. This mass murder was the work of a white supremacist who was filled with hate against Muslims.

In the aftermath of this horrific Islamophobic attack, Bilal Rahall and Nusaybah Al-Azem, spokespersons for the London Muslim Mosque, called on all three levels of government to hold an Emergency National Action Summit on Islamophobia and address individual and systemic issues Canadian Muslim communities are facing on a daily basis – whether it's their personal safety, physical, mental and economic well-being or the education of their children.

(CCMW, 2021, p. 2)

This act of intentional violence against a model family in a modest-sized and seemingly peaceful Canadian city quickly captured provincial and national attention, provoking recognition that fear and hatred could have fatal consequences, and that in this respect the Canadian experience was not unlike that of other nations which had witnessed similar atrocities.

Due to this horrific event, awareness was spread, actions were initiated, and policies were created about Islamophobia in Canada at federal, provincial, and municipal levels as well as in post-secondary and secondary schools. Here are some examples of this response:

- Members from all major parties from federal and provincial governments (including Prime Minister Justin Trudeau, NDP Leader Jagmeet Singh, Conservative Leader Erin O'Toole, Green Party Leader Annamie Paul, Bloc Québécois Leader Yves-Francois Blanchet, Premier of Ontario Doug Ford, Ontario NDP Leader Andrea Horwath, Ontario Liberal Leader Steven Del Duca, and Ontario Green Party Leader Mike Schreiner) joined London mayor Ed Holder and members of London city council at the London Muslim Mosque on June 8, 2021, for a vigil in support of the family. There were also communities across the country who organized vigils to commemorate the family.[21]
- London, Ontario city council unanimously supported a motion, put forward by Ward 3 Councillor Mo Salih and Ward 13 Councillor Arielle Kayabaga, to denounce the attack in London, denounce Islamophobia, and commit to working with the local Muslim community in London and other stakeholders "to help end Islamophobia and report back on the outcomes of that work" (City of London, 2021).
- On June 29, 2021, Ontario Education Minister Stephen Lecce announced the province's decision to commit $300,000 in funding to educational programs to combat Islamophobia in schools ($225,000 to the Muslim Association of Canada to create digital resources for educators, students, and parents to raise awareness about Islamophobia, and $75,000 to the National Council of Canadian Muslims to help Muslim newcomers navigate their new country and to help new students prepare for school in September).

- The House of Commons unanimously passed a nonbinding motion from London-Fanshawe NDP MP Lindsay Mathyssen for the federal government to convene an emergency national action summit on Islamophobia before the end of July, 2021.
- British Columbia Parliamentary Secretary for Anti-Racism Initiatives, Rachna Singh, and British Columbia Minister of Education, Jennifer Whiteside, released a joint statement on July 22, 2021, on the National Summit on Islamophobia, announcing the launch of a province-wide anti-racism awareness campaign and "funding for Islam Unravelled to work with communities on ways to stop faith-based hate."[22]
- Post-secondary institutions, school boards, professional associations, non-profit organizations, Muslim charities, municipalities, and religious institutions across the country issued statements of support and solidarity, condemning the attack and sharing mental health, spiritual care and support resources to support students, staff, and community members.[23]

All of these responses are influencing policy recommendations and funding decisions, and are causing the formation of new coalitions. For example, the following organizations submitted policy recommendations for the National Action Summit on Islamophobia that was held on July 22, 2021:[24] Canadian Council of Muslim Women;[25] National Council of Canadian Muslims;[26] Noor Cultural Centre; International Civil Liberties Monitoring Group;[27] and Muslim Association of Canada.[28] As part of the National Summit on Islamophobia, the federal government issued a list of commitments, including: (1) Engaging with Muslim communities on the government's next anti-racism action plan, looking at adjusting some programs – like the security infrastructure program – for effectiveness and to be more responsive to community needs, improving digital literacy and tackling misinformation (Major, 2021); and (2) Minister of Diversity and Inclusion and Youth in 2021, Bardish Chagger, also announced funding for eight projects[29] through the Anti-Racism Action Program to address Islamophobia. The National Summit on Islamophobia was not without criticism: The virtual summit was scheduled at short notice during Eid al-Adha (an inappropriate time to meet for some Muslims), there is ongoing skepticism over whether the government's policy recommendations are actionable, and the proposed policies were ultimately affected by the federal election which was called on September 20, 2021 (Rodriguez, 2021).[30]

The breadth and intensity of responses to a highly visible and dramatic act of hatred underscores the dynamic nature of contemporary experiences, as well as shared stakes experienced by Muslim women across their many differences. In addition, for all the divisiveness that surrounds controversial issues such as those analyzed in the chapters of this volume, social capacity to understand the dangers inherent in prejudicial attitudes clearly exists.

Progress toward deeper embrace and inclusion is not fully assured – recent decades have also witnessed reversals – yet political action by Muslim women is not without consequence.

Conclusion

Certain seasoned scholars of "women and Islam," such as Lila Abu-Lughod (2013) and Leila Ahmed (2011), have argued that any monolithic image of the Muslim woman is inherently flawed: There is a desperate need to diversify understandings of what it means to be a Muslim woman. This chapter has sought to contextualize this message, underscoring the diversity of Muslim women and the many issues they face in 21ˢᵗ century North America, and the impossibility of a "single narrative" about the meaning of their experiences. As is reflected in the demographics of ethnic, cultural, sectarian, or interpretive differences found in America and Canada, each Muslim woman ultimately negotiates and navigates the experience of the sacred in their own unique and authentic way. At the same time, certain overarching issues and pressures confront North American Muslim women on a daily basis, inviting analysis of similarities and differences in their experiences as female members of a minority religious community that is grappling with how to engage traditions of liberal democracy as well as persistent forms of Islamophobia. The following chapters will explore these issues – the inherent diversity of Muslim women, the inevitability of contestation over identity and meaning, similarities and differences between national contexts, and the high stakes of struggles for recognition and acceptance – as they manifest in relation to a series of controversial issues that have become focal points for debate. Throughout, attention will be given not only to sources of polarity and division, but also to emergent developments that might enable the discovery or creation of common ground, or the unfolding of new possibilities in response to "tipping point" events. Although the challenges posed by divergent positions (among Muslims, as well as within the larger societies) will not be minimized, it is important to approach controversies in a way that also acknowledges potential for "convergent horizons" and new understandings.

To approach controversies as much as possible within a framework that seeks to clarify divergent understandings, this book will be informed by scholarship grounded in the principle and practice of dialogue. The next chapter will therefore examine scholarship informed by a dialogical epistemology that analyzes the ebb and flow of social life as a relational process through which understandings, norms, and identities are continually shaped and reconstituted. Scholars working on the basis of dialogical epistemologies have offered compelling insights into ongoing negotiation across Islamic and Western identities and cultures – insights that are of value for understanding lives that take shape at the meeting of polarities, and for examining how a great many American and Canadian Muslims are constructing identities defined by complex nuances of meaning. Consciously or unconsciously, these Muslims are seeking to defy binaries and embrace what GhaneaBassiri (2010) calls "messiness" instead of the closure and limitation that are embedded in conflicting narratives.

Notes

1 For many Persians, a copy of the Qur'an (the holy book for Muslims) is found in an elevated place in one's home and next to it is often found the *Divan* of Hafiz (also known as "the second Qur'an" for Persians). Shams al-din Hafiz (d. 1390) is recognized as one of the "immortal poets" of Persia.

2 For information about the survey methodology, refer to: https://www.pewresearch.org/fact-tank/2017/08/16/muslim-americans-methods/

3 Given the voluntary nature of the National Household Survey, which replaced the mandatory long-form census, there are significant gaps in the data. For example, the survey does not provide a breakdown of type of Muslims living in Canada (Postmedia News, 2013). Additionally, the National Household Survey, 2011 "does not account for the growth of the Canadian Muslim population nor the growth of certain segments within the Canadian Muslim population" (Shah, 2019, p. 34).

4 Similarly, in the United States, there are no federal or state statistics on religious identity. Pew Research Center notes that its "periodic Religious Landscape Study aims to fill this gap through massive surveys that detail the nation's religious composition and changing religious dynamics" (Pew Research Center, 2021).

5 See more on "sub-Ummahs" in my book, *Encountering the Transnational* (2008, p. 30).

6 In the United States, conversion has not significantly impacted the size of the Muslim population because of comparable numbers of Americans who leave the faith (Mohamed, 2018). As a researcher at Pew Research Center points out, "while about one-in-five American Muslim adults were raised in a different faith tradition and converted to Islam, a similar share of Americans who were raised Muslim now no longer identify with the faith" (Mohamed, 2018). Survey data indicates that approximately eight-in-ten U.S. Muslims say that they have always been Muslim, while 21% self-identify as converts to Islam (Pew Research Center, 2017b). Additionally, religious switching to Islam from another faith tradition (including Protestant, Catholic, Orthodox Christianity, Judaism, and Buddhism) or from being religiously unaffiliated is more common among Muslims born in the United States than those who have immigrated from other places: 95% of Muslim immigrants surveyed responded that they have always been Muslim, while 54% of U.S.-born Muslims said the same (ibid.). Two-thirds of U.S.-born Black Muslims said they have not always been Muslim (ibid.).

7 In Canada, there is limited data available on religious affiliation in general. The Census collects information on religion every ten years – the most recent was the 2011 Census. While the Environics 2016 Survey of Muslims in Canada offers some updated demographic information, it does not cover religious switching or conversion. In 2014, a preliminary report on conversion to Islam in Ontario was published (Flower & Birkett, 2014). However, since this report was based on qualitative methods (participant observation and ethnographic interviews) and a small sample (25 Muslim converts), generalizations cannot be drawn.

8 See Marcia Hermansen's and Karin van Nieuwkerk's chapters in *The Oxford Handbook of Religious Conversion* (2014). Many English-speaking converts to Islam prefer to be called 'reverts' because of an Islamic concept known as *fitra* which recalls

an event known as the Primordial Covenant where all souls recognized God in pre-eternity. It is also in reference to the Islamic belief that "Everyone is born sinless and by becoming Muslim you return to that original sinless state in which God created him or her."

9 For example, before 1961, the Muslim community in Canada constituted a small minority with low rates of immigration. During the 1980s and 1990s, Canada saw a high growth rate of Muslim immigrants. Muslims in Canada more or less reflect the global profile of Muslims, and thus for a heterogeneous population, "highly diversified in terms of ethnic, national and sectarian affiliations, and degrees of religious convictions" (Mogedessi, 2006, p. 24).

10 As Hermansen points out, other aspects of the Progressive Muslim movement include mosque and state separation, non-literal Qur'anic interpretation, interfaith dialogue, embracing modernity, and emphasis on the arts (2004, p. 81). See also Safi (2003).

11 Refer to Sharify-Funk (2010 and 2011).

12 One issue that illustrates these tensions is the right to pray in public schools. According to the Environics Survey of Muslims in Canada, 75% of respondents "believe that Muslim students should have the right to pray in public schools, compared with 13% who do not agree, and a comparable proportion who say it depends (e.g., on circumstances) (8%) or cannot offer an opinion (4%)" (Environics, 2016). Support for this right is particularly strong among Ontario residents (83%), women (82%), Muslims under age 45 (80%), Canadian-born Muslims (91%), respondents who identify primarily as Muslim (87%) – versus those who identify primarily as Canadian – and respondents who visit mosques for prayer at least once per week (81%) (Environics, 2016, p. 29). On the other side, "opposition to Muslims praying in schools is most evident in Quebec (47%) and increases with age (17% among those 18 to 34, rising to 38% among those 55 and older)" (ibid.).

13 In particular, under the Trump administration during 2017–2021, nativism and white nationalism became prominent themes for the construction of American identity politics in which there are no special efforts to promote equity or accommodation for minority cultural or religious groups.

14 Refer to Husain & Howard (2017); Khan (2014); Welborne et al. (2018); Shams (2018); Saleem and Ramasubramanian (2017); Dana et al. (2019); Perry (2015); Bakht (2013); Elsheikh et al. (2017); Helly (2016); Rockenbach et al. (2017); Perry (2014); Zempi (2016); Alimahomed-Wilson (2017); Ontario Human Rights Commission (2012); and Tiflati (2017).

15 In a CCMW report based on data from the National Household Survey of 2011 – the most recent Census data in Canada that includes religion as a variable – Muslim women encountered more difficulties in the labor market than other communities with similar sociodemographic profiles, and in spite of the favorable changes in the Muslim female labor force, the labor market outcomes have not improved for them. Unemployment among Muslim women was high and persistent: "Some 16.7 per cent of Muslim women 15 years of age and older were unemployed in 2011, a figure more than double the national average of 7.4 per cent for all Canadian women. They fared poorly compared with other faith communities. Only the women practising traditional spirituality (Aboriginal) faced higher unemployment than Muslim women and girls. This is in spite of the fact that proportionately twice as many Muslim women as all Canadian women specialize in STEM and twice as many use both official languages at work" (CCMW, 2014, p. ix).

16 The study of Islamophobia has emerged since the beginning of the 21ˢᵗ century with a diverse range of scholars and activists. There are a variety of academic programs studying Islamophobia that have developed. One example is The Islamophobia Research and Documentation Project (IRDP) and the *Islamophobia Studies*

Journal, both initiatives in the Center for Race and Gender at the University of California, Berkeley. The IRDP focuses on "a systematic and empirical approach to the study of Islamophobia and its impact on the American Muslim community." See their website: https://www.crg.berkeley.edu/research/islamophobia-research-documentation-project/. Additionally, prominent book titles on Islamophobia are *Islamophobia: Making Muslims the Enemy* (2008); *Islamophobia: The Challenge of Pluralism in the 21st Century* (2011); *Islamophobia: The Ideological Campaign Against Muslims* (2011); and *The Islamophobia Industry: How the Right Manufactures Fear of Muslims* (2012); *Under Siege: Islamophobia and the 9/11 Generation* (2022).

17 Marcia Hermansen, in her chapter on "The Evolution of American Responses to 9/11" in *Islam and the West Post 9/11,* discusses Sherman A. Jackson's observation that "after Sept. 11th the door to American whiteness was closed to immigrant Muslims" (2004, p. 88). Hermansen then analyzes this thought that Jackson is pointing out that many "Muslim immigrants who had previously thought that by falling into the 'Caucasian' category they would be able to 'pass, the situation had fundamentally changed. A new distrust of the foreign and explicitly the Muslim, he proposed, would permanently exclude them from the American national consensus'" (p. 88). Jackson's observation highlights a destabilization of racial categories, and ways in which full acceptance in an American context depends on a variety of factors including racial appearance as well as religion.

18 For more on this topic, refer to Chapter 4 section on "Women's Emancipation as a Focal Point."

19 In response to a variety of mental and physical health issues, many "helplines" or "mental hotlines" for Muslim women have emerged within the 21st century. *Naseeha* is an example of one popular helpline that supports both Canadian and American callers. See Javed (2017).

20 There have been more events around the same time, such as on July 12, 2021, when a Muslim mother and daughter, both wearing *hijab*, were nearly hit by a vehicle in a Shoppers Drug Mart parking lot in Hamilton, Ontario. The driver used racist slurs toward the Muslim community and threatened to kill the two women (Hristova, 2021). On July 14, 2021, the Bai'tul Kareem Mosque in Cambridge, Ontario, was vandalized, costing thousands of dollars in damage (Nielsen, 2021).

21 See https://www.nccm.ca/londonvigils/. In Manitoba, more than 60 faith leaders signed a statement of grief and support, extending condolences to the family in London and to Muslim communities, and denouncing Islamophobia: http://westworth.ca/2021/06/interfaith-statement-of-grief-and-support/. Refer to CBC News (2021).

22 See BC Gov News (2021).

23 Halton Hills was one municipality that issued a statement. Universities that issued statements included Carleton University, University of Toronto, York University, Western University, Bishop's University, University of Windsor, Mount Saint Vincent University, University of Waterloo, University of Calgary, the University of British Columbia Department of Physical Therapy, McMaster University, Wilfrid Laurier University Students' Union, the Ontario College of Art & Design Faculty Association, and University of Ottawa. Schools and school boards that issued statements included Toronto District School Board, University of Toronto Schools, and Durham District School Board. Professional associations included the Ontario Confederation of University Faculty Associations and the Canadian Sociological Association. Nonprofit organizations included Ontario Association of Children's Aid Societies, The Salvation Army, SickKids, United Way East Ontario (United for All Coalition), Flemingdon Health Centre and The Neighbourhood Organization, Alliance for Healthier Communities, Fred Victor, Imagine Canada, and the Ontario Council of Agencies Serving Immigrants. Muslim charities included

Muslim Association of Canada (MAC) and National Council of Canadian Muslims (NCCM). Religious institutions included the United Church of Canada, Canadian Conference of Catholic Bishops, and the Evangelical Fellowship of Canada.

24 See different submissions that were compiled by the National Council of Canadian Muslims (2021a).

25 See CCMW's recommendations (2021), which were informed by the CCMW Young People's Roundtable on Islamophobia, hosted July 16, 2021, in collaboration with the Honourable Bardish Chagger, Minister of Diversity and Inclusion and Youth, and the Honourable Maryam Monsef, Minister for Women and Gender Equality and Rural Economic Development.

26 Refer to the National Council of Canadian Muslims (2021b) to learn about their 61 policy recommendations for federal, provincial, and municipal governments – including an investigation into how national security agencies deal with white supremacist groups, reviewing school curricula with an anti-Islamophobic lens and providing resources for telling Muslim stories, providing national support funding for survivors of hate-motivated crimes, and amendments to municipal bylaws regarding harassment and the Criminal Code to better address hate crimes. These recommendations were generated through consultation sessions with mosques and community organizations across Canada.

27 Azeezah Kanji and Tim McSorley's proposals include releasing and collecting disaggregated race- and religion-based data by the government, and reviewing how the Canada Revenue Agency works with national security agencies to conduct audits (International Civil Liberties Monitoring Group, 2021).

28 Muslim Association of Canada (MAC) submitted a proposal to the National Action Summit on Islamophobia, calling the government to "1. Establish a federal office to implement an anti-Islamophobia strategy; 2. Immediate moratorium on CRA RAD audits of Muslim charities pending a review of the division; 3. A commitment to reform and oversight of the CBSA and eliminate the profiling of Muslims" (2021).

29 See details of projects at Canadian Heritage (2021).

30 Prime Minister Justin Trudeau called for a federal election in August 2021, and the election was held on September 20, 2021. The results – a Liberal minority government, led by Trudeau – remained largely unchanged from the 2019 federal election.

References

Abu-Lughod, L. (2013). *Do Muslim women need saving?* Harvard University Press.

Ahmed, L. (2011). *A quiet revolution: The veil's resurgence, from the Middle East to America.* Yale University Press.

Al Wazni, A. B. (2015). Muslim women in America and *hijab*: A study of empowerment, feminist identity, and body image. *Social Work, 60*(4), 325–333.

Alimahomed-Wilson, S. (2017). Invisible violence: Gender, Islamophobia, and the hidden assault on U.S. Muslim women. *Women, Gender, and Families of Color, 5*(1), 73–97. https://doi.org/10.5406/womgenfamcol.5.1.0073

Allison, K. (2013). American Occidentalism and the agential Muslim woman. *Review of International Studies, 39*(3), 665–684.

Amirani, S. (2012, September 29). Tehrangeles: How Iranians made part of LA their own. *BBC News.* https://www.bbc.com/news/magazine-19751370

Aslan, E., Hermansen, M. K., & Medeni, E. (2013). *Muslima theology: The voices of Muslim women theologians.* Peter Lang AG.

Bakht, N. (2013). Veiled objections: Facing public opposition to the *niqab*. In L. G. Beaman (Ed.), *Reasonable accommodation: Managing religious diversity* (pp. 70–108). UBC Press.

Barlas, A. (2005). The excesses of moderation: Colloquium on "moderate Islam," University of Utah, Feb. 21–22, 2004. *American Journal of Islam and Society, 22*(3), 158–165.

BC Gov News. (2021). *Joint statement on National Summit on Islamophobia.* https://news.gov.bc.ca/releases/2021AG0047-001422

Birani, A. (2017). *Toward an inclusive Islamic identity? A study of first- and second-generation Muslims in Canada.* [Doctoral dissertation]. The University of Western Ontario. https://ir.lib.uwo.ca/etd/4582

Canadian Council of Muslim Women (CCMW)/Le conseil canadien des femmes musulmanes (CCFM). (2021, July 21). *National Action Summit on Islamophobia: Submission & recommendations.* https://static1.squarespace.com/static/5b43ad2bf407b4a036d27f06/t/60f9d93e6e68dc3b8886d4d8/1626986815351/CCMW+National+Action+Summit+Final-3.pdf

Canadian Council of Muslim Women (CCMW)/Le conseil canadien des femmes musulmanes (CCFM). (2021). *CCMW's National Action Summit on Islamophobia recommendations.* https://www.ccmw.com/media-room-1/2021/7/22/ccmws-national-action-summit-on-islamophobia-recommendations

Canadian Council of Muslim Women (CCMW)/Le conseil canadien des femmes musulmanes (CCFM), & Hamdani, D. (2014, September). *Canadian Muslim women: A decade of change - 2001 to 2011.* https://static1.squarespace.com/static/5b43ad2bf407b4a036d27f06/t/5c4756816d2a73efe1f498b9/1548179076001/Canadian-Muslim-Women.pdf

Canadian Heritage. (2021, July 22). *The Government of Canada concludes National Summit on Islamophobia.* https://www.canada.ca/en/canadian-heritage/news/2021/07/the-government-of-canada-concludes-national-summit-on-islamophobia.html

CBC News. (2021, June 10). *More than 60 Manitoba interfaith leaders sign letter denouncing Islamophobia after London, Ont., attack.* https://www.cbc.ca/news/canada/manitoba/interfaith-letter-support-muslim-london-attack-1.6060713

City of London. (2021, June 9). *Re: Emergent motion – Hyde Park Road terrorist attack.* https://pub-london.escribemeetings.com/filestream.ashx?DocumentId=81796

Cole, J. (2009). *Engaging the Muslim world.* St. Martin's Press.

Dana, K., Lajevardi, N., Oskooii, K. A. R., & Walker, H. L. (2019). Veiled politics: Experiences with discrimination among Muslim Americans. *Politics & Religion, 12*(4), 629–677.

Elsheikh, E., Sisemore, B., & Ramirez Lee, N. (2017). *Legalizing othering: The United States of Islamophobia.* Haas Institute for a Fair and Inclusive Society at UC Berkeley. haasinstitute.berkeley.edu/islamophobia

Flower, S., & Birkett, D. (2014). *(Mis)understanding Muslim converts in Canada: A critical discussion of Muslim converts in the contexts of security and society.* TSAS: Canadian Network for Research on Terrorism, Security and Society. https://www.tsas.ca/publications/misunderstanding-muslim-converts-in-canada/

Gecewicz, C. (2017, August 7). *In many ways, Muslim men and women see life in America differently.* Pew Research Center. https://www.pewresearch.org/fact-tank/2017/08/07/in-many-ways-muslim-men-and-women-see-life-in-america-differently/

GhaneaBassiri, K. (2010). *The history of Islam in America.* Cambridge University Press.

Haddad, Y. (2011). *Becoming American? The forging of Arab and Muslim identity in pluralist America.* Baylor University Press.

Haji, R., Cila, J., & Lalonde, R. N. (2020, September 14). Beyond sectarian boundaries: Dimensions of Muslim Canadian religiosity and the prediction of sociocultural attitudes. *Psychology of Religion and Spirituality*, 1–10. Advance online publication. https://doi.org/10.1037/rel0000393

Hamdani, D. (2015). *Canadian Muslims: A statistical review.* Commissioned by The Canadian Dawn Foundation. https://muslimlink.ca/pdf/Canadian-Muslims-A-Statistical-Review-Final.pdf

Hammer, J. (2012). *American Muslim women, religious authority, and activism: More than a prayer.* University of Texas Press.

Helly, D. (2016). Islamophobia in Canada? Women's rights, modernity, secularism. In F. C. Gonzalez & G. D'Amato (Eds.), *Multireligious society: Dealing with religious diversity in theory and practice.* Routledge Publishers.

Hermansen, M. (2004). The evolution of American Muslim responses to 9/11. In R. Geaves, T. Gabriel, & J. I. Smith (Eds.), *Islam and the West post 9/11.* Routledge Publishers.

Hermansen, M. (2014). Conversion to Islam: Historical and theological perspectives. In L. R. Rambo, & C. E. Fahadian (Eds.), *The Oxford handbook of religious conversion* (pp. 632–666). Oxford University Press.

Hristova, B. (2021, July 20). 'Mom, he's following us, run!' - Hamilton imam fears for family after man charge with hate crime. *CBC News*. https://www.cbc.ca/news/canada/hamilton/imam-hamilton-hate-crime-1.6105528

Husain, A., & Howard, S. (2017). Religious microaggressions: A case study of Muslim Americans. *Journal of Ethnic & Cultural Diversity in Social Work*, 26(1–2), 139–152. https://doi.org/10.1080/15313204.2016.1269710

Hussein, S. (2019). *From victims to suspects: Muslim women since 9/11.* Yale University Press.

International Civil Liberties Monitoring Group. (2021, July 16). *Brief to the National Action Summit on Islamophobia.* https://iclmg.ca/wp-content/uploads/2021/07/ICLMG-Brief-to-the-National-Action-Summit-on-Islamophobia.pdf

Javed, N. (2017, January 2). GTA-based helpline for Muslim youth overwhelmed by U.S. callers. *Toronto Star.* https://www.thestar.com/news/gta/2017/01/02/gta-based-help-line-for-muslim-youth-overwhelmed-by-us-callers.html

Keshani, H. (2018). Doctrine and design: Two Islamic centres in Burnaby, Canada: A photo essay. *BC Studies*, Vancouver Issue 198, 37.

Khalil, M. (2018). *Voices of Muslim women in America: Identity and Islamophobia.* [Master's thesis]. University of Akron. http://rave.ohiolink.edu/etdc/view?acc_num=akron1524492381353179

Khan, S. (2009). *Of hockey and hijab: Reflections of a Canadian Muslim woman.* TSAR Publications.

Khan, S. R. (2014). Post 9/11: The impact of stigma for Muslim Americans. *Peace and Conflict: Journal of Peace Psychology*, 20(4), 580–582.

Kymlicka, W., & Walker, K. (2013). *Rooted cosmopolitanism: Canada and the world.* UBC Press.

Major, D. (2021, July 22). Trudeau calls out federal agencies during national summit on Islamophobia. *CBC News.* https://www.cbc.ca/news/politics/national-summit-islamophobia-1.6111405

McCloud, A. B. (2004). Conceptual discourse: Living as a Muslim in a pluralistic society. In Z. H. Bukhari, S. S. Nyang, M. Ahmad, & J. L. Esposito (Eds.), *Muslims' place in the American public square: Hopes, fears, and aspirations* (pp. 73–83). Rowman & Littlefield.

Mirsepassi, A., & Fernée, T. G. (2014). *Islam, democracy, and cosmopolitanism: At home and in the world.* Cambridge University Press.

Mogedessi, H. (2006). *Muslim diaspora: Gender, culture, and identity.* London: Routledge Publishers.

Mohamed, B. (2018, January 3). *New estimates show U.S. Muslim population continues to grow.* Pew Research Center. https://www.pewresearch.org/fact-tank/2018/01/03/new-estimates-show-u-s-muslim-population-continues-to-grow/

Mohamed, B., & Diamant, J. (2019, January 17). *Black Muslims account for a fifth of all U.S. Muslims, and about half are converts to Islam.* Pew Research Center. https://www.pewresearch.org/fact-tank/2019/01/17/black-muslims-account-for-a-fifth-of-all-u-s-muslims-and-about-half-are-converts-to-islam/

Muslim Association of Canada (MAC). (2021, July 19). *Proposal submission to the National Action Summit on Islamophobia.* https://www.macnet.ca/2021/07/19/proposal-submission-to-the-national-action-summit-on-islamophobia/

National Council of Canadian Muslims. (2021a). *Appendix: Formal submissions from community organizations.* https://www.nccm.ca/wp-content/uploads/2021/06/Appendix-NCCM_final.pdf

National Council of Canadian Muslims. (2021b). *NCCM recommendations: National Action Summit on Islamophobia.* https://www.nccm.ca/islamophobiasummit/

Nielsen, K. (2021, July 15). Cambridge mosque broken into, vandalized on Wednesday afternoon in 'act of hate.' *Global News.* https://globalnews.ca/news/8030471/cambridge-baitul-kareem-mosque-vandalism/

Nyang, S. S. (2004). Introduction. In Z. H. Bukhari, S. S. Nyang, M. Ahmad, & J. L. Esposito (Eds.), *Muslims' place in the American public square: Hopes, fears, and aspirations* (pp. xiv–xlii). Rowman & Littlefield.

Ontario Human Rights Commission. (2012). Discrimination experienced by Muslims in Ontario. *Diversity Magazine, 9*(3). http://www.ohrc.on.ca/en/creed-freedom-religion-and-human-rights-special-issue-diversity-magazine-volume-93-summer-2012/discrimination-experienced-muslims-ontario

Page, S.-J., & Shipley, H. (February 2021). Understanding young adult Muslim and Christian attitudes toward queer identity: A Canadian and UK comparison. *Sexualities.* Online First. https://doi.org/10.1177/1363460721995756

Perry, B. (2014). Gendered Islamophobia: Hate crime against Muslim women. *Social Identities: Journal for the Study of Race, Nation and Culture, 20*(1), 74–89. https://doi.org/10.1080/13504630.2013.864467

Perry, B. (2015). 'All of a sudden, there are Muslims': Visibilities and Islamophobic violence in Canada. *International Journal for Crime, Justice and Social Democracy, 4*(3), 4–15. https://doi.org/10.5204/ijcjsd.v4i3.235

Pew Research Center. (2011). *Region: Americas. The future of the global Muslim population.* https://www.pewforum.org/2011/01/27/future-of-the-global-muslim-population-regional-americas/

Pew Research Center. (2017a, July 26). *Demographic portrait of Muslim Americans.* https://www.pewforum.org/2017/07/26/demographic-portrait-of-muslim-americans/

Pew Research Center. (2017b, July 26). *Religious beliefs and practices.* https://www.pewforum.org/2017/07/26/religious-beliefs-and-practices/

Pew Research Center. (2021, July 29). *Quarterly update from the President* [email newsletter].

Postmedia News. (2013, May 8). *Survey shows Muslim population is fastest growing religion in Canada.* National Post. https://nationalpost.com/news/canada/survey-shows-muslim-population-is-fastest-growing-religion-in-canada

Pratt, D. (2005). *The challenge of Islam: Encounters in inter-faith dialogue*. Ashgate Publishers.

Rahmath, S., Chambers, L., & Wakewich, P. (2016). Asserting citizenship: Muslim women's experiences with the *hijab* in Canada. *Women's Studies International Forum, 58,* 34–40.

Rahnema, S. (2006). Islam in diaspora and the challenges to multiculturalism. In H. Moghissi (Ed.), *Muslim diaspora: Gender, culture, and identity* (pp. 23–38). Routledge Publishers.

Rockenbach, A. N., Mayhew, M. J., Bowman, N. A., Morin, S. M., & Riggers-Piehl, T. (2017). An examination of non-Muslim college students' attitudes toward Muslims. *The Journal of Higher Education, 88*(4), 479–504. https://doi.org/10.1080/00221546.20 16.1272329

Rodriguez, J. (2021, July 22). Canadian Muslims have doubt, cautious hope anti-Islamophobia summit will bring real change. *CTV News.* https://www.ctvnews.ca/canada/canadian-muslims-have-doubt-cautious-hope-anti-islamophobia-summit-will-bring-real-change-1.5519423

Safi, O. (2003). *Progressive Muslims: On justice, gender and pluralism*. Oneworld Academic.

Saleem, M., & Ramasubramanian, S. (2017). Muslim Americans' responses to social identity threats: Effects of media representations and experiences of discrimination. *Media Psychology, 22*(3), 373–393. https://doi.org/10.1080/15213269.2017.1302345

Shah, S. (2019). *Canadian Muslims: Demographics, discrimination, religiosity, and voting*. Institute of Islamic Studies, University of Toronto. http://hdl.handle.net/1807/96775

Shams, T. (2018). Visibility as resistance by Muslim Americans in a surveillance and security atmosphere. *Sociological Forum, 33*(1), 73–94. https://doi.org/10.1111/socf.12401

Sharify-Funk, M. (2008). *Encountering the transnational: Women, Islam and the politics of interpretation*. Ashgate Publishing, Ltd.

Sharify-Funk, M. (2010). Muslims and the politics of 'reasonable accommodation': Analyzing the Bouchard-Taylor report and its impact on the Canadian province of Québec. *Journal of Muslim Minority Affairs, 30*(4), 535–553. https://doi.org/10.1080/13 602004.2010.533451

Sharify-Funk, M. (2011). Governing the face veil: Québec's Bill 94 and the transnational politics of women's identity. *International Journal of Canadian Studies, 43*(Spring), 135–164.

Siddiqui, H. (2008). Muslims and the rule of law. In N. Bakht (Ed.), *Belonging and banishment: Being Muslim in Canada* (pp. 1–16). TSAR.

Statistics Canada. (2016). *Canadian Demographics at a Glance*. https://www150.statcan.gc.ca/n1/pub/91-003-x/2014001/section03/33-eng.htm

Terman, R. (2017). Islamophobia and media portrayals of Muslim women: A computational text analysis of US news coverage. *International Studies Quarterly, 61*(3), 489–502. https://doi.org/10.1093/isq/sqx051

The Environics Institute. (2016). *Survey of Muslims in Canada 2016: Final report*. https://www.environicsinstitute.org/docs/default-source/project-documents/survey-of-muslims-in-canada-2016/final-report.pdf?sfvrsn=fbb85533_2

Tiflati, H. (2017). Muslim youth between Quebecness and Canadianness: Religiosity, identity, citizenship, and belonging. *Canadian Ethnic Studies, 49*(1), 1–17. doi: 10.1353/ces.2017.0000

van Es, M. A. (2016). *Stereotypes and self-representations of women with a Muslim background: The stigma of being oppressed*. Palgrave Macmillan.

van Es, M. A. (2019). Muslim women as 'ambassadors' of Islam: Breaking stereotypes in everyday life. *Identities: Global Studies in Culture and Power, 26*(4), 375–392. https://doi.org/10.1080/1070289X.2017.1346985

van Nieuwkerk, K. (2014). 'Conversion' to Islam and the construction of a pious self. In L. R. Rambo, & C. E. Fahadian (Eds.), *The Oxford handbook of religious conversion* (pp. 667–686). Oxford University Press.

Welborne, B. C., Westfall, A. L., Russell, ÖÇ, & Tobin, S. A. (2018). *The politics of the headscarf in the United States.* Cornell University Press.

Zempi, I. (2016). 'It's a part of me, I feel naked without it': Choice, agency and identity for Muslim women who wear the niqab. *Ethnic and Racial Studies, 39*(10), 1738–1754. https://doi.org/10.1080/01419870.2016.1159710

Zine, J. (2022). *Under siege: Islamophobia and the 9/11 generation.* McGill-Queen's University Press.

Chapter 2

Living the Dialogical
Negotiating Identity and Meaning

At the end of the 20th century and the beginning of the 21st century, scholars of Islamic-Western relations, such as Fred Dallmayr and Roxanne L. Euben, have sought to reimagine religion in relation to social and political theory within a global, intercultural and inter-civilizational context, in ways that enhance understanding of transnational conversations concerning identity, values, worldview, and meaning. In contrast to scholars, like Samuel P. Huntington, who perceived religious and cultural differences primarily as a source of division and conflict, and in distinction from the approach of postcolonial theorists who maintain a pessimistic stance on the possibilities for fruitful cross-cultural dialogue in a world of power imbalances, scholars focusing on "dialogical" interactions across and between cultures have sought to create a new basis for empirical analysis as well as normative reflection. As a lens for empirical investigation, a dialogical approach takes note of tensions and asymmetries while also drawing attention to the complexity of cross-cultural interactions. In the process, dialogical analysis underscores dynamics that are also emphasized in the field of relational constructivism: Interactions across cultural boundaries are by no means merely collisions between static, oppositional entities; rather, they are infused with both conflict and cooperation, and have a profound impact on the way each party constructs identity and meaning. From a normative perspective, the "dialogical" construes these insights as a rationale for ruling out intellectual closure and metaphysical triumphalism for any particular worldview, knowledge system, or episteme. Rather than inviting closure, it highlights the potential for transformative and communicative interaction in which symbolic identity politics are suspended in favor of genuine effort to explore resonances *and* dissonances.

This book analyzes a range of different controversies shaping Muslim women through a dialogical lens to reveal complexities of religious, cultural, and political dynamics in contemporary North America. Without privileging the voice and worldview of either visible Muslims or their critics, this book seeks to shed light not only on common rhetorical claims concerning Islam and Muslims in America and Canada, but also on the diverse ways in

DOI: 10.4324/9780429341151-3

which different actors position themselves vis-à-vis cultural and intellectual conflicts, which are themselves shaped by collective fears, political calculations, and substantive value concerns. In the process, attention is drawn to the manner in which identities are being defined and redefined through ongoing, cross-cultural negotiations – a reality that need not lead only to negative, "us vs. them" contrasts. These negotiations have the potential to produce new syntheses within which cultural minorities and/or newcomers integrate values and symbols of their new home, and in which defenders of past North American cultural syntheses make space within their identities and worldviews for constructively engaging what was once regarded as irreconcilably "other."

This chapter is a preliminary investigation into the tendencies of the dialogical in Western-Islamic scholarship, which can be used to understand the complexity of identity construction that Muslim women in North America navigate and negotiate. In particular, this chapter analyzes and critiques specific themes and identifies major features of the "dialogical" as an outlook and as an approach to humanist and social scientific analysis. First, as connected to the emergence of relational thinking, this chapter explores how the term "dialogue" is experiencing a renaissance in contemporary scholarship of social and political theory. Then, it investigates the cross-cutting themes of the dialogical with cosmopolitanism and, lastly, explores the idea of the dialogical self as a composite of complementary contradictions.

The (re)turn toward the "dialogical" and relational understanding

Traditionally, social science inquiry has sought to reflect the natural sciences. In recent decades, however, alternative epistemological and methodological positions have emerged, offering new ways of interpreting human behavior and seeking social knowledge. Though the ensuing debates remain unresolved, a new ethos of epistemological and methodological pluralism has provided support to those who are asking new questions about the role of *meaning* in human endeavors: To what extent is social change driven by external conditions, and to what extent is it a religiously and culturally specific process? How do debates and dialogues within and across religions and cultures shape social practices? How do *texts*[1] – written words as well as humanly created codes and structures that give intelligible form to social life – define our collective existence? Are the social sciences also *human*, interpretive sciences? What does it mean to be a humanist social scientist? Are there social hermeneutics?[2]

In the late 20th century, one can witness in a variety of disciplines, from religious studies to sociology to international relations, a renaissance of "relational thinking" in social and political theory.[3] In such scholarship, social reality is no longer imagined in terms of static substances that constitute fundamental units of inquiry; rather it is a construction that is dynamic and continuous, with unfolding relations in which members are in constant negotiation over meaning. Society too is not a collection of autonomous-sovereign self-sustaining entities, but rather an intersectional web of diverse networks of social relations and temporal ideational processes.

The social ontology suggested by relational thinking has far-reaching implications for key analytical concepts. Rather than existing as a resource or currency possessed or held by key social actors, power instead emerges out of patterns of relations as well as conversations within the actors themselves. Human agency and social structure are seen as co-constituted, with a heightened awareness that humans are not merely objects or subjects of inquiry but intersubjective beings immersed in, saturated by, and negotiating with social meaning.[4] A key intention of those who advance these definitions is to "open" the humanities and social sciences in ways that invite reflexive and reflective understanding, and to foster a vision of social reality as an organic, interactive, and continually creative process rather than as a collection of cold, objective facts independent of the observer. In addition, several influential scholars have sought to utilize these understandings in ways that nurture new orientations and conversations in theory and method, such as cross-cultural scholarly dialogue that compares Western and non-Western understandings.

On the eve of the 21st century, Fred Dallmayr, an American philosopher and political theorist who is the Packey J. Dee Professor Emeritus in Political Science with a joint appointment in Philosophy at the University of Notre Dame, brought together scholars from around the world and from diverse religious and political traditions in an edited volume entitled, *Border Crossings* (1999). This volume was to "inaugurate or help launch a new field of academic inquiry": Comparative political theory (Dallmayr, 1999, p. 1). As stated by Dallmayr:

> In contemporary academia, comparative political theory or philosophy is either completely nonexistent or at best an embryonic and marginalized type of endeavor. As practiced in most Western universities, the study of political theory or philosophy involves basically the rehearsal of the 'canon' of Western political thought from Plato to Marx or Nietzsche... Only rarely are practitioners of political thought willing (and professionally encouraged) to transgress the canon, and thereby the cultural boundaries of North America and Europe, in the direction of genuine comparative investigations.
>
> (1999, pp. 1–2)

With six of the twelve chapters focusing on Islamic topics, Dallmayr's volume applies a comparative lens to shed light on different topics that have a bearing on contemporary Islamic-Western relations. In the process, he and his colleagues stress the necessity of thinking in the plural. As contributor

Hwa Yol Jung concludes, this ultimately means challenging any arrogant ethnocentrism, "whether it be Eurocentric, Sinocentric, Indocentric, or Afrocentric" (1999, p. 288). While enjoining "mutual interrogation, contestation, and lateral engagement," Dallmayr and the contributing scholars of this volume offer an example of a form of inquiry that the late Raimon Panikkar (d. 2010) would term as "imparative" (instead of comparative) – an approach to scholarship centered in mutual learning, and that is not "imperative" or "commanding" from one particular perspective (1999, p. 2). As reflected in one of the concluding statements of the volume, stated by Hwa Yol Jung, a globalized search for truth(s) within "the context of postmodernity":

> [...] is the result of a cross-cultural intertwinement or chiasm in which one culture can no longer be a 'negative mirror' of another... [T]he question [is] not merely of discovering a Plato, an Aristotle, a Machiavelli, a Descartes, a Kant, or a Hegel in the non-Western world but also of finding a Confucius, a Mencius, a Nishida, a Watsuji, a Hu, a Tagore, or a Radhakrishnan in the West.
>
> (1999, p. 288)

For the purposes of this book, in this ever-growing field of comparative social and political theory, one finds a "hermeneutic (re)turn" to the concept of *the dialogical*. Ever since Plato began recording his reflections on the teachings of Socrates, "dialogue" has been a constant fixture in not only the human society but also the academy. All of Socrates' and Plato's knowledge was conveyed through the form of dialogue. Searching for knowledge and wisdom through direct, person-to-person encounters was the purpose of dialogue. Socrates and Plato set a precedent that, though often celebrated, has seldom been perceived as an epistemological or methodological model. Even in the humanities and social sciences, the "Socratic method" is more often viewed as a teaching device (whereby the "learned" professor tests the knowledge of students) than as an actual means of knowing or being. For Socrates, however, dialogue was a means of bringing the search for knowledge into everyday life through conversation and constantly being "in-relation" *with* others.[5] Contrary to a popular misconception, the meaning of *dia-* in the word dialogue is "with" rather than "through"; thus, to be in dialogue is to be "in relation." When dialogue becomes more of an epistemological stance than a simple technique or posture, the understanding of knowledge itself begins to change – from a more or less static commodity that can be accumulated to a dynamic pursuit of wisdom and transformation in relation with the self and others. From a deeply Socratic perspective, the pursuit of meaning, or *logos*, becomes a constant process of construction and negotiation within the context of relationships.[6] No matter how different the understandings of self and other, the implicit emphasis is on the relationships of those differences and how they create conversation and, ultimately, wisdom.

Even though dialogue can be seen as the root of most intellectual traditions (i.e., for it is in the act of dialoguing that knowledge claims are to be questioned rather than blindly accepted), it is fascinating that a dialogical epistemology is only recently finding more salience in North American and European scholarship.[7] Notably, since the beginning of the 21st century, there has been a growing body of comparative social and political theorists in North America, like Dallmayr, who are pointing to the significance of the dialogical when it comes to contemporary Western-Islamic relations and "the global village."[8]

The dialogical has permeated through Dallmayr's scholarship, as reflected in such works as, *Dialogue among Civilizations* (2002) and *Being in the World* (2013). In these books and others, he emphasizes the importance of global interconnectedness and dialogical understanding. He rejects intellectual isolationism and seeks enrichment and solidarity through constructive engagement with "Western" (e.g., German philosophical hermeneuticists) and "non-Western" (e.g., Muslim and Confucian philosophical scholars) intellectual traditions. In the process, he brings new interpreters and texts within the purview of his original intellectual tradition and subverts tendencies toward insularity and confrontation.

Gleaning from Martin Heidegger's and Hans Georg Gadamer's thoughts on "dialogical hermeneutics," Dallmayr reflects on the significance of understanding the intricacies of "being-with," which recognizes that we are all products of "symbiotic" relationships *between* tradition and modernity, *between* global and local, *between* West and East.[9] This relational symbiosis is the act of living together in a more intimate association or close union of dissimilar otherness, whether temporal or spatial. This open-ended nature of dialogue works against intellectual closure, and stresses that no one has definitive or final answers. Rather, as aptly summarized by Dallmayr:

> [...] dialoguing here involves not only an act of questioning but also the experience of being questioned or being "called into question" – often in unsettling and disorienting ways. The openness of dialoguing means precisely the readiness of participants to allow themselves to be "addressed" and challenged by the other: particularly the stranger, the different, the exile... Hence... dialogical understanding as the 'true locus of hermeneutics' always hovers in the 'in-between': between self and other, familiarity and strangeness, presence and absence.
>
> (2002, p. 27)

Transcending the bifurcation of the world based in *static, separated, preconceived* concepts of self and other, dialogical thinking encourages more organic awareness of a pluralized identity as an ever-changing whole with endless frontiers (Dallmayr, 2010, pp. 2–8).

Dallmayr's idea of "being-with," which he would later connect with the concept of "integral pluralism,"[10] regards the other's texts and contexts as sources of knowing that must be interpreted in a dialogical manner; in so doing, an opening is created for those moments of understanding that Gadamer described with the phrase, "fusion of horizons."[11] When arrived at through shared inquiry into common problems of human existence, such a hermeneutic process can develop a sense of common, inclusive identity across cultural boundaries. Self and other become a nexus rather than a dichotomy – a dynamic relationship that is influenced but not fixed by past assumptions and understandings. The process of inquiry shifts from an insular and retrospective justification of the self toward an open and prospective attitude toward the self-other relationship.

In E. Ilieva's critique of Dallmayr, she points out that "the attention shifts to questioning and remaining open to being questioned (be it by the text or by another person)". She then adds, "the openness of dialogue implies that we also expose ourselves to suffering... we risk our prejudices, we risk critique, and we risk being misunderstood" (Ilieva, 2015, p. 24). Accounting for one's own experience of self in relation to others is ultimately allowing the other to be with and in one's own existential and social being, creating a fluidity of being and experience that is not bound by particular borders of alterity.

Similar reflections are found in Xavier Guillaume's text, *International Relations and Identity* (2014), in which he too explores the significance of the dialogical in the context of identity formation within the continuous processes of alterity:

> Dialogue is a way for the self to avoid the condition of "splitting," but it is up to the self to locate the "other within" through a moment of sympathy, of co-suffering with the other. The responsibility to the other, to difference, is crucial as oppression 'seems to depend on evading or refusing the call to find in the other a source of critical self-reflection'.
>
> (p. 41)

This imperative of being aware of the "co-suffering with the other" is what distinguishes the dialogical form of relational thinking. As will be discussed in the following chapters, the many divisive controversies shaping contemporary Muslim women's experiences in North America consistently create and reinforce distinct binaries of different selves and others. When these binaries and oppositions are taken to be more real and important than human connections and existential commonalities, there is a lack of recognition in the complexity of suffering as a relational experience:

> Dialogic criticism and intercultural dialogue should therefore offer ways to comprehend self/other relations by looking at the "other" as an equal that is different, as an alter-ego. The self should strive to recognize in

difference the suffering for which it might be responsible... Recognition of the other's suffering and of the self's responsibility is a pre-condition for fulfilling a dialogic situation that requires the self to transcend the alienation and denial... [created by] othering....

(Guillaume, 2014, p. 41)

Self-responsibility connected to the experience of "co-suffering" is also what makes dialogical social theory a distinct form of relational thinking. There is a recognition of personal meaning in the other's truth: Meaning that ultimately cannot be evaded without a deepening rupture between self and other, and an exacerbation of conflict.

Such interdependent conceptions of self and other have profound consequences. For example, Guillaume's dialogical call to appreciate the difference of the other and thereby practice responsibility for the self is a challenge both to classical and "post-modern" international relations theory and epistemology.[12] In contrast to both positivist and post-structuralist perspectives on the notion that "knowledge is power," scholars such as Guillaume perceive knowledge as something that must be created or co-constituted through dialogue of self and other. For these dialogical thinkers, knowledge for human agency is derivative of relationships – of dialogical ways of knowing, being, and doing. Power is not something one can own, control, or possess in a binary opposition; rather it emerges as a manifestation of complex relationships which symbiotically reconstruct self and other.

A dialogical approach enables us to study the relations between a multitude of potential and possible articulations of an identity in order to see how, across time, emerging hegemonic collective political identities, as well as their alternatives, are in continuous transaction with alterity and among themselves. These transactions cannot only be considered through binaries and dichotomies.

(p. 138)

In a chapter entitled "Unveiling the International," Guillaume reflects on what he calls the "French veil affair" and the relevance of understanding identity dialogically. By highlighting the complexity of understandings connected to the Muslim *hijab* (the female Muslim headscarf) and questions of French citizenship, he emphasizes the need for scholarship of the international that is "intersecting, multiple, and overlapping," stressing the rationale for "process-based approaches over a substantialist conceptualization" (2014, pp. 142–143). Such scholarship helps to redefine the international and identity by reimagining power as "not something one possesses but a constellation of relations in which one is enmeshed" (2014, p. 139). Also, that social phenomenon is too complex and nuanced to be conceptualized as "static units";

rather, ongoing transformation is inherent within the construction of social reality. Thus, for Guillaume, knowledge is "process-based" with an inherent dynamism in which self and other are not static entities but living, complex conversations.

Dallmayr and Guillaume then would likely agree that a dialogical perspective on intergroup relations can enhance understanding of how the worldviews and authority structures of groups change over time, based on how each group "reads" a communal canon. Groups that are bonded by a strong sense of communal identity (whether, religious, tribal, or ethnonational) constitute these bonds in no small part through the development of an intertextual fabric of interpretations and understandings, from which the group identity is woven and symbolized. This fabric of interpretations, however, is not static and can change over time. More profound encounters among members of different groups can help to overcome solipsistic tendencies, and shed light on the likelihood that ideational exchange has been occurring across cultural boundaries, in a manner that likely contravenes assumptions about a sharply bounded, non-porous communal identity.

By rejecting the idea of a past, "pure" state – "untainted" by contact with the other – a dialogical perspective supports a more dynamic reading of collective identity and societal values, according to which new and changing contexts impact the interpretation of core communal texts. Because interpretation can never be fixed and is responsive to changing contexts, a principled openness to others – and even to the ways in which these others read one's own communal canon – can provide new experiences and insights. Ethnocentric contextuality that preserves or reinforces boundaries is not the objective of the dialogical; rather it aspires toward innovative intercultural understandings that open identity to ever new experiences of the self and other. Although political and communal authority has often been derived in no small part through practices of exclusion and boundary maintenance, social movements that seek to include others can generate new patterns of meaning that correspond with inclusion, and with forms of authority that are predicated on this value. Creating dynamic, shared meaning across cultural contexts can form the basis to confront shared problems.

Abdul Aziz Said (d. 2021), former occupant of the Mohamed Said Farsi Chair of Islamic Peace at American University, in *The Dialogue of Healing*, states that, "shared meaning is the foundation of the social whole we seek to heal.[13] To heal the 'social' is to reinvigorate the ability of individuals to be capable of the act of unity through logos. In other words, *we find meaning through each other*" (Said, 2003, p. 2). For Said, the dialogical is a means to reimagine social reality as a flow of meaning permeating throughout self and other, in which communal and cultural understandings are constantly under reflection and negotiation. It is this dynamic renewal of meaning that enables creative rethinking of societal norms and practices. To support his musings, Said later quotes from *On Dialogue* (1990) by David Bohm,

> [Bohm] defines dialogue as, "…a stream of meaning flowing among and through us and between us. This will make possible a flow of meaning in the whole group, out of which will emerge some new understanding. It's something new, which may not have been at the starting point at all. It is something creative. And this shared meaning is the 'glue' or 'cement' that holds people and societies together.
>
> (p. 6)

As the malleable "glue," the dialogical to Said is also the means to question our own understandings and interpretations as well as assumptions. In being in-relation, we ultimately are constantly reflecting on our past assumptions and whether they "no longer serve us or reflect our emerging shared values, goals, or ideals" (2003, pp. 3–4).

In the edited volume, *Contemporary Islam* (2006),[14] Said, Abu-Nimer, and Sharify-Funk describe the dialogical as an affirmative means to complexify the living relations between the communal conceptions of "Muslims and Westerners." In particular, the authors emphasize how new meaning needs to be sought out in their "common tragedy of estrangement" and through reconsidering "traditional ways of construing values in dichotomous terms – i.e., 'individualism vs. community,' 'reason vs. passion,' 'science vs. faith,' 'materialism vs. spirituality,' 'efficiency vs. hospitality,' 'freedom to do vs. freedom to be'" (2006, p. 7). Ultimately, by arguing that Islamic-Western realities have never been "out of relationship," it is a way to reimagine the solipsistic as well as ethnocentric tendencies found "in-relationship."

The dialogical and cosmopolitanism

In addition to recognizing the fluidity of knowledge and identity construction, Dallmayr, Guillaume, and Said point out that the dialogical is fundamentally connected to an analytical perception, on the one hand, and a normative prescription, on the other. First, a deep analysis of dynamics of interaction between parties reveals linkages of interdependence and mutual influence at the level of social meaning. Second, given the manner in which interpretations of and orientations toward the other shape relations, efforts to evoke "good will" on the part of both the self and the other can be vital for constructive social relations based on sound perceptions and understandings. While some realist and postcolonial sceptics would be wary of such normative prescriptions in social and political theory, Dallmayr, in particular, argues that the dialogical challenges the fear of normative prescription by evoking Gadamer's use of *"eumeneis elenchoi"* – a concept found in the works of Plato which is defined as "the hermeneutical attitude of openness, of acknowledging that we may have something to learn from the other" (Ilieva, 2015, p. 24).[15]

"Hermeneutics of openness" implies an attitude of humility and not knowing the totality of reality. In other words, reality is too vast and multifaceted to understand exhaustively and completely, and even the diversity of meanings within a single text or social context is open to multiple interpretations. Despite these limitations, exposure to multiple perspectives and angles of vision has the potential to generate new learning from any given text or context. To access a potential epistemological benefit from multiple perspectives, however, humility is required. To this basic openness of humility, some dialogical thinkers have also added an attitude of affirmation, embracing the open-endedness of knowledge itself within a reality that never ceases to reveal new aspects of itself to those who engage in collaborative inquiry. Some might call this "affirmation (not negation) of a perpetual beginner" and/or embracing "the child of the moment" – always seeking the mystery (the unknown) which is never solved but has never-ending possibilities to explore.

The "dialogical" ultimately begins with recognition of complexity, both in the world and in the textual sources of moral guidance for navigating the world. Typically, this recognition arises in combination with an apprehension that the assumptions behind solipsistic understandings of self and other may be too comfortable to be true. What follows is a sincere effort to counteract misperceptions and potential double standards, according to which one expounds an ethical principle while failing to uphold it consistently, at the very least in the eyes of those whose position in the world affords a different angle of vision. Recognizing that experiences, perceptions, and insights differ in accordance with the positionality of self and other leads to questioning moral self-images and immoral other-images, and allows space for refined perceptions that are closer to reality. To arrive at such a recognition, however, one must put brakes on habits of contrasting one's own cultural ideal (be it "freedom" or "faith") with the other's practice. In other words, the act of the dialogical is to orient oneself toward "the good" in relation to the self and the other. As reflected by Dallmayr,

> [...] the prevalent global discourse is a discourse of the market and, to some extent, a discourse of science, technology, and the media. What is lacking is a discourse about deeper existential and practical-moral concerns: a discourse about the meaning structure of the global village, about proper modes of living and sharing together, or about what Aristotle called the 'good life.' To this extent, our time is suffering from a global 'cultural lag'.
>
> (1999, p. 1)

Roxanne L. Euben, a Professor of Political Science at Wellesley College, has also emphasized the importance of inviting normative reflection within a context of dialogue and relationship. Her writings recognize that interpretive dialogue across cultural boundaries makes it possible for members of different communities to not only challenge notions of self and other, but also to rediscover their own traditions from a dynamic perspective. By questioning predominant interpretations and seeking ways of understanding that accommodate present realities and truths revealed through external criticisms, practitioners of the dialogical allow their texts to speak to new contexts. In the process, they gain access to more sympathetic readings of other cultural systems, in ways that permit a rediscovery of the self – and of textual foundations of self-identity – within a broader and more inclusive framework of knowledge. Though this need not mean sacrificing one's own original textual loyalties and communal affiliations, at a minimum it does require more "inter-contextual" habits of reading: Reading other contexts and experiences into one's realities, rather than out of them.

Euben started exploring such ideas of the dialogical in her book, *Enemy in the Mirror* (1999a). Similar to Guillaume and his analysis of the controversial French veil affair, Euben also engages with the divisive and often polarized worlds of opposing fundamentalisms – whether Islamic or Western. In doing so, she posits the following questions: What are the limitations (as well as projections) of modern Western rationalist analyses of Islamic fundamentalism? What can interpretive analyses of Islamic fundamentalist discourses tell us about the "blind spots" of modern Western rationalist analysis, and about the motivations and ideas of fundamentalists – whether Islamic or Western? To explore answers to these questions, Euben utilizes a "dialogic model of interpretation" which orients her comparative social and political inquiry with the assumption that truth cannot be monopolized and must concomitantly enable "an openness to other meanings" (1999a, pp. 36–37). Like Dallmayr, she gleans from Gadamer's often used idea of dialogue as a "fusion of horizons":

> Given the limits of rationalist explanations [...], a dialogic model of interpretation may be usefully employed to generate a "better" understanding of fundamentalism... Abandoning the notion of a neutral observer is simultaneously an abandonment of a positivist epistemology that sustains a conception of understanding as discovering the objective and final truth. Instead, understanding comes to be seen as a dialogue between two horizons of meaning, neither of which can claim a monopoly on truth.
>
> (Euben, 1999a, p. 36)

For Euben and others, neutrality is not an option in dialogue; rather there is an insistence of being aware of one's own biases in order for the experience of otherness to occur and (ultimately) relate to the truth of the other. Euben argues for dialogical understanding then challenges the rationalist analyses of "The West and the Rest" and "Us vs. Them" in which scholars of social and political theory have created a divide, "a clash," or as she says, a "historical antagonism" of opposing identities between Western, rational, secular, universalistic, and modern perspectives (connected to such concepts as democracy, individualism, human rights, free markets, equality, etc.) and putatively Eastern, irrational, "Oriental," particularistic, and archaic perspectives (connected to such concepts as vicegerency, hierarchy, tradition, etc.).

Euben concludes by arguing that "a dialogic approach does not entail relinquishing standards of objectivity, but rather the rejection of positivist standards of objectivity in favor a view of understanding as a reciprocal, transformative, and, perhaps above all, ongoing process" (1999a, p. 157). In disaggregating the concept of fundamentalism and the different manifestations of it in Islamic-Western relations, Euben calls for a transcultural discussion on modernity and an understanding of comparative epistemologies and political ideologies. Ultimately, she also argues for "multiple-modernities" by acknowledging the different ways of understanding modernity.[16]

Additionally, Euben also explores the relationship between the dialogical and the development of theory. To this end, she evoked ancient meanings of the word "theory" to preface and frame her comparative approach to political theory:

> Theory at… [the time of ancient Greeks] connoted the act of observing, seeing, witnessing; more particularly a theorist (*theoros*) was, as Sheldon Wolin describes it, 'a public emissary dispatched by his city to attend the religious festivals of other Greek cities.' Over time, 'theory' was linked to observation of different and often alien lands, institutions, and practices, a journey that not only produced knowledge of other political worlds, but also 'could eventually issue in a critical sense toward the particularity, even arbitrariness of [one's] own culture and stimulate a drive to find higher unity or reality beneath the particularity of appearances, whether in nature, being or human nature.' This suggests that theory was and still is an inherently comparative enterprise at least in part because it is through comparisons that we are led to question the 'naturalness' of our own perspective. Such questioning both presupposes and makes possible a critical distance toward everyday practices, a distance crucial to self-knowledge, learning about others, and making sense of the world in general.
>
> (Euben, 1999a, p. 11)

Once again, an "attitude of openness" which shifts or questions the "naturalness" of the familiar is present not only in Dallmayr, Guillaume, and Said but also Euben's approach, and informs the manner of relating to, analyzing, and understanding patterns of social thought (and in the case of Euben, patterns that are present in Islamic fundamentalism and modern Western rationalism).

Interest in the dialogical and the deeper meaning of *theoria* inspired Euben to articulate her understanding of these terms in more detail in another text, *Journeys to the Other Shore* (2008). In it, Euben explores in more depth the Greek practice of *theoros* and examines the imperative that "the acquisition of knowledge requires not detachment from the world but movement in and through it" (2008, p. 23). Through historical cases, she finds that this dialogical approach has enabled Muslim and Western travelers (e.g., Ibn Battuta and de Tocqueville) to experience disclosures as well as closures in self, society, and humanity as a whole.

In *Journeys to the Other Shore*, Euben also reflects on the act of dialoguing as a means to help in constructing what she calls a "new cosmopolitanism," which she defines as "a protean category that at the very least signals an attempt to rethink the scope and scale of moral and political obligations among human beings whose identities and loyalties are no longer coextensive with the modern nation-state" (2008, p. 175). In painting a picture of Islamic and Western travelers who sought to understand "foreign" cultures of unfamiliarity while experiencing critical distancing from all that was familiar, Euben discovers the imaginary world of these travelers and their sense of belonging to the world as global citizens rather than just their "native" lands. She concludes her book by reclaiming the cosmopolitan from the clutches of imperial powers, and reconnecting to the original Greek meaning of the word, "citizen of the world."

Euben's connections between the dialogical and the ancient concept of the "cosmopolitan," or "citizen of the world," are also present in works of other scholars. Like dialogical theory, "cosmopolitanism" has also had a renaissance in North American scholarship on Islamic-Western relations in the early 21st century.[17] In one of his later works, *Being in the World* (2013), Dallmayr elaborates on the relationship between dialogue and cosmopolitanism, and actually coins the concept "dialogical cosmopolitanism":

> [In] the absence of a homogenous global community, [our situation] mandates the resort to an interactive or dialogical cosmopolitanism. Such an interactive approach involves multiple forms of border-crossing – between self and other, familiarity and unfamiliarity – with the aim not of excluding or annihilating, but of "befriending the stranger." This notion of befriending or cross-cultural friendship stands in stark contrast to the dominant global "politics of fear," which, in essence, is anchored in the assumption of radical interhuman enmity.
>
> (2013, p. 5)

Dallmayr prefers to use the term "dialogical cosmopolitanism" rather than "dialogical universalism" in order to avoid any "liberal" aspirations that have been associated with the limitations of past historical practices, within which particular "Western" solutions to problems of politics and social reform were regarded as universal, and in which genuine encounters with non-Western voices and cultures were precluded.

By employing "dialogical cosmopolitanism" as a framework for transforming human relations, Dallmayr ultimately is pointing out that power *with* the other is a far more promising way forward in Western-Islamic relations than power *over* an "alien" culture. Ideally, such egalitarian cultural engagement should not merely be an elite endeavor, but rather a more broadly participatory process in which members of estranged cultures reread and rediscover their respective texts, traditions, and motivations. Rather than focus primarily on the negative task of debunking stereotypes (as these distorted images manifest in tendencies of Orientalism and its opposite, Occidentalism), dialogical cosmopolitanism seeks to develop new, mutual understandings on a shared complementary basis.

Dialogical understandings from Dallmayr and other scholars can significantly reframe ways of understanding how the world is organized. In conventional international relations thinking, Guillaume has observed, "questions of identity and citizenship are generally situated among states, or in relation to an inside (the citizens) and outsiders of the sovereign state (immigrants)" (2011, p. 141). The result is a static, binary conception that neglects dynamics associated with the fluidity of meaning between and within communities. From a dialogical perspective, however, "citizenship can be treated as a constellation of symbolic representations defining who, how, and why one should belong to an imagined social and political community" (2011, p. 141). Going beyond purely legal and state-centered concepts of citizenship, Guillaume seeks to highlight how the *meaning* of citizenship is negotiated over time, such that particular minority communities within a national state might come to be regarded as somehow less legitimate members of the political community than members of other groups. Similarly, the same political community might define the meaning of its corporate identity, and of the normative identities of individual citizens, through certain understandings of both internal and external "others."

Additionally, the dialogical, according to Dallmayr and Euben, is not premised on the idea that one needs to abandon particularism or preference for the value system of one's own community. All that is necessary is recognition that developing a realistic and constructive relationship with the other is impossible without dynamism and *cultural empathy*: The ability to suspend one's own frame of reference long enough to enter and experience the other's world of values, experiences, and meanings. In doing so, one is aware of the inevitability of experiencing the other's world and how that experience in turn influences one's own understandings (Dallmayr, 2013).[18]

In the context of Western-Islamic relations, both Dallmayr and Euben are suggesting that cultural rivalry is not the result of cultural "essences" but rather of political and cultural relations inspired by solipsistic rather than eth-norelative tendencies. Ultimately, although obsession with viscerally evoc-ative symbols and slogans at the expense of disciplined analysis has led to a polarization of identities, the present impasse need not be understood as inevitable or final. If dialogue were preferred to coercive measures, areas of shared meaning might be found.

As will be reflected in Chapter 3, dialogical thinking also recognizes that, in the mirrors of our solipsistic Western and Islamic imaginations, stereo-typical representations of the other are often used to comfort or flatter us, in ways that proclaim our own advancement and virtue, and the other's com-parative primitiveness and moral lassitude. Such imaginings provide us with a sense of boundaries within which we can pull ourselves together and create a semblance of inner unity by symbolically exiling qualities we attribute to the other. Others provide us with ways of defining ourselves and asserting a collective sense of selfhood. They can create a useful foil, and even ways of diverting attention from conflict among members of the in-group by evok-ing fear or condemnation of a familiar out-group. Through processes that psychologists define as externalization and projection, they help us to live with blessed illusions and even with lies.

Whenever we slide into the consciousness of solipsistic thinking – that is, of preoccupation with our own particular experience and story, particu-larly at times when fresh input from and about the other is needed – we find that it is remarkably easy to become fixated on "either/or" value dichoto-mies that split the world into opposing camps. This occurs first by positing two "pure," abstract qualities, and then by elevating one quality above its presumed opposite. As a result, important aspects of human experience (in the case of "the West," spirituality, faith, contentment and quiescence, and in the case of "the world of Islam," materiality, science, ambition, and creative dynamism) are denied or repressed, and regarded largely as distin-guishing characteristics of the other. In the absence of effort to investigate and reclaim denigrated values, the putative virtues of each culture become narrow and limiting.

To escape such an interpretive cul-de-sac, the dialogical suggests that we need to provide a voice for the other in the process of understanding our-selves, our world, and even our most cherished values and texts. Attempting to account for the authentic experiences and perspectives of the other has the potential not just to correct cultural and communal blind spots, but also to expand ideas about what a community is or might become. Communal identities – be they national, ethnic, or religious – are never fully formed, and can always be rewoven in ways that include new claims and insights. Because it is such a valuable corrective to selective perceptions and moti-vated biases, input from the other can enhance the way we see the world, adding depth to the field of vision in a manner akin to stereoscopic vision. Perceiving the world in such a manner, however, may require a shift on the basis of authority from exclusion to inclusion, and willingness to adopt a more porous sense of boundaries and identity that permits enrichment by the other.

Clearly, the dialogical offers a vigorous counterpoint to the hubris and disdain associated with triumphalist conceptions of innate cultural superiority. Rather than pit one cultural context against another through self-versus-other value dichotomies, it seeks points of convergence and complementarity. In other words, it seeks to counteract the distortion and devaluation of presumably "alien" traits without seeking to stigmatize or deconstruct ideas of patterned cultural difference.

As previously mentioned, one way in which the dialogical can seek understanding is by reframing the value oppositions that have long colored Western representations of Islamic cultural reality, such as "science vs. obscurantism," "progress vs. stagnation," "individuality vs. conformism," "democracy vs. authoritarianism," "liberty vs. tyranny," and "civilization vs. barbarism." Such oppositions incline their adherents to locate virtue in the West and vice in the East, just as a contrary set of oppositions (e.g., "religious values vs. materialism," "faith vs. infidelity," "traditional authority vs. egocentrism," "self-restraint vs. self-indulgence," "community vs. chaos") emerges in an Islamic context when the subject of cultural relations with the West arises.

Hwa Yol Jung[19] in Dallmayr's edited volume, *Border Crossings*, points out the necessity to distill new meaning by embracing our complexity of difference and being "wary of 'ethnocentric chauvinism'… and 'faceless universalism'." He continues by stating,

> For it is the result of cross-cultural intertwinement or chiasm in which one culture can no longer be the 'negative mirror' of another. As differentiation is thoroughly relational… hermeneutics in search of lateral or cross-cultural universals must be truly 'cosmopolitan' (cosmopolitical) nature, of the new 'Orient of the mind'… which allows the fusion of horizons both temporal (past/old and present/new) and cultural (Western and non-Western) to take place, i.e., cosmopolitanism or cosmopolitics, which incorporates difference…. [Harmonization]… – like making music together – is not inimical to difference; it *is* rather the play of difference(s), of heterogeneity, not of homogeneity. […] The confluential humanism of postmodernity… exists only in the lateral relationships of all cultures including emerging ones in which the echoes of each awaken and are resonant with the others.
>
> (p. 288)

Jung, like Dallmayr, Guillaume, Euben, and Said, is acknowledging there are no dichotomies and yet there is (com)possibility that humans are characterized by all of their relations making the world a place of pluralized selves who can ultimately exist together.

Self and other as a dynamic composite
of complementary contradictions

Although identity is often construed as something static and stable, the scholarly perspectives explored thus far in this chapter propose that identities are continually subject to ongoing negotiation and reinterpretation – even when social actors believe that they are asserting a way of being in the world that is deeply rooted in history. Rather than reify identities by uncritically accepting the self-representations of individuals and groups, dialogical scholars examine identities in relationship and in motion. Instead of categorical certainties evoked by simple labels, these scholars see both continuity and change in the hermeneutics and politics of identity, and observe ways in which self-knowledge and other-knowledge transform together within a process of dialogical relationship. Though a sense of similar themes evades these writings on the dialogical, each author's narrative suggested that identity cannot easily be "boxed." To the contrary, identity is a complex, dynamic composite of multiple relational elements and currents, including aspects that are existential, cultural, social, political, economic, and educational, just to name a few.

Conceiving of identity in open, dynamic, and relational terms can be challenging, yet it has become a major issue in contemporary Islamic thought. Precisely to the extent that such an approach can undermine a sense of closure, certainty, and integration, it can be psychologically uncomfortable and inimical to the narrower and more exclusive formulations of identity that are preferred by many social actors in times of rapid change and political contestation – particularly within communities that have experienced marginality or colonial imposition. Tendencies to understand the past through a settled, tightly woven, and highly coherent narrative also generate resistance to acknowledging ways in which a particular communal experience has always existed in relationship with other communities and experiences. In many respects, new strands of contemporary Islamic interpretation are concerned precisely with this challenge of reimagining and rediscovering the past, and with recognizing plural voices and interpretations within a historical intellectual experience that has often been represented in monolithic confessional terms. To the extent that colonial and postcolonial experiences have produced a tendency to either "reflect or reject" the West while defining the essence of Islamic experience (Said et al., 2006, p. 6), the task has been rendered all the more difficult and politically sensitive. Acknowledging this dynamic, however, is an essential step toward taking a more encompassing view of the conditions under which Islamic interpretation proceeds, and for reviewing Islamic intellectual history with greater openness to past syntheses and visions that are compatible with self-reflexive and pluralistic thinking.

Just as Euben and Dallmayr have questioned overly simplistic understandings of "the West" and of its potential relationships with other cultural and civilizational traditions, so too have many Muslim intellectuals sought to transcend the notion that a singular and definitive Islamic discourse can appropriately circumscribe contemporary or premodern Muslim identities. To this end, they have embraced engagement with global conversations, seeking bases for maintaining "open intellectual horizons." Some have gone so far as to invite a "multiplex epistemology" and "open ontology" (Senturk, 2001, p. 101) – that is, a more complex vision of the world that can accommodate different kinds of truths, including the truths of modern physical, social, and human sciences as well as those of premodern and traditional metaphysical beliefs. A dialogical approach to understanding not only allows for the sharing of perspectives across diverse intellectual communities, but also allows space for metaphysical questions in which sacred meaning is sought amid cultural, historical, social, and political relations. Though inadmissible in some global and Western secularist discourses, questions of sacred meaning are integral to specifically religious worldviews and essential Islamic communal understandings. As articulated by Dallmayr and Euben, a dialogical approach to understanding the world's religions and cultures in relation to one another necessarily involves digging more deeply into historical intellectual traditions. The process of comparative social and political thought is necessarily connected to dialogue with past thinkers who shaped the horizons of a given community.

Significantly, a dialogical epistemology and worldview enables efforts to heal historical ruptures – within as well as between communities – and privileges past intellectual contributions that are particularly well suited to this task. Although eager to find points of connection across differences, dialogical scholarship cannot afford to bypass powerful contemporary voices who underscore the need for postcolonial and decolonial thinking, by centering experiences of harm caused by uneven power relations, discrimination, identity loss, and racism (Dallmayr, 1996, 2004).[20] At the same time, dialogical thinking also seeks to root responses to present realities deeply in affirmative historical visions, by accessing internal resources that enable the manifestation of a tradition's own "particular universalism" (Said & Funk, 2004) that have the potential to resonate profoundly across the boundaries of race, religion, culture, and nationality. Such visions invite reflection on transformational possibilities and potential for peaceful change.

In their search for underappreciated historical figures with visions that are expansive enough to bridge divides among contemporary Muslims as well as between Muslims and other religious and cultural communities, contemporary Muslim intellectuals have turned to a number of different exemplars. Recognizing the destructive nature of the divide between traditionalist and revivalist formulations of Islam, some have sought to reinvigorate scholarship on Abu Hamid al-Ghazali, the great 12th-century jurist and philosopher who sought to bridge and integrate orthodox and mystical formulations of Islam.[21] Explicitly Arab nationalist Muslim thinkers have often turned their attention in another direction, to the contributions of Ibn Rushd (d. 1198), an Arab Andalusian philosopher whose intellectual contributions were particularly influential among European thinkers seeking renewed appreciation for Aristotle and for bases of naturalistic and scientific thinking (Abu Zayd, 2005; al-Jabri, 1999; Bano, 2020). Another thinker whose value has been recognized by a growing number of contemporary thinkers is Ibn Rushd's contemporary, the Andalusia-born mystical philosopher and metaphysician Muhyi ad-din Ibn al-'Arabi (d. 1240) who developed a synthesis of Sufi thought that had a profound impact on Muslim cultures for many centuries, while also shaping discourse on Islamic theology, philosophy, cosmology, psychology, and other pre-modern sciences. Although best known among scholars who have specialized in Islamic mysticism (e.g., Chittick, 1989, 1998; Chodkiewicz, 1993, 2004; Corbin, 1969), appreciation for Ibn al-'Arabi's dynamic and encompassing worldview has been cited with increasing frequency among scholars disillusioned with simple, binary thinking about "self" and "other," as well as in ecumenical, interfaith contexts and discourses on modernity (e.g., Coates, 2002).

There are numerous reasons for the renewed attention to Ibn al-'Arabi. One reason pertains to the breadth and internal diversity of Ibn al-'Arabi's thinking, which became "a conciliation between theological, philosophical and mystical parameters" (De Cillis, 2014, p. 168). Another reason can be found in analogies between the turbulence Ibn al-'Arabi was forced to navigate in his own times and the unsettled character of contemporary social and political realities. He too lived in an age of uncertainty in which efforts to reinforce conservative understandings, boundaries, and differences were prevalent. Yet in response to others who sought to construe Islam in narrow, exclusive, and reductionist terms, he offered an encyclopedic synthesis that supported not just mystical communion with the divine and recognition of the diversity of Islamic thought but also identification with creatures of the broader natural world and with the diverse religious other.

Many aspects of the dialogical that have been previously discussed are also present in Ibn al-'Arabi's writings. Similar to dialogical thinkers in the early 21st century, Ibn al-'Arabi lived in an age of great divides between different schools of epistemological thought (most notably, rationalists and traditionalists) and promoted what we might call a "hermeneutics of openness" to multiple ways of knowing. Within his overarching epistemological stance, he gave special importance to experience and to ways of knowing that have an affinity to phenomenology – a key theme underscored in dialogical thinking (Godrej, 2017). Another common thread is the emphasis on human potential present in Ibn al-'Arabi's worldview, expressed in terms of spiritual and moral capacity as well as in ways that strongly affirm the standing of women. Yet another characteristic emphasized in Ibn al-'Arabi's work, non-duality, also speaks powerfully to the dialogical outlook, notably through a vision that sees purpose in seemingly opposing positions and that proposes the existence of "complementary contraries."

Experience, phenomenology, and a hermeneutics of openness

To be committed to dialogue is in many respects to be bound by the assumption that the full depth and meaning of specific realities cannot be comprehended "from a distance," outside of relationship, connection, and communion with that which is to be known. To the extent that one's experience is limited, so too will be the scope of one's deeply assimilated knowledge. With respect to knowledge of other human beings and their articulations of truth, connection with the other – and indeed empathic insight into the other's experiences and perceptions – is necessary to accurately understand the import and significance of what they are saying. Thus, experience of the other and of the subject in question must necessarily come before critique and meaningful exposition.

In emphasizing experience over mere cognition, Ibn al-'Arabi found it useful to employ an analogy from human sensory experience through his conception of *dhawq*, or "direct tasting." Though exposition can point us in the direction of experiential knowledge and of new experiences, written communication is no substitute for direct experience. As he states:

> The knowledge of tasting given by each existent thing cannot be given by any other existent thing. The human may find in himself a distinct taste in each bite of an apple not found in any other bite. The apple is one, yet he finds a sensory distinction in each bite, even if he is not able to explain it.
>
> (Ibn al-'Arabi, quoted in Chittick, 1989, p. 220)

Thus, for Ibn al-'Arabi, knowledge is participatory in the sense that each act of knowing is connected to the knower of the act. To know something is in an important sense to come into communion with it. When this connection between subject and object is established, the knower does not observe something external to themselves. Rather, there is an immersion of self into the knowing.

An implication of this perspective is that when our experience is limited, so too is our knowledge. To know something, we must be open to it rather than preoccupied solely with what is already known. Knowing is living knowledge in the present moment that is negotiating with the knowing of the past. Writing on the subject of religious knowledge and spiritual experience, Ibn al-'Arabi remarked that:

> Every author is under the authority of his own choice – even if he is compelled in his own choice – or he is under the authority of that particular science which he transmits in a specific way... We are only hearts clinging onto the door of the divine Presence, waiting for it to be open. We are poor and deprived of any knowledge.
>
> (Ibn al-'Arabi, quoted in De Cillis, 2014, p. 171)[22]

The experience of "opening" is prevalent throughout Ibn al-'Arabi's thought. Notably, in specific contexts, Ibn al-'Arabi testified to experiences of opening to and communing with sacred symbols of other faiths – experiences which he did not regard as contrary to his own spiritual and communal commitments (Chittick, 1994; Sharify-Funk, 2018). In his commentaries on powerful experiences of openness and connection, Ibn al-'Arabi's "multi-dimensional understandings which convey a multiplicity of perspectives" (De Cillis, 2014, p. 171) can be compared to those of contemporary interreligious dialogue scholar Raimon Panikkar, who spoke of an "imparative" spirit in the construction of knowledge as previously discussed in this chapter.

In affirming different ways of knowing and degrees of knowing, and highlighting bases for knowledge that stand beyond linear rational thought processes, Ibn al-'Arabi stands in distinction from forms of Western thought that uphold rational manipulation of language and symbols – backed by empirical measurement – as the only way of knowing. His stance is not, however, alien to the approach of dialogical thinkers such as Dallmayr, who was himself influenced by phenomenology, in which "concrete experience of the world comes first, world-critique second; openness to and understanding of the other is prior to critical opposition" (Godrej, 2017, p. 2). Particularly, Dallmayr "rejects the objectivism of the detached consciousness gazing at the world and insists on the embeddedness of this gazing subject within the world" (p. 2). Furthermore, an additional point of connection between Dallmayr and Ibn al-'Arabi can be found in Dallmayr's insistence on the value of reconnecting social and political theory to understandings of spiritual and metaphysical realities.[23]

Human potentiality

In their embrace of comparative exploration of normative beliefs and worldviews within a global context, dialogical thinkers reject a narrow view of human subjects as self-interested actors captive to parochial interests – a view that is implicit if not explicit in much social and political theory. By affirming the value of moral visions and ethical systems, they underscore the potential of humans to enact these visions and norms – if not perfectly, still in more fulsome ways that might secure a pluralistic and sustainable global community.

Ibn al-'Arabi's conception of human potential was articulated primarily in the context of spiritual development and moral agency, but offers strong affirmation of the human capacity to uphold a moral order that is congruent with the overarching structure of reality.[24] In so doing, Ibn al-'Arabi invited the spiritual maturation of the individual into a "complete" or "perfected" human being who has polished the "mirror" of their heart sufficiently to see in it a reflection of the divine and of the entire cosmic order. This realization of deep identity with the whole of existence becomes a foundation of moral action and of service.

Notably, Ibn al-'Arabi distinguished himself from many of his contemporaries by clearly stating that this highest station of human development was by no means an exclusive province of men. Rather, women are equally tasked as human beings to fulfill their spiritual and moral potential. Suad al-Hakim of the Lebanese University offers the following commentary:

> It is astonishing that a colossal Islamic scholar, Muhyiddin Ibn 'Arabi (AH 560–638), who lived more than eight centuries ago, should have declared that woman and man are absolutely equal in terms of human potentiality… [He] presented a new vision in the history of Islamic culture…
>
> Ibn 'Arabi's positive and unadulterated view of woman is astonishingly modern when compared to contemporary perspectives, be it those of some Muslim extremists who treat women as a lesser being, or those of people who demand a reassessment, historical, linguistic, legal, theological, etc. of woman's place in both the East and the West, according to some other kind of limitation.
>
> This view shows the humanity of Islam, cleansed of all the oppression, coercion and persecution of women that has been attributed to it. Indeed, the vision of Ibn 'Arabi extends far beyond the sixth-century Hijrah to fill woman with sanctity – and she is in dire need of it today – and to restore truly Islamic principles, which have been banished by the passage of years and masked by personal interests.
>
> (2006, pp. 1, 13)

For Ibn al-'Arabi, human potential is not limited to gender differences; rather, the experience of opening and knowing is at the core of all human beings, dignity and responsibility.[25]

Non-duality

As his epistemological emphasis on "tasting" (*dhawq*) suggests, Ibn al-'Arabi's cosmology places a strong emphasis on non-duality and on attaining knowledge through the communion of subject and object. In underscoring non-duality and the fundamental unity of all things within a divine context, Ibn al-'Arabi did not seek in any way to diminish the diversity and dynamism of the world. Indeed, he maintained that the very diversity of the cosmos was a sign of its underlying unity. To put this in terms of contemporary dialogical thinking, there is one world we share, but never one experience of it. Recognition of this impels us to allow space for diverse experiences and articulations of the one reality in its infinite facets and manifestations. By attending to the diversity of human experiences and expressions, we can come to know our shared reality more fully and comprehensively.

Such an understanding underpins Ibn al-'Arabi's teachings on religious diversity, which are striking in their emphatic assertation that denying the capacity of other religions to manifest truth is a spiritually damaging position. Such a stance, Ibn al-'Arabi proposed, limits our understanding of reality:

> Beware of being bound up by a particular religion and rejecting all others as unbelief! If you do that you will fail to obtain a great benefit. Nay, you will fail to obtain the true knowledge of the reality. Try to make yourself a (kind of) Prime Matter for all forms of religious belief. God is wider and greater than to be confined to a particular religion to the exclusion of others.
>
> (Ibn al-'Arabi, quoted in Izutsu, 1983, p. 254)

To the extent that negation of the other's religious beliefs and identity is at the heart of much contemporary strife, this teaching retains profound contemporary relevance. Another aspect of Ibn al-'Arabi's teachings on non-duality, and the expression of the divine in the many different parts of a single whole, pertains to deep knowledge of the self as a basis for knowledge of reality. One's own being is, as expressed by Ibn al-'Arabi, unlimited Being (wujud) transforming through temporal unfolding. It is through our self, our being that we come to know the transcendent source or ground of existence. For Ibn al-'Arabi, all knowledge is ultimately established in self-knowledge, which is inextricably interconnected with other-knowledge. To truly know the other, one must also come to know the self. And yet discovering the truth of the other still requires relationship and encounter because each person, at each moment, has a unique experience of Reality. Or, put alternately, Being manifests to each person, at each moment in a new and different way. Creation is forever new; Being's self-manifestation is forever changing. This idea of divine-Being is later reflected in the Muslim axiom, La takrar fi'l-tajalli – "There is no repetition in self-disclosure" (Chittick, 1989, p. 103). Such an understanding of God, Being and the world has profound implications for appreciating different cultural beliefs, religions, and philosophies, and lays the groundwork for a radical pluralism.

For Ibn al-'Arabi, human dignity and potential are defined in light of the Quranic and Biblical understanding that humankind was created in the divine Being's image. "To find" Oneself in the multiplicity of creation is a significant aspect of understanding existence. Self-knowledge is existence. As Ibn al-'Arabi notes, the Arabic word for existence, wujud, derives from the trilateral Arabic root verb, wajada, "to find." This term is derived from the same linguistic root as wajd, which means ecstasy. It is interesting to note the link between the origin of the words "static" and "ecstatic" – the former "unchanging" and the latter "dynamic." For Ibn al-'Arabi, being is also dynamic, ever-changing, and yet has connection to that which is impermanent.

By implication, then, existing, finding, and dynamism are deeply interrelated. For Ibn al-'Arabi, to exist is to find and vice versa constantly. The unicity of being is intertwined with the perpetual fluctuation and transmutation of time. As stated by William C. Chittick (1989), *wujud* is ultimately related to the continual dynamic search for the origin of self and relation to other. If God-Being manifests in all things, in all beliefs, to all people, in different ways, then each human witnesses and remembers God in and through all of these forms. Accordingly, Ibn al-'Arabi writes:

> God discloses Himself perpetually, since changes are witnessed perpetually in the manifest things and the nonmanifest things, the unseen and the visible, the sensory and the intelligible. His task is self-disclosure, and the task of the existent things is change and passage from one state to another state. Among us there are those who recognize this and those who do not recognize it. Those who recognize it worship Him in every state. Those who do not recognize it deny Him in every state.
>
> (Chittick, 1989, p. 103)

This notion of radical dynamism is another connection to dialogical thinking as reflected in the works of Dallmayr, Euben, Guillaume, and Said.

Complementary contraries

For Ibn al-'Arabi, the plurality of existence expresses a deeper unity, through infinite manifestations of the One and Only Being. However, human minds cannot grasp the whole and instead perceive reality as a plurality of things. The knower is veiled from the realization of this unifying vision of the human reality and lives in what he calls "complementary contraries."[26]

"Complementary contraries" is derived from the English translation of the original Arabic phrase, *jama'ta bayna-l mutaqabilati*, found in the Friday evening prayer of Ibn al-'Arabi's collection of daily and nightly prayers, also known as his *Wird*, supererogatory devotional acts in addition to the five daily Muslim prayers:

> O my God... You are Lord [of all] absolutely. You unite *the complementary contraries*, for You are the Majestic, the Beautiful. There is no end to Your sheer delight in Your Essence, as there is no end to Your witnessing of Yourself...
>
> I ask of You, by the mystery with which You unite *the complementary contraries*, that You bring together for me all that is disunited of my being, in such union that I may contemplate and witness the Oneness of Your Being.
>
> (2000, p. 115, emphasis added)

In Arabic, this phrase literally means the union, gathering, or joining between things facing each other in opposition, hence opposed or opposite from one another, and yet facing each other as in conversation or dialogue – indeed, derivatives of *qa-ba-la*, the trilateral root of the last word, can mean conversation or meeting. Such a framing of differences invites reflection on the possibility that certain opposites or contraries may actually be *complementary* insofar as they are in dialogue with each another, and have in their natures the possibility (or ultimate necessity) of being united or joined.[27] For Ibn al-'Arabi, this notion of complementary contradiction is a defining feature of God and reality (and for him there is no ultimate difference between the two). God unites opposites: Reality is both approachably beautiful (*jamal*) and assertively majestic (*jalal*); Reality is the one (*wahid*) and the many (*kathira*); Reality is the hidden (*batin*) and the apparent (*zahir*); Reality is both changeless essence and ever-dynamic, changing form. And because the human self and the cosmos are expressions of Reality, they too express complementary contradictions.

As a concept with spiritual roots but clear implications for affirming the inescapable diversity of the world, "complementary contraries" invites an attitude of openness and curiosity toward the multitude of differences inherent in social, historical, cultural, and physical phenomena. The idea also supports a tolerant and magnanimous stance toward beliefs that differ from one's own. William Rory Dickson, author of *Dissolving into Being* (forthcoming), describes the implications of Ibn al-'Arabi's vision in the following terms:

> In his *Futuhat al-Makkiyya* he [Ibn al-'Arabi] writes that, when one can appreciate where each person is coming from, the place from which they speak, one can see that their beliefs about reality are correct according to their own experience of it (their experience being determined by their own self, which is shaped by God's self-disclosure), such that "there is absolutely no error in the cosmos" (Chittick, 1994, p. 140).
>
> Anyone who exists has a perspective on Reality that is at least *somewhat* valid. However, each person sees Reality from a particular standpoint that simultaneously veils the seer from Reality as it appears from other positionalities. Hence every philosophy, ideology, religion, belief, understanding, or perspective, *is simultaneously true and false* (though each in different ways and in varying degrees). Put differently, each individual's belief is true from one standpoint, and false from another. Hence, the more one can perceive the singular Reality underlying various beliefs, and the ways in which each belief is true and false, with its own perfections and limitations, the more forms of God one can recognize and worship, and the more complete one's understanding of God's dynamic, multifaceted reality is. The famous nineteenth century Algerian Sufi, anti-colonial hero, and close student

of Ibn al-'Arabi's, 'Abd al-Qadir al-Jaza'iri (d. 1883), summed this perspective up nicely:

If you think and believe that [God] is what all the schools of Islam profess and believe – He is that, and He is other than that! If you think that He is what diverse communities believe ... Christians, Jews, Mazdeans, polytheists and others – He is that and He is other than that! And if you think and believe what is professed by the Knowers *par excellence* – prophets, saints, and angels – He is that! He is other than That! (Chodkiewicz, 1995, pp. 127–128).

As Coates also observes, Ibn al-'Arabi maintained that "All human knowledge is perspectival, conditioned, and relative..." (Coates, 2002, p. 15). Thus, our own worldview can never be complete, and can always benefit from consideration of truths embedded in other worldviews. The implications for dialogical engagement with the other are clear and profound, suggesting ever-present potential for learning and transformation.

Such a perspective is implicit in commentary by Abdul Aziz Said and Nathan C. Funk on current polarization between Islamic and Western cultures. Rather than remain mired in narratives of cultural contradiction and political confrontation, Said and Funk call for a "new story of complementarity" in Islamic-Western relations premised on mutual learning efforts to move beyond the "scarcity paradigm of truth," which maintains that the truth of one side necessarily negates the claim of the other.

Security is no longer the private good of a particular state and nation that may be purchased at the expense of others, but a public good that can only be achieved through the cultivation of consensus, collaboration, and reciprocity within a framework of dialogue and mutual engagement.

(2004, p. 23)

Only active engagement through "sustained dialogue" can help to discover common humanity concealed by symbols and obscured by fear, anger, and insecurity. Humans need to affirm forms of ever-changing reconciliation which evoke the dynamic ideal that "the whole world needs the whole world" or as Said and Funk have stated:

We have moved from a humanity that experienced its collective life as fragments of the whole to a humanity that must experience itself as a whole – a humanity that must come to terms with realities of interdependence in all the spheres of life.

(2004, p. 23)

Ultimately, this open outlook as seen in such dialogical thinking is a message of profound hope that is based in the theory of the mutually transformative nature of humans.

Conclusion

A dialogical and "open" approach to identity enables us to study the relations between a multitude of potential and possible articulations of an identity in order to see how, across time, emerging hegemonic collective political identities, as well as their alternatives, are in continuous transaction with alterity and among themselves. These transactions cannot only be considered through binaries and dichotomies. By focusing analysis on tensions as well as resonances within social discourse, contemporary "dialogical" theorists provide a useful framework for (re)examining controversies in Muslim – majority community relations, and provide a constructive basis for teasing out divergent beliefs and claims about social values while also highlighting ways in which different claims are not always fundamentally incompatible.

This transformational nature of Muslim public experience has been described in a variety of ways, and some of the recurring characteristic tendencies include notions of open identity toward differences and dynamism. As reflected in Dallmayr's *Border Crossing*, the dialogical provides a means of enhancing knowledge about self and others, in an atmosphere that suspends standard tropes of self-referential discourses about identity. It is an attitude of openness and rediscovery, an affirmation of the possibilities that are inherent in contemporary cross-cultural encounters and interpretive processes. More specifically, it becomes possible to conceive one's own authenticity as emerging from a rediscovery and affirmation of – rather than a negation of – the other, or to imagine tradition and modernity as realities that can be *within* each other. It also becomes possible to imagine the essence or ideals of a religious tradition as emergent and potentially dynamic rather than as static and rooted in a distant historical reality.

As will be explored in this book, there are a variety of divisive controversies and biases when exploring the subject of Muslim women in North America. In acknowledging and problematizing the limitations within polarized understandings, the author gleans from the scholarship of the dialogical within the cacophony of voices who seek to define Western-Islamic relations. By reflecting on the writings of Dallmayr, Euben, Guillaume, Said, and others, this chapter highlights the presence of voices that seek to transcend divisive discourses and invite new projects in social and political theory as well as global citizenship – projects that acknowledge the damage caused by closed discourses and international power imbalances, while inviting forms of humanistic thought that are not freighted with colonial baggage. They also challenge scholars to be willing to suspend past certainties in the pursuit of knowledge by revisiting the core meaning of theory within a context of encounter with difference.

By reclaiming and reaffirming both dialogue and the idea of the cosmopolitan, thinkers such as Dallmayr and Euben offer no easy solutions, yet they do succeed in opening new horizons of possibility. Precisely at a time when profound conflict is driven by notions of ineluctable "otherness," intellectual discourse that imagines a genuine encounter with otherness – an encounter that has the power to unsettle past certainties and provoke new questions – is profoundly humanizing and necessary. The merits of dialogical as it manifests in the works of Dallmayr and Euben as well as others, deserve a great deal more attention among engaged scholars who seek a way forward, beyond intellectual closure and toward a more open and humane future.

While deeply held convictions and (in many cases) fears concerning the status of women in Islam may not in every case resolve into complementary opposing positions, including ideas from Ibn al-'Arabi such as "complementary contradictions" provides an important supplement for the analytical framework, the value of which is particularly evident when one considers the extent to which differences are frequently inflamed, exaggerated, or misconstrued on the basis on sensationalist coverage and in many instances misinformation. Utilizing this concept and others helps to highlight ways in which opposing discourses exist interdependently, accentuating different potential conclusions about truth, morality, and authenticity as well as the limitations of human understanding and the value of relationship. Applied to controversies surrounding contemporary Islam, this concept invites consideration of the potential for coherence and complementarity between competing claims which may at first appear dissonant and contradictory. With respect to the specific debates explored in this book, where "anti" and "pro" divisions animate discourse on issues ranging from veiling to female religious leadership, this book attends not just to genuinely incompatible (and sometimes misinformed) views, but also to truth and value claims held by different camps that are in many cases not as contradictory as the most partisan protagonists may believe. Analysis often reveals that surface contradictions can give way to deeper patterns of coherence and compatibility, or at least differences that can in good conscience be sustained by individuals who share one or more common concerns. Thus, contradictory stances, though "seated" opposite to one another and hence in some sense opposing, are also facing one another and ideally ought to be placed in dialogue and conversation.

Finding complementarity in seemingly contradictory positions, however, often requires considerable effort to move beyond preconceptions rooted in a totalizing or closed narrative. The next chapter takes note of how commonplace such "clash" narratives have become, and examines key assumptions that are associated with a rejection of dialogue on matters pertaining to Muslim communities and cultures. Although authors of "clash" narratives do not express interest in sitting across the table on matters of contention, and are unlikely dialogue partners, awareness of conceptual "memes" and themes that arise from "clash" thinking can be useful for those seeking to navigate contemporary intellectual and social landscapes.

Notes

1   I am using the term "text" in an inclusive manner, with reference both to the written word and to forms of cultural production that are transmitted largely by oral means. "Texts" in this latter (metaphorical) sense include sociocultural narratives that give authoritative meaning and structure to human interactions. Using "text" as a primary analytical device is quite relevant to the study of Islamic cultures, which place great weight on the importance of allusions to "the book" (i.e., the Qur'an and other sacred texts). Understanding of Islamic cultures is incomplete, however, without recognition of the significance of oral transmission, memorization, and recitation. Before being reproduced in a literary manner, the Qur'an and the sayings of the Prophet were orally transmitted, in ways that overlapped with other forms of traditional wisdom which were often embedded in narratives about exemplary practitioners of the faith. In many Muslim communities, the spoken word transmitted directly remains as influential as direct reading from the most profoundly authoritative texts. Remembering that texts can be both oral and written is crucial if the analyst is to avoid falling into the traps of disregarding or devaluing oral cultures.

2   For more on the idea of "social hermeneutics," see the author's chapter, "Toward a Global Understanding of Pacifism" (2019).

3   In particular, see the works of "relational sociologist" Mustafa Emirbayer, who was heavily influenced by Norbert Elias and others. Also see works of relational theorist of International Relations, Naeem Inayatullah (i.e., his work with David Blaney, *International Relations and the Problem of Difference*).

4   The term and concept "intersubjectivity" has been used in a variety of disciplines from psychology to philosophy. In particular, German philosopher and sociologist Jurgen Habermas proposed intersubjectivity to counter atomistic conceptions of the individual in the world, which he found even among his predecessors in the Frankfurt school. He saw rationality and social progress as things that arise when people intersubjectively strive for understanding and shared goals together. Habermas' thought would influence many of the scholars (i.e., Dallmayr and Euben) mentioned in this chapter.

5   It is interesting to point out that Plato warned in the book of *Phaedrus* that the written can destroy "the living soul," implying that a written text is susceptible to being dead whereas the oral word through human dialogue is alive and open to further examination. In comparison, the significance of the "oral" in the construction of early Muslim identity was also emphasized over the written. "Living memory" of conversations was not to be lost to simple repetition. For more about dialogue in Plato's works and in Qur'anic experience, see Fischer & Abedi (1990).

6   Ultimately, Socrates was skeptical about the prospects for accumulating the variety of knowledge sought by scholars, expressing more confidence in his ability to know love – that which dwells in-between the cognized and the cognizer. Throughout the writings of Plato, Socrates only mentions one teacher: Diotima of Mantineia, "a wise woman" who taught him "the only subject in which [he] professed to have any knowledge," that being "love" (Plato 1993, p. 6). According to Diotima, "Love is the mean between wisdom and ignorance... [it] is the power which interprets and conveys to the gods the prayers and sacrifices of men, and to men the commands and rewards of the gods; and this power spans the chasm which divides them, and in this all is bound together..." (1993, p. 26).

7 In the last century, the word "dialogical" acquired renewed meaning for increasingly diverse groups of scholars, from philosophers and peace educators to policy analysts. See the works of such philosophers: David Bohm (1990); Hans Georg Gadamer (2002); and M. Bakhtin (1981). See the works of such peace educators: Raimon Panikkar (Prabhu, 1996) and Abdul Aziz Said (2003).

8 Many of the scholars whose ideas are explored in this chapter and others (i.e., Dallmayr, Euben, Guillaume) are gleaning from the works of 20th century philosophers and their investigations into the "dialogic" or "dialogical" (see previously mentioned scholars in endnote 7).

9 The late John Shotter (d. 2016), an Emeritus Professor and Philosopher of Communication Studies at the University of New Hampshire, also emphasized the idea of "being with." In *Getting It* (2011), Shotter elaborated on the relevance of the dialogical and the concept of "witness-thinking" in reimagining the process of thinking and how knowledge is constructed,

> ...witness-thinking [is a] contrast with our much more usual style of exploratory thought in which we think *about* things in terms of some kind of representation, that is, picture, of them. It involves imaginatively thinking *from within* a moment of acting, *with* the voice of another or *with* a detailed concrete circumstance in mind (p. 2).

For Shotter, the dialogical was not "aboutness (monologic)-thinking... [that] is unresponsive to another's expressions" (2011, p. 214), rather it is "open to being affected in an uncontrolled fashion by the rest of our surroundings, and as we turn to produce an intended effect elsewhere, we open ourselves to being affected by the very original aspect of our concern."

10 See Dallmayr's *Integral Pluralism* (2010).

11 Gadamer's search for a "fusion of horizons" permits us to enter into conversation with the intention of *experience with* the other. In the process of conversation, we are open to new understandings as *experienced in* the dynamic interaction between text, context, and interpreter. According to Gadamer's dialogical hermeneutics, there is no objective position from which to see the "truth" of the text or, indeed, of our present sociohistorical reality; rather, interpretation is a continuous and open-ended exposition of meaning based on the interpreter's present reality. The result, *living the transformation*, is a combination of intersubjective and experiential/existential transformation. See Gadamer (2002), pp. 309, 374.

12 See other works by Xavier Guillaume (i.e., 2002a; 2002b).

13 If interested in learning more about the life and scholarship of Abdul Aziz Said, please see Funk & Sharify-Funk (2022).

14 This edited volume was a result of an invitation-only scholarly conference that was held in October 2003 at the Library of Alexandria in Egypt. The conference attendees, who ranged from Grand Muftis (like H.E. Grand Mufti Mustafa Ceric of Bosnia and Herzegovina) to professors of Islamic thought and identity (like Dr. Mohammed Arkoun).

15 In her article about Dallmayr, Ilieva quotes from Gadamer to elucidate this ancient concept: "One does not go about identifying the weakness of what another person says in order to prove that one is right, but one seeks instead as far as possible to strengthen the other's viewpoint so that what the other person has to say becomes illuminating" (2015, p. 24).

16 For a more thorough engagement with the idea of "multiple modernities," see Euben's chapter in *Border Crossings* (1999b).

17 Euben and Dallmayr are not alone when it comes to resurrecting the Greek concept of *kosmopolitikos* in order to address the questions of contemporary Islam, pluralism, and living in an ever-increasing global world. For some more examples, see the works of Bruce Lawrence (2021), Carl W. Ernst and Richard C. Martin (2012), and Karim H. Karim (2012).

18 The English word "empathy" is connected to the German word, "Einfuhlung," which means "in-feeling." This term reflects both the inner/internal worlds of the self as innately and inherently intertwined with the outer/external worlds of the other.

19 Jung (b. 1931) is an Emeritus Professor of Moravian College in Bethlehem, PA. See his work, *Transversal Rationality and Intercultural Texts* (2011).

20 The decolonial world-systems analysts (i.e., Ramon Grosfoguel) prioritize dialogues on the periphery at this point in history. They argue for more dialogues between Aboriginal Australians and Nigerians, Vietnamese and Chileans, Mexicans and Moroccans, Muslims and Hindus, etc., and indeed conversations from multiple peripheral perspectives than core/periphery dialogues. From a decolonial perspective, "The West" needs to speak less for a while and listen to the conversations others are having about the world-system. Additionally, the decolonial world-systems analysts do not talk of comparison or incommensurable cultural differences since humans are all speaking from different locations within the same global system. Thus, humans all experience the same system, but in different ways. This is why dialogue about this system, which is a common reference, is the priority, rather than a comparative analysis.

21 Hamza Yusuf is the cofounder of Zaytuna College and has given a variety of talks about the critical importance of Abu Hamid al-Ghazali's thought in our contemporary times. He started the al-Ghazali Children Project with Fons Vitae Publishers which offers resources on al-Ghazali and courses: https://ghazalichildren.org/about-the-project/

22 The experience of opening, for Ibn al-'Arabi, was the experience of divine inspiration and, ultimately, enabled him to be a "translator of spiritual 'openings'" as reflected in the title of his magnum opus, *Futuhat al-Makkiyyah* (*The Meccan Openings*) (De Cillis, 2014, p. 171).

23 This relationship between the social and spiritual is reflected in many areas of Dallmayr's thought, one example being in an essay, *Conversation across boundaries*:

> …'thick conversation' or a 'thick dialogue,' that is a communicative exchange willing to delve into the rich fabric of different lifeworlds and cultures. The appeal in such exchanges is no longer merely to the rational-cognitive capacity of participants, but rather to the full range of their situated humanity, including their hopes, aspirations, moral, or spiritual convictions, as well as their agonies and frustrations.
>
> (2002, pp. 155–156)

24 Due to the vastness of Ibn al-'Arabi's metaphysical positioning, Peter Coates argues that:

> Human existence… is to be understood as a potential which has an order, ground and meaning… we have to find out and know who and what we are… And the way of finding is "to know ourselves" in order to know God, of which we are, Ibn 'Arabi insists, in reality no other. This is the fundamental logic of Ibn 'Arabi's deployment of the concept of Being.
>
> (2002, p. 32)

25 In Sharify-Funk's chapter on "Ibn al-'Arabi and the Virtues of 'Holy Envy in Islam'" (2018), the author explores the concepts of *insan al-kamil* (the perfected human being) and *awliya-Allah* (the friends of God) and how Ibn al-'Arabi affirms again and again, "[t]here is no spiritual quality belonging to men to which women do not have equal access" (Chodkiewicz, 1993, p. 30). The author also points out that while studying with numerous Sufi teachers in Muslim medieval Spain, Ibn al-'Arabi specifically mentions that some of the most realized of souls were his female teachers.

26 William Rory Dickson, Merin Shobhana Xavier, and the author started to explore this concept in their book, *Contemporary Sufism* (2018).

27 Sachiko Murata, in her article, "Yin/Yang Complementarity in Islamic Texts" (1996) observes the significance of complementarity in Sufi thought:

> The more I studied a variety of Islamic texts, the more I found that many Muslim thinkers, especially in the fields of Sufism and philosophy, employ an approach similar to that of Chinese sages in that they look at the whole of reality as determined by complementary principles. No matter what such thinkers discuss, they tend to speak of complementarity and equilibrium among different powers or forces.
>
> (pp. 65–66)

References

Abu Zayd, N. (2005). *Rethinking the Qur'an: Towards a humanistic hermeneutics.* Humanistics University Press.

al-Hakim, S. (2006). Ibn 'Arabi's twofold perception of woman: Woman as human being and cosmic principle. *Journal of the Muhyiddin Ibn 'Arabi Society, 39*, 1–13.

al-Jabri, M. A. (1999). *Arab-Islamic philosophy: A contemporary critique* (Aziz Abbassi, Trans.) University of Texas Press.

Bakhtin, M. (1981). *The dialogic imagination: Four essays* (C. Emerson & M. Holquist, Trans.). University of Texas Press.

Bano, M. (2020). *The revival of Islamic rationalism: Logic, metaphysics and mysticism in modern Muslim societies.* Cambridge University Press.

Bohm, D. (1990). *On dialogue.* David Bohm Seminars.

Chittick, W. C. (1989). *The Sufi path of knowledge: Ibn al-'Arabi's metaphysics of imagination.* State University of New York Press.

Chittick, W. C. (1994). *Imaginal worlds: Ibn al-'Arabi and the problem of religious diversity.* State University of New York Press.

Chittick, W. C. (1998). *The self-disclosure of God: Principles of Ibn al-'Arabi's cosmology.* State University of New York Press.

Chodkiewicz, M. (1993). *Seal of the saints: Prophethood and sainthood in the doctrine of Ibn 'Arabi.* The Islamic Texts Society.

Chodkiewicz, M. (1995). *The spiritual writings of Amir 'Abd al-Kader.* State University of New York Press.

Chodkiewicz, M. (2004). *The Meccan revelations* (Vol. II). Pir Press.

Coates, P. (2002). *Ibn 'Arabi and modern thought: The history of taking metaphysics seriously.* Anqa Publishing.

Corbin, H. (1969). *Creative imagination in the Sufism of Ibn 'Arabi*. Princeton University Press.

Dallmayr, F. (1996). *Beyond orientalism: Essays on cross-cultural encounter*. State University of New York Press.

Dallmayr, F. (2002). *Dialogue among civilizations: Some exemplary voices*. Palgrave Macmillan.

Dallmayr, F. (2004). Beyond monologue: For a comparative political theory. *Perspectives on Politics, 2*(2), 249–257.

Dallmayr, F. (2010). *Integral pluralism: Beyond culture wars*. University Press of Kentucky.

Dallmayr, F. (Ed.). (1999). *Border crossings: Toward a comparative political theory*. Lexington Books.

Dallmayr, F. R. (2013). *Being in the world: Dialogue and cosmopolis*. University Press of Kentucky.

De Cillis, M. (2014). *Free will and predestination in Islamic thought: Theoretical compromises in the works of Avicenna, al-Ghazali and Ibn 'Arabi*. Routledge.

Dickson, W. R. (Forthcoming). *Dissolving into being: Understanding Sufism and Islam through the Fusus al-Hikam*.

Ernst, C. W., & Martin, R. C. (2012). *Rethinking Islamic studies: From orientalism to cosmopolitanism*. University of South Carolina Press.

Euben, R. L. (1999a). *Enemy in the mirror: Islamic fundamentalism and the limits of modern rationalism: A work of comparative political theory*. Princeton University Press.

Euben, R. L. (1999b). Mapping modernities, 'Islamic' and 'Western'. In F. R. Dallmayr (Ed.), *Border crossings: Toward a comparative political theory* (pp. 11–37). Lexington Books.

Euben, R. L. (2008). *Journeys to the other shore: Muslim and Western travelers in search of knowledge*. Princeton University Press.

Fischer, M. M. J., & Abedi, M. (1990). Qur'anic dialogics: Islamic poetics and politics for Muslims and for us. In T. Maranhao (Ed.), *The interpretation of dialogue* (pp. 120–153). University of Chicago Press.

Funk, N. C., & Sharify-Funk, M. (Eds.). (2022). *Abdul Aziz Said: A pioneer in peace, intercultural dialogue, and cooperative global politics*. Springer-Verlag Publishers.

Gadamer, H. G. (2002). *Truth and method* (2nd revised ed.) (J. Weinsheimer & D. G. Marshall, Trans.). Continuum Publishing Co.

Godrej, F. (2017). *Fred Dallmayr: Critical phenomenology, cross-cultural theory, cosmopolitanism*. Routledge Publishers.

Guillaume, X. (2002a). Foreign policy and the politics of alterity: A dialogical understanding of international relations. *Millennium: Journal of International Studies, 31*(1), 1–26.

Guillaume, X. (2002b). Reflexivity and subjectivity: A dialogical perspective for and on international relations theory. *Forum: Qualitative Social Research, 3*(3), Art. 13. https://www.qualitative-research.net/index.php/fqs/article/view/826/1794

Guillaume, X. (2014). *International relations and identity: A dialogical approach*. Routledge Publishers.

Ilieva, E. (2015). Philosophical hermeneutics and comparative political theory. *Journal of Dialogue Studies, 3*(2), 5–29.

Inayatullah, N., & Blaney, D. (2004). *International relations and the problem of difference*. Routledge.

Izutsu, T. (1983). *Sufism and Taoism: A comparative study of key philosophical concepts*. University of California Press.

Jung, H. Y. (1999). Postmodernity, Eurocentrism, and the future of political philosophy. In F. R. Dallmayr (Ed.), *Border crossings: Toward a comparative political theory* (pp. 277–296). Lexington Books.

Jung, H. Y. (2011). *Transversal rationality and intercultural texts: Essays in phenomenology and comparative philosophy*. Ohio University Press.

Karim, K. H. (2012). Cosmopolitanism: Ways of being Muslim. In A. B. Sajoo (Ed.), *A companion to Muslim cultures* (pp. 201–220). I.B. Tauris.

Lawrence, B. (2021). *Islamicate cosmopolitan spirit*. Wiley-Blackwell.

Murata, S. (1996). Yin/Yang complementarity in islamic texts. *Cosmos, 12*, 65–81.

Plato (1993). *Symposium and Phaedrus*. Dover Publications.

Prabhu, J. (Ed.). (1996). *The intercultural challenge of Raimon Panikkar*. Orbis Books.

Said, A. A. (2003). *The dialogue of healing* [Paper presentation]. On the Frontiers of Social Healing: An International Learning Community, Palestres, Cyprus.

Said, A. A., & Funk, N. C. (2004). Islam and the West: Narratives of conflict and conflict transformation. *International Journal of Peace Studies, 9*(1), 1–28.

Said, A. A., Abu-Nimer, M., & Sharify-Funk, M. (Eds.). (2006). *Contemporary Islam: Dynamic, not static*. Routledge Publishers.

Senturk, R. (2001). Toward an open science and society: Multiplex relations in language, religion, and society. *Islam: Arastirmalari Dergisi (Turkish Journal of Islamic Studies), Sayi, 6*, 93–129.

Sharify-Funk, M. (2018). Ibn al-'Arabi and the virtues of 'holy envy' in Islam. In H. Gustafson (Ed.), *Holy envy: Learning from traditions other than our own* (pp. 37–52). Palgrave Macmillan.

Sharify-Funk, M. (2019). Toward a global understanding of pacifism: Hindu, Islamic, and Buddhist contributions. In J. Kustermans, T. Sauer, T. D. Lootens, B. Segaert, & B. Switzerland (Eds.), *Pacifism's appeal: Ethos, history, politics* (pp. 129–131). Palgrave Macmillan.

Sharify-Funk, M., Dickson, W. R., & Xavier, M. S. (2018). *Contemporary Sufism: Piety, politics and popular culture*. Routledge Publishers.

Shotter, J. (2011). *Getting it: Withness-thinking and the dialogical – In practice*. Hampton Press.

Chapter 3

Pervasive Anxiety about Islam and Muslims

"Clash Literature" in North America[1]

Since Samuel Huntington posited the now infamous "Clash of Civilizations" theory in a 1993 essay published in the journal *Foreign Affairs*, much academic controversy has flared around his assertion that cultural and religious differences will become the main source of international conflict in the post–Cold War era. Although Huntington's thesis has been frequently criticized by a broad spectrum of academics for its extremely broad-brush approach to conflict analysis and its vulnerability to manipulation as a conflict-intensifying cliché, the events of September 11, 2001, catapulted his ideas beyond the academy and into the heart of contemporary discourse.[2] His predictions that civilizational conflicts would be especially prevalent between Muslims and non-Muslims received particular attention, as did his effort to shift discussion of international affairs from the ideological geopolitics of the Cold War to resurgent religio-cultural identities rooted deep in history. With statements on political geography, such as "Europe ends where Western Christianity ends and Islam and Orthodoxy begin," Huntington proposed that religiously based civilizations constitute the largest meaningful framework for human loyalty. He also emphasized the frailty of political projects with broader scope and ambition, from the European Union to the United Nations. Huntington arguably contributed to an intellectual atmosphere within which many less disciplined writers felt greater freedom to write their own manifestos linking contemporary concerns about terrorism to a primordial struggle between "Islam and the West."

While most academics ignore writings which might be construed as combative popularizations of Huntington's clash theory, the proliferation of exactly this variety of *clash literature* since September 11, 2001, constitutes a phenomenon worthy of investigation and analysis. This broader clash literature, which proclaims an intent to break the shackles of "political correctness" and tell the truth about Islam and the West, contains many volumes which have risen to best-seller heights. In content as well as tone, this literature is decidedly alarmist and insistently polarizing.[3] Leaving behind the subtler forms of Orientalist derogation critiqued by Edward Said in his influential thesis on the subject,[4] the new clash literature represents Islam and the West[5] as irreconcilable entities

DOI: 10.4324/9780429341151-4

locked into ideological and sometimes actual warfare for decades if not centuries. Dismissing dialogue and relying on strident "us vs. them" rhetoric, the literature actively seeks to interfere with the development of relations between Muslims and non-Muslims. Though produced by authors of varied backgrounds, the written products display striking consistencies in core premises and ultimate conclusions, as "ex-Muslims" who generalize from negative personal experiences find common cause with atheists who warn against religious resurgence as well as with theologians who worry that apocalyptic demographics will displace their religious heritage once and for all.

Given the astronomically higher sales of such books (e.g., *Infidel, Surrender, America Alone*) when compared to writings espousing dialogue and coexistence, themes from the clash literature have undeniably infiltrated the public imagination in Europe and North America, amplifying negative perceptions of Islam and Muslims and reinforcing popular anxieties. Though emphasis varies across texts and authors, books from the clash literature consistently encourage a culture of suspicion within which Islam and Muslims constitute a threat to Western societies. Islam is portrayed as the religious heritage of a dysfunctional and misogynist "tribal" society that prevents Muslims from adapting to modern settings and leaves all Muslims vulnerable to indoctrination with radical ideology. Such texts suggest that because Islam is incompatible with cultural and political liberalism, Muslim immigrants cannot be integrated into Western culture, and the "ghettoization" of Muslims in Western societies is self-inflicted rather than driven by adverse social, economic, and political factors.

While acknowledging differences in emphasis and focus within the clash literature, this chapter analyzes and critiques prominent shared themes found throughout these books. Particular attention is given to what might be described as the overarching narrative that informs the clash literature. According to this narrative, "the West" and Western liberalism embody humanity's highest achievements, which are manifest in societies, structures, and norms that underscore individual freedom and political secularism. Rather than push Muslims and Muslim societies to adopt these ideals, however, Western elites have lost confidence in the fundamentals of their own traditions and succumbed to patronizing forms of "good will" and practices of political correctness, epitomized by policies that promote multiculturalism and ignore the pathologies of immigrant cultures. By opening the gates of society to large-scale Muslim immigration and failing to require assimilation, this approach has put Western and especially European societies on a path that will eventually lead to the demise of Western culture. Demographic factors linked to differential marriage and fertility rates will now lead to an inexorable decline or "slow suicide" of Western civilization as we know it. The only way to correct this decline and avoid a "last days" scenario, these authors suggest, is to assertively condemn Islamic culture and promote women's emancipation within Muslim communities.

After identifying and illustrating key themes of this narrative within multiple clash texts, analytical attention is directed not so much to specific exaggerations and distortions inherent in this literature as to the overarching mode of argument and the way in which key themes are intended to speak to North American readers. Although there is no denying that many purveyors of clash literature have political motives[6] and are reproducing, in exaggerated form, classic tropes of Orientalism[7] that run counter to much empirical evidence,[8] the clash literature is also worth probing for what it reveals about contemporary "Western" identity insecurities. Clash authors rely heavily on pessimistic extrapolations and cherry-picked facts in ways that serve to advance a dehumanizing image of Islam and Muslims, all the while articulating a clear intent to sharpen polarization and dispel hope that relational engagement might transform or mitigate conflict. The fact that tendentious arguments purveying dehumanized enemy images have led to remarkable book sales should arouse concern.[9] By taking contemporary identity insecurities seriously but not succumbing to discourse rooted in dualism, blame, or scapegoating, scholars who pause to reflect on the meaning of the clash literature have the potential to expand academic and popular conversations. The very appeal of the clash literature points to a profound need for new dialogical arguments and visions – for accessible but not unsubstantial literatures that seek to stretch human imagination beyond the simplistic dichotomies and reactionary impulses that have come to define the "post-9/11" era.

The West as a threatened savior: Western liberalism vs. Islamic authoritarianism

At the core of the new clash literature is an attempt to define Western values and identity in relation to a threatening Islamic "other." "The West" is portrayed as a fundamentally sound civilization, embodying the peak of idealism and human achievement, whereas Islam is characterized as a confounding, diseased tradition that is rotten to the core.[10] Whereas the West is inherently benign, peaceful (there is no critique of colonialism and imperialism), and focused on the liberation of human potential, Islam is equated with violence, an irrational drive toward world domination, and an absence of human liberty. For each attributed virtue or positive quality of the West, Islam provides an idealized foil or contrast. The West appears without the taint of historical errors or injustices, while Islam is essentialized as the West's antithesis or shadow.

Robert Spencer, a prominent American conservative blogger who has been officially banned from Britain for his provocative advocacy against Islam,[11] articulates this approach to contrasting Islam with the West in vivid terms. In his *Religion of Peace?*, Spencer argues that the core of Islam, including sharia laws, is built on the fundamentals of violence and domination. He therefore urges all other religious orders to align against this "common enemy" of

"Islamic supremacy" (2007, p. 204). In making such arguments, Spencer and most other clash authors establish a fundamental distinction between their own discourse and arguments made in conventional post-9/11 anti-terrorism discourse. Whereas the former asserts directly that Islam is fundamentally flawed in ways which predispose followers toward violence, the latter differentiates between extremist and mainstream positions within the Muslim community.[12]

A related theme of clash literature is that, despite the obvious hostility of Islam and Muslims, most Westerners are unaware of the gathering danger posed by Islamic infiltration of European and North American societies. As Bruce Bawer argues in *Surrender*, "We in the West are living in the midst of a jihad, and most of us don't even realize it…" (2009, p. 3). Bawer proposes that because violence and Islamic supremacy are intrinsic to the Islamic faith, Muslims living in the West are necessarily engaged in jihad to dominate Westerners and deprive them of individual freedom. To lend credence to this position, he utilizes individual stories of trauma and pain in which Islam can be identified as the perpetrating factor. These personal narratives of victimization and themes related to how Islam is identified as the perpetrating factor will be explored in Chapter 4.

The denial of Muslim moderation

To maintain this vision, writers of clash literature need to persuade readers that Muslims are far more alike in their tendencies than unalike, and that they cannot be trusted either to harmonize with Western social norms or implement their own religious reformation. Many are quite blunt in asserting that, though Muslims may differ somewhat in the means that they choose, there are not significant differences between the goals of mainstream Muslims and those of terrorists. Mark Steyn, Canadian author of the 2006 *New York Times* bestseller, *America Alone*, argues that a large majority of Western Muslims support terrorists' strategic goals. He substantiates this by citing a poll in which "over 60 percent of British Muslims" articulated a desire to "live under *shari'a* in the United Kingdom" (2006, p. 76). Though this is certainly an unsettling statistic for many non-Muslims, its significance is less obvious than Steyn implies, given that Muslims differ quite profoundly in their understandings of *shari'a*. Furthermore, many Muslims' desire to make their personal lives (particularly matters such as marriage, intimate relations, funerals, and divorce) compliant with traditional Islamic norms need not necessarily imply a totalizing theocratic threat to the "Western" way of life. Like statistics concerning the number of Americans and Canadians who question evolutionary theory or who believe that end times are imminent, the number cited by Steyn does not immediately lend itself to a definitive, let alone alarming, interpretation. Sounding an alarm is, however, a definite intention behind works like *America Alone*. Steyn's book addresses the relationship among America,

Europe, and Islam. Writing within the overall context of the global war on terror, Steyn places particular weight on recent demographic statistics that signal population trends in predominantly Muslim and non-Muslim countries: Muslim immigration, birth rates, fertility rates, and marriage rates. He raises the prospect that Europe will fall to Muslim domination, leaving only America to uphold Western values in the face of a Muslim opposition that lacks true moderates. The text, incidentally, was recommended by former U.S. president George W. Bush to his staff.[13]

For Steyn and other clash authors, the West has no trustworthy allies within the Muslim world, except for those who place themselves on or beyond the outer margins of Islamic faith and belief. Creating a vision within which an authentic Muslim cannot be truly moderate, they portray Islam itself as an extreme religion that prevents assimilation and compromise. Those who seek to paint a different picture of an Islam that is dynamic and flexible or endowed with positive values are discounted as "apologists." In *Why I am Not a Muslim*, a writer known as Ibn Warraq (reputedly a former Muslim) dismisses those who represent Islam positively and equates Islam with the worst events in Muslim history, which are presumably far worse in magnitude than persecutions organized by followers of other religions. Apologists of Islam, to Ibn Warraq, still insist on perpetuating the myth of an Islam that accorded equality to non-Muslim subjects: They talk of a time when all the various religious communities lived in perfect harmony in the Islamic lands. The same apologists minimize, or even excuse, the persecution, the discrimination, the forced conversions, the massacres, and the destruction of the churches, synagogues, fire temples, and other places of worship (1995, p. 214). For Ibn Warraq, as for other clash authors, Islam is an exception in the domain of religions, intrinsically intolerant and aggressive. Implicitly, Muslims who insist otherwise are either being dishonest or they are not truly Muslims.

Many clash authors appear to favor the former interpretation, that so-called "moderate Muslims" are actually hiding the extent of their support for radical Islamic ends. Rhetorically, Steyn attacks the credibility of his intellectual opponents by associating their views with those of terrorists. The language is inflammatory, and seeks to discredit all Western Muslim commentators as potential enemies within: "Given the very few degrees of separation between very prominent Western Muslims—ambassadors, princes, professors—and the terrorists, it seems likely that many prominent figures in these parties will be supportive of terrorists ends" (Steyn, 2006, p. 204). Bawer uses a similar approach to characterize his adversaries, suggesting that even the most "assimilated" or liberal of Muslims living in the West harbor elements of the Islamic worldview, which, by their nature of being Islamic, clash irreconcilably with those of the secular Western worldview. "No, there's no guarantee," states Bawer, "that western Muslims, in meaningful numbers, will ever openly and actively champion freedom and defy jihadists; to do so, after all, is alien to every value with which many of them were raised" (Bawer, 2009, p. 276).

Significantly, the pronouncements of clash authors are themselves based on an interpretation of Islam that equates religious extremism with religious authenticity. Spencer's proposal for a religious alliance against Muslims to defend the West clearly reveals this equation:

> Islam seeks the conversion, subjugation, or death of not only Christians but also all non-Muslims. Thus it is imperative that all the victims or potential victims of Islamic jihad—Christians, Jews, Buddhists, Hindus, atheists, secular Muslims, and all others—recognize that...we must all hang together, or we shall indeed hang separately.
>
> (2007, p. 9)

For Spencer, the beliefs of the most extreme and inflexible Muslims are to be taken as normative and long-standing, while the beliefs of other Muslims are discounted and treated as either insincere or insignificant. Islam, he proposes, has not historically embraced "peaceful coexistence between Muslims and non-Muslims" (2018, p. 11) and cannot accommodate moderation, so it must be resisted. Spencer's work reflects similar rhetoric to Bill Maher, Sam Harris, Christopher Hitchens, Richard Dawkins, and others who identify with New Atheism – including an emphasis on the prevalence of fundamentalist perspectives in predominantly Muslim societies, and on widespread tolerance among Western liberals for Islamic fundamentalist views (Ingraham, 2014; Malik, 2018).

Some authors of clash literature affect a less strident and more nuanced attitude toward Islam, while conveying a generally negative evaluation of the religion and its adherents. Christopher Caldwell, former Senior Editor at *The Weekly Standard* and a regular contributor to the *Financial Times*, casts serious doubt on the Muslim capacity for adaptation, and points to disproportionate incarceration rates among European Muslims (2009, p. 135). In his popular book, *Reflections on the Revolution in Europe*, skepticism about Islam is conveyed less directly:

> Reaching out to so-called "moderate Muslims" is the cornerstone of European strategy against terrorism. Moderate Muslims are the people who can be trusted not to "distort Islam", or at least to distort it is a positive way-by building a "European islam" that can interact with the continent's political institutions without breaking them.
>
> (2009, p. 283)

By inserting the adjective "so-called" before the term "moderate Muslims" and using a lowercase letter for "European islam," Caldwell casts doubt on the authenticity of accommodating Muslim responses to Western culture and institutions. In the clash literature, the mark of authenticity is applied to forms of Islamic practice that appear most incompatible with the idealized Western model with which they are compared.

Demise of the West: Muslim demographics and the loss of faith

Demographics is a salient theme in a variety of clash texts, and one of the primary areas in which the authors perceive the West to be vulnerable. Drawing upon a variety of trajectories, projections, and conjectures, the authors paint a picture in which Muslims gradually overcome their non-Muslim counterparts and achieve by high immigration levels and birthrates what they could not accomplish by military means: A "Muslim Takeover" of the West (i.e., Europe, America, and Canada). They accomplish this "Takeover" with the complicity of liberal elites attached to welfare and multicultural policies that impede assimilation and foster an atmosphere of political correctness that stifles protest.

Concern about new classes of immigrants who cannot be assimilated is by no means a new phenomenon. In the United States, large-scale immigration of Catholics from Ireland and southern Europe generated great anxiety in the late 19th and early 20th centuries, leading to arguments about fertility rates and questionable religious loyalties that parallel those made about contemporary Muslim immigration to Western contexts.[14] The validity of such comparisons is not obvious to clash authors, however, who view the opening of immigration to Muslims through a dark lens.

In *Decline and Fall*, Bruce Thornton goes so far as to describe Europe's accommodation of a Muslim presence as "suicide by immigration" – not just resignation in the face of an "invasion" (2008, p. 80), but "a complete capitulation and betrayal of Western civilization" (2008, p. 80). This betrayal reveals the extent to which "cultural toxins" have infected the West since World War II, especially "fashionable self-loathing guilt over supposed Western crimes like racism, imperialism, colonialism." This guilt weakens Europeans and emboldens "invaders" (2008, p. 80).

Caldwell's language is less pointed, but advances similar undertones of Muslim invasion. When Europeans opened their doors to mass immigration in the wake of World War II, they began a monumental experiment without any consideration of the long-term consequences or "hidden costs." As a result, the face of Europe is changing:

> Muslims now either dominate or vie for domination of certain important European cities…. Such places may, as immigration continues and the voting power and political savvy of the Muslims already there increases, take on an increasingly Muslim character.
>
> (Caldwell, 2009, p. 118)

As soon as it became obvious that certain immigrants proposed to establish foreign cultures on European lands, immigration – and Muslim immigration a fortiori – appeared in a different light. It appeared in the light of a project to claim territory.

(Caldwell, 2009, p. 132)

Using government statistics, social surveys, think-tank reports, novels, and newspapers in eight languages, Caldwell argues that changes are underway which will fundamentally change the character of the European experience, providing lessons in failed government policies that have increased the challenge of merging newcomers who were already resistant to assimilation into the continent's established cultures and values.

Walter Laqueur's *The Last Days of Europe* (2013) explores similar themes, but with added emphasis on the unplanned and uncontrolled nature of Muslim immigration, as well as on what he regards as the dysfunctional impact of welfare policies. Like Caldwell and other authors, he bemoans the idea that Europe's once dominant place in the world is a thing of the past. Continued decline, he suggests, appears inevitable; changes in the European landscape associated with the large influx of Muslim immigrants are both a consequence of this decline and a major contributing factor.[15]

Laqueur points out that the first wave of immigration had much to do with the dissolution of Empires (e.g., West Indians, Pakistanis, Indians from India, and Indians from Uganda going to the United Kingdom; North Africans migrating to France) and was generally assumed to be a temporary phenomenon regulated by work permits. Many of these immigrants, however, managed to stay on legally or illegally, "and the host governments were not willing to enforce the law against those who broke it" (2013, p. 33). Thus, major foreign communities were developing in Europe at the same time as the oil crisis of 1973, which reinforced trends toward high unemployment (2013, pp. 34–35). The growth of Asian, African, and Middle Eastern immigrant communities, then, had less to do with genuine opportunity than with high birthrates, success in bringing dependents to Europe (legally or illegally), the transformation of illegal immigration into an organized business, and the proliferation of asylum seekers fleeing imprisonment or political turmoil. To underscore the rapid pace of population growth and its transformative impact, Laqueur cites a variety of data that indicates the doubling and tripling of Muslim communities across Europe from the 1980s to 2006 (2013, pp. 36–37).

In Laqueur's view, these changes bode ill for the future of Europe, for a variety of reasons. In addition to the fact that many immigrants have been unable to find steady and gainful employment, European countries were not well prepared to absorb large-scale immigration by foreigners emanating from wholly different cultures (Laqueur, 2013, p. 170). Though Laqueur does not go as far as Bawer in emphasizing undesirable values held by new immigrants who were not prepared to play by established rules and respect European institutions,[16] he does suggest that European countries were to some degree taken advantage of by immigrants whose primary motivations were economic, and whose ranks included a criminal element:

> [E]ven though the majority of these immigrants, probably the great majority, were not political refugees but economic immigrants in search of a better life for themselves and their children. Among the political asylum seekers there were islamists or even terrorists who were indeed in danger of being arrested in their native countries, but for reasons that had nothing to do with the struggle for democracy and freedom... also asylum seekers were criminals and came to establish criminal gangs.
>
> (2013, p. 35)

In permitting large-scale immigration, therefore, European nations allowed the infiltration of Islamists, terrorists, and others who were in danger of being arrested in their own countries. The latter established criminal gangs specializing in the drug trade, prostitution, car theft, and other illegal activities in their new home countries. A significant proportion of immigrants came to depend on European welfare services "from the day of their arrival." State authorities should have instead directed them to "productive labour" (2013, p. 172). Laqueur finds it particularly upsetting that some Muslim immigrant religious leaders were inclined to incite their followers "against the decadent and sinful Western way of life" and believes these figures should have been deported. "They should have been expected to behave in accordance with the law of the land and the values and prevailing norms. If these laws and norms were not according to their convictions, they would have been free to leave" (2013, p. 172).

Steyn's treatment of this subject echoes that of other clash authors, underscoring Europe's low birth rates and generous welfare state. These factors have weakened the continent and made it dependent upon immigrants, largely Muslims, to work and maintain the social benefits for the elderly non-productive social sector. The European "nanny state" has therefore played a central role in transforming Europe into "Eurabia" (Thornton, 2007). Even as many immigrants work to support the welfare state, however, many others become dependent on its services in ways that support the maintenance of state-subsidized enclaves that cannot assimilate to mainstream culture.

Thornton agrees with Steyn that Europe impedes the progress of immigrants by lavishing welfare benefits on them, and further elaborates on the idea of "Eurabia" by drawing on Bat Ye'or's definition of the term: "Europe's evolution from a Judeo-Christian civilization, with important post-Enlightenment secular elements, into a post Judeo-Christian civilization that is subservient to the ideology of jihad and the Islamic powers that propagate it" (2007, p. 90). Thus, again borrowing from Bat Ye'or, Europe is becoming a "civilization of dhimmitude" (2007, p. 90) – that is, a civilization that is subservient to Muslim rule. Thornton associates this condition with the decline of Christianity and Europe's failure to protect Western Christianity:

> In the past, Europe's resistance to Islamic imperial ambition was fired by Christian faith... But having abandoned God and country, where will Europe find the spiritual resources to assert the rightness of the Western civilization Christianity helped to create, and fight back vigorously against those who wish to destroy it?
>
> (2007, p. 130)

In Thornton's account of the situation, secularism has created a politics void of religious conviction. In the absence of such conviction, the void is being filled by outsiders hostile to Europe's unique religious heritage.

Intriguingly, this call to respect and protect Europe's Christian heritage finds an echo in Ayaan Hirsi Ali, whom some call a Muslim atheist.[17] Hirsi Ali calls on Muslims to learn from and perhaps convert to Christianity, largely on account of modern, post-Enlightenment Christianity's superior treatment of religious dissenters:

> I would by far rather live in a Christian than a Muslim country. Christianity in the West today is more humane, more restrained, and more accepting of criticism and debate. The Christian concept of God today is more benign, more tolerant of dissent. But the most important difference between the two civilizations is the exit option. A person who chooses to opt out of Christianity may be excommunicated from the Church community, but he is not harmed; his destiny is left to God. Muslims, however, impose Allah's rules on each. Apostates—people, like me, who leave the faith—are supposed to be killed.
>
> (2010, p. 244)

Hirsi Ali goes on to represent the involvement of Christian groups as perhaps the most crucial element in integrating Muslim immigrants and stopping the spread of radical Islam: "the clash of civilizations can be won through religious competition" (2010, p. 253). In an interview for *The Wall Street Journal*, Hirsi Ali argues that the United States needs to fight against the political ideology of Islamism to protect constitutional rights such as gender equality and tolerance for diverse sexual orientations (2017, p. A11).

Virtually all clash authors blame the West for lacking an appropriate strategy to deal with Muslim immigration; some also credit Muslims for having a dangerously coherent and effective strategy for infiltrating and asserting control over Western nations. William Wagner's *How Islam Plans to Change the World* (2012) is such a text. "In analyzing the Muslim strategy," Wagner states, "I have come to the conclusion that they have a three-pronged plan, which is as follows: jihad, da'wah, and mosques" (2012, p. 12). According to Wagner,[18] Islam becomes a threat and danger to the entire Western world and more importantly the Christian world, through their forms of proselytization, holy struggle and visibility.[19] Wagner refers to Islam as a more or less unified and monolithic entity driven by the objective of world domination: "In the search for world dominance, *Islam* will use truth as *they* understand it even if it conflicts with the Christian understanding of the term... Both the concepts of truth and fear have proven to be helpful in the *overall Islamic strategy*" (2012, p. 136, emphasis added).

Wagner dedicates a whole section of his book to the Islamic process of *da'wah*, or missionary work. One of his key concerns is that Christians are not competing vigorously enough with their Muslim counterparts: "These 'propagators' also carry the title of being *daa'i*. Sometimes these Islamic missionaries are fully funded... Most likely, there are more *daa'is* preaching Islam in the West than there are missionaries in the Muslim countries preaching Christianity" (2012, p. 42).

Though Wagner believes Christians are falling behind Muslims in the missionary enterprise, he remains convinced that Christian missions are morally superior to Islamic *da'wah*, and dedicates an entire section within his text to the differences between the two religious approaches. One of the contrasts, for instance, is the greater Christian emphasis on charitable enterprises: "Christian Missions engages in the establishment of schools, hospitals and other benevolent institutions through cooperative methods (2012, p. 44)" whereas "Islamic *Da'wah* stresses the construction of a mosque and then establishes its ministries" (2012, p. 44). This argument is pitched toward a relatively narrow audience and neglects to acknowledge the extensive social services provided by Muslim revival organizations within Muslim-majority societies, but provides insight into how some Western Christian groups perceive interreligious relations within the context of the broader clash literature.[20]

The failure of Muslim immigrant assimilation

According to most clash authors, the failure to assimilate Muslim immigrants is the Achilles' heel of Western civilization. The following quotation illustrates this concern with assimilation:

> [T]he spectacular failure of integration has brought some nations to the verge of social chaos and is leading others steadily in that direction.
>
> (Kepel, 2008, p. 233)

The European failure to assimilate immigrants, as Timothy Garton Ash notes, may contribute to a "downward spiral which will be the curse of the national politics of Europe for years ahead..." (in Thornton, 2007, p. 45). Clash authors project that immigrant Muslim youth will increasingly become involved in Islamist extremism and outright terrorism, as happened in Madrid and London, thereby reinforcing native-born resentments and fears. Almost without exception, contemporary clash authors paint a highly pessimistic picture of Europe and, ultimately, North America's future, within which youth riots and incidents of delinquency and terrorism become ever more frequent.

Notably, clash authors steer clear of in-depth sociological analysis. Many thinkers who frame their analysis in terms other than those of the clash literature have argued that failures of integration are at least to some extent caused by barriers within European and North American societies, which for decades desired guest workers for economic reasons and yet created legal and social obstacles to citizenship and full participation. Marginalization was therefore an outcome of specific policy choices, and the inability to overcome job discrimination or invest appropriate resources. Clash authors, however, take the position that European and North American nations have been far too accommodating. Laqueur, for example, argues that individual European citizens "had never been asked whether they wanted millions of new neighbors in their country... [and] about this very essential issue no one had ever consulted them" (2013, p. 171). As a result, European governments and societies found themselves in a position in which they were unable to provide guidance to newcomers but were instead "highly permissive." Social and political elites had lost their self-confidence; among the establishment, cultural and moral relativism rather than pride prevailed. Thus "newcomers to these countries were bound to gain the impression that prevailing laws and norms could safely be ignored" (Laqueur, 2013, p. 172). Caldwell amplifies this point about ignoring prevailing Western norms and laws, stating that, "Islam in Europe is different... Since its arrival half a century ago, Islam has broken or required adjustments to or rearguard defenses of a good many of the European customs, received ideas, and state structures with which it has come in contact" (Caldwell, 2009, p. 13).

In addition to the general concerns about the failure of assimilation, the ghettoization of European and North American Muslims is a major concern of clash thinkers. A number of authors stress that this condition is self-imposed by the Muslim community, and that religious leaders are particularly culpable. In these respects, Muslims are perceived as different from other ethnic communities:

> Muslim newcomers apparently like to stick longer with their coreligionists than do other groups of immigrants, and they are encouraged by the preachers to do so. This is true even with regard to India, where there is more ghettoization than in Europe; even middle-class Muslims seem to be reluctant to leave the areas where members of their community live.
>
> (Laqueur, 2013, p. 42)

Muslim religious leadership has a vested interest in keeping Muslims in ghettos because it allows them to have better control in ensuring that "there is little, if any, contact between the faithful and the infidel" (Laqueur, 2013, p. 206).

Of central concern is that areas of concentrated Muslim settlement become intensely conservative and resist cultural influences from the larger society. Most authors express concern that these new Muslim ghettos are "breeding grounds" with major demographic consequences, as reflected in high marriage and fertility rates. Because these rates are significantly higher than in the general population, the authors express grave concern that Europe and North America will be overwhelmed demographically from within, and not only in comparison to other world regions with rapidly growing populations.

It is against this backdrop of stated concerns that Steyn proclaims his thesis that, as central as America may be to saving the world, concerted action is now necessary to save America. Calling his production "a doomsday book with a twist" (2006, p. 15), Steyn uses demographics to demonstrate Europe's inept and suicidal social politics, and to warn Americans about Europe's demise. He wants America to resist the gradual "Islamization" that has penetrated the developed lands of Europe. In his view, more Muslims in Europe correlate directly with more terrorism, honor killings, and polygamy, and inversely with individual and political freedom. To save America from such a fate, it must refashion its traditional role as the land of opportunity for newcomers, and avoid giving minorities too many rights. America, he proposes, is the West's last chance, and faces nothing less than an ideological war to preserve the "Western way of Life."[21]

The problems of political correctness and multiculturalism

Another central theme of the clash literature is that Western elites have betrayed their mother culture, by indulging in excesses of self-criticism and self-doubt. These habits of thought and intellectual attitudes have led to an undervaluation of Western culture and to the rise of multiculturalism, which has been exploited by a Muslim adversary who benefits from pluralism without practicing it in relation to others. Because the West now faces a powerfully motivated and implacable foe, clash authors assert, the West needs to recover faith in its past greatness and cultural heritage, as well as its willingness to engage in critique of other cultures.

Spencer blames political correctness for current problems. Building on Bernard Lewis's judgment that Europeans "have no respect for their own culture," Spencer argues that political correctness has led to a double standard according to which the majority culture and religious traditions affiliated with this culture are subjected to scholarly and societal criticism: "Americans and Europeans... need to stop apologizing for all our forefathers allegedly and actually did wrong, and for the culture they built and remember what they did right, recognizing what Judeo-Christian civilization has brought to the world" (Spencer, 2007, p. 3). Rather than focus guiltily on historical misdeeds committed in the name of culture and religion, Spencer proposes, Western education and social commentary need to restore a sense of cultural pride or patriotism to collective consciousness. Without such a shift to a different way of being, Spencer believes that the West will ultimately lose the "War on Terror" (2007, p. 4).

Closely associated with this theme of political correctness is the idea of moral equivalency. Clash authors argue passionately in favor of Western moral superiority vis-à-vis Islam, and accuse Western elites of fostering a false perception that all religions and cultures are equal. Spencer, for example, argues that the present state of society and academia in the West has permitted the rise of a perception that Islam is "morally equal" to Christianity (2007, p. 1) – a perception with which he emphatically disagrees. Whereas an attitude of moral equivalency conceals the flaws of immigrant Muslim culture, respect for Western values demands an unwavering critique. Gilles Kepel elaborates on this point, specifically arguing that it was "the multicultural elite [who] was, almost without exception, allied with the Islamic right… [in] explaining away delinquency, suppressing reports of violence, standing up for the hijab, and so forth" (2008, p. 212). Multiculturalism, this logic proposes, leads elites to stand up for the "other" even when the practices of this other are not acceptable in light of modern societal standards.

Bawer argues that Muslims pose a grave threat to liberal values in the Western countries where they live. The inability of Western leaders to uncompromisingly assert the priority of these values over the dictates of multiculturalism, integration, and cultural and religious accommodation (which forces compromise with Muslim immigrants' expectations), may be the factor that will ultimately result in the demise of Western liberal values. Bawer is especially concerned with what he perceives as the vulnerability of the right to free speech, and believes Western countries have taken too accommodating a response to Muslim offences during the past two decades, including rioting, death threats against critics, and murders of non-Muslims. Free speech is in a crisis. To respond with the "accommodation" recommended by so many journalists, politicians, and intellectuals would be simply to submit to abandon freedom, embrace dhimmitude, and hope for the best from our new overlords (Bawer, 2009, p. 276).

For Bawer, multiculturalism is an evil that has forced Westerners into complacency with foreign cultural norms. It has blinded intellectuals to the threat that Islam poses to Western democracy, while simultaneously empowering Muslim immigrants and allowing them to resist adaptation to the ideals of the Enlightenment. To put the matter in even stronger terms, it has enabled Muslims to wage cultural warfare against the West from within the heart of Western societies. In Bawer's view, Muslims living in the West are engaged in a "cultural jihad" and will stop at nothing to bring the West into the "House of Submission," or "Dar al-Islam" (2009, p. 3).[22] Bawer alleges that "the pernicious doctrine of multiculturalism" motivated non-Muslims to support Muslims in targeting Salman Rushdie, as multiculturalism "teaches free people to belittle their own liberties while bending their knees to tyrants... which... has proven to be so useful to the new brand of cultural jihadists that it might have invented Osama Bin Laden himself" (2009, p. 5).

A similar polemic against multiculturalism appears in Ibn Warraq's *Why I am Not a Muslim*. According to Ibn Warraq, multiculturalism has lowered cultural defenses and enabled newcomers to make excessive demands. He equates multiculturalism with one or two attitudes with respect to human values – a false universalism or a harmful relativism:

> The implications of Muslim demands on the wider British are enormous. Unless great vigilance is exercised, we are all likely to find British society greatly impoverished morally, and all the gains, social and moral, may well be squandered in an orgy of multicultural liberalism.
>
> (1995, p. 353)

> Multiculturalism is based on some fundamental misconceptions. There is the erroneous and sentimental belief that all cultures, deep down, have the same values; or if these values are different, they are equally worthy of respect. Multiculturalism, being the child of relativism, is incapable of criticizing cultures, of making cross-cultural judgments. The truth is that not all cultures have the same values, and not all values are worthy of respect.
>
> (1995, p. 356)

At the core of this argument is the contention that Muslim values overlap very little with Western liberal values, and that multicultural tolerance is one of the central factors perpetuating certain practices that are especially problematic from a Western liberal point of view. Rather than an attitude of respect and dialogue which invites reciprocity and coexistence, Ibn Warraq sees in multiculturalism an inability to engage in critical thinking, as well as a racism of low expectations: "Multiculturalists are incapable of critical thought, and in a deep sense are more racist than the racists they claim to fight" (1995, p. 354).

Bruce Thornton's *Decline and Fall* embellishes on this theme of multiculturalism as a key causal factor that prevents assimilation. Thornton's overarching thesis is that Europe is becoming "Eurabia" due to "cultural toxins" imported by Muslim immigrants. This process is facilitated by a doctrine of multiculturalism that permeates the thinking of Western elites. The essence of multiculturalism is not the call to recognize and respect the values and contributions of other cultures, something which he believes the West has been doing for centuries. Rather, openness to the cultural "other" and willingness to criticize one's own ways have degenerated into a naïve idealization of the non-Westerner and a corresponding hatred of the West (2007, p. 96).

Thornton explains that modern multiculturalism in the West began with Europeans admiring the "noble savages" they encountered, including American Indians, South Sea Islanders, Africans, and Arabs. These peoples seemed to embody a simpler, more humane existence that the West had abandoned in its pursuit of power and profit. This explanation is reflected in Romantic complaints, such as the following by Wolfgang von Goethe in 1828:

> We other Europeans are ailing. Our styles of life are far from the healthy state of nature, and our social relations lack charity and benevolence. ... I often wish I were one of those so-called savages born in the islands of the South Seas, so that at least once I could savor human experience in its purity, without some artificial aftertaste.
>
> (2007, pp. 97–98)

Thornton contends that such attitudes have dominated the art and literature of the West for the last two centuries, eroding cultural certainty and self-confidence.

Another key factor in Thornton's critique of elite attitudes that have undermined the West is Marxism. He notes that, like the Romantics, Marxists similarly complained about the West in their writings on the destructive effects of industrial capitalism, which Marx himself represented as a system which had replaced the humane, organic relations between people with the alienating, dehumanizing power of the contract, private property, wage labor, and the profit motive (2007, p. 98). Such assumptions, Thornton alleges, caused the West to give more credit to precapitalist non-Western societies than was warranted. Idealization of the non-West also found reinforcement in later Marxist analyses of imperialism and colonialism. This led to the idealization of the Third World as "history's instrument for transforming the wicked West; because of this, resistance to immigration, demands that immigrants assimilate to their new homes, and expressions of national pride have all become 'fascist,' tainted with Nazi racism and the Holocaust" (2007, pp. 99–100).

Echoing many other conservative thinkers and clash theorists, Thornton argues that Western intellectual elites have destructively wedded themselves to "self-hating" ideas. Leftists, he believes, have used naïve idealizations of the Third World as the basis for pursuing the liberation of the oppressed, while ignoring the very brutal imperialist ambitions of the Soviet Union as well as the current expansionist ambitions of jihadists. The currently reigning mode of thought is "Third Worldism," the doctrine that "every Westerner is presumed guilty until proven innocent" (2007, p. 100). This way of thinking is the product of a combination of noble-savage idealism and Romantic discontent with Marxist-Leninist theorizing and post-Marxist multiculturalism. The result is a suicidal self-hatred among many Westerners, who, convinced of their guilt, do not have the cultural resources for defending their way of life: "These days, the successor of Europe is Eurabia" (2007, p. 101).

Because of multiculturalism, then, Muslim immigrants have been allowed to perpetuate their cultures no matter how alien to the values of Western civilization even as the European nations make it difficult for those who wish to assimilate. Immigrant communities are allowed to create their own standards of behavior, educational curricula, social mores, and public practices – indulgences not allowed native born-citizens of host countries (2007, p. 101). Multiculturalism, then, creates too much space for difference. To back up this claim, Thornton uses the following examples:

- In Sweden, the legal age of marriage is 18, but for immigrants there is no minimum age.
- Turkish and Pakistani immigrants in Germany are exempted from the usual intrusive procedure that a German who wishes to marry someone not from an E.U. member state has to undergo in order to prove that the relationship is legitimate, on the assumption that their marriages are arranged.
- In France, public swimming pools are segregated by sex to appease Muslim sensibilities.
- Some British retailers have stopped selling mugs that depict the character Piglet because Muslims find pigs offensive.
- Burger King's chocolate ice cream swirls were banished in some places because they reminded Muslims of Arabic writing.
- After the murder of Theo van Gogh, Dutch schoolchildren were not allowed to wear Dutch flags on their backpacks lest Muslims find them provocative.

(2007, pp. 101–102)

Thornton categorically rejects the notion that at least some bias toward Muslim immigrants is based on prejudice and ignorance. He characterizes "Islamophobia" as a new thought-crime, a variation on the "racist" charge used by multiculturalists to forestall criticism or silence those who speak of uncomfortable facts. Such oversensitivity, he proposes, illustrates how far the European establishment has gone in abandoning its own values such as freedom of speech and respect for truth in order to appease a vocal minority (2007, p. 103). Thornton rejects charges of Islamophobia for his own beliefs, and maintains that many of the supposedly false prejudices about Islam are true. He maintains, for example, that Islam is responsible for the mistreatment of women and for intolerance toward other faiths (2007, p. 104).

A core theme of the clash literature is that, rather than accommodate Muslim identity, Westerners need to assert Western identity. Western eagerness to be politically correct results in efforts to accommodate Muslims at any cost. It gives Islam an advantage and adversely affects Western policy and the Western way of living. Whereas a focus on accommodation and mere integration contributes to an erosion of Western identity, a reemphasis on assimilation might help to correct a creeping tendency toward Muslim domination (Steyn, 2006, p. 60). Steyn frames the reassertion of a more exclusive Western identity as a matter of "Cultural Will": The Western majority culture needs to use the power it still has, and demonstrate that it is not weak.

Discussion and the necessity of the dialogical: Narrative tendencies across the clash literature

Despite variations in emphasis and in the precise structure of arguments, the clash literature manifests a number of consistent tendencies that express the profound anxiety of many authors with respect to Islam, and that signal serious challenges for protagonists of intercultural dialogue and coexistence. First, the literature as a whole appears to be driven by deep-seated identity insecurity, not just in relation to an "intrusive" and seemingly monolithic Islam that is wholly "other," but also in relation to an idealized but now receding West that is being threatened from within by what the authors perceive as a corrosive over-extension of their civilization's ethos of critical reason. The remarkably broad generalizations and sharp dichotomies used in the literature are best understood not just as efforts to define an enemy, but also as attempts to recapture or define an "authentic" identity that has become internally contested. Thus, the arguments are not just about Islam, but also about the West. Second, in their critiques of Islam, the clash authors rely heavily on extrapolation from past demographic data trends and from provocative incidents, with only limited consideration of complex causal factors that might provide a much richer context for understanding the phenomena in question. In this sense, the literature appears to be more alarmist than analytical in nature and intent. Third, to the extent that the authors surface some genuinely problematic issues within Muslim cultures (immigrant and otherwise) and Islamic-Western relations, the insistence on polarization and "winning" manifested by their writings actively pushes against collaborative and complementary solutions predicated on dialogue and relational engagement.

Arguments rooted in insecure identity

The arguments of clash authors manifest not just a profound fear of Islam, but also a powerful anxiety about threats to the future of "the West" that predates current controversies. In other words, the clash literature's call to arms against Islam and Muslim immigration is not simply a matter of Islamophobia, though certainly the discourse is permeated with deep distaste for all things that purport to be Islamic. Rather, it is also an expression of a longstanding debate about what the West is and should be. The fact that "the West" is so consistently represented in unproblematic, uncontested, essentialized terms – even as Western tendencies such as multiculturalism, Romanticism, or leftism are denounced – is itself a signal that, whatever else concerns the clash authors, they are fundamentally engaged in Western identity politics. In this sense, Islam enters the equation both as a substantive concern (there is no reason to doubt the genuineness of the authors' fears) and as a foil, a useful "other" for defining what the "self" ought to be or not to be. The clash authors' simplistic, essentialized, and almost entirely negative representations of Islam, therefore, serve the purpose of defining basic us/them distinctions that have an import which transcends intercultural relations.

In a real sense, the clash authors are deeply insecure about and uncomfortable with what the West has become: hybrid, diverse, contested, culturally plural, and religiously diverse. This discomfort has been a long time in the making. The issue of Islam brings this discomfort to the surface, producing discourse that seeks to save what the authors fear they are losing, and to that end seeks to draw sharp dichotomies that reassert cultural boundaries and amplify debate about what it means to be "Western." The result is a discourse that privileges an idealized Western and European culture, juxtaposed with willfully undifferentiated representation of Islam as a static, unchangeable, and threatening adversary culture. Unreflective use of the term "Eurabia" manifests a sharply reductionistic tendency to equate Islam as a whole (a faith that spans continents and cultures) with Arabia and Arabia with Salafist extremism. The diversity within both of these "macro-identities" is purposefully downplayed and the relevant scholarly literature on this diversity is ignored. Europe is presented as the human Christian civilization that gave birth to skeptical humanism, and Islam as a universal, authoritarian, misogynist ideology without significant internal conflicts, schisms, and interpretive or legal debates. In seeking to galvanize Europeans against Islam and Americans against the European response to Islam, the authors seek to call Westerners back to fundamentals and undermine adversaries within their own context. Some readers may detect notes of envy in clash authors' characterizations of strong Muslim identities and doctrinal certitudes. Caldwell, for example, emphasizes the strength, confidence, and cohesion of Muslim culture, which in his view is an inherent threat to a more loosely anchored and "malleable" European culture (2009, p. 349). This imbalance, he believes, works to the detriment of Europeans, who are easily overwhelmed by strong immigrant cultures.

To be sure, certain issues are more salient for some clash authors than for others. For some, security and terrorism remain the preeminent issues, while for others a greater sense of motivation may arise from a sense of threats to individual freedom (including freedom from religion) or from a sense that traditional allegiance to Christianity or Judeo-Christian civilization has been betrayed by intellectual elites. In the issue of Islam, however, clash authors find common cause and a push to renegotiate among themselves a "pure" Western identity that is in many respects a new construction. In the process of renegotiating this identity, there is an opportunity and a need to affix blame to those who have let the "barbarians" through the gates.

Insofar as the clash literature is not only about "them" (Muslims) but also about "us" (people of the West and their existential discomfort with a changing world), the genre is arguably more symptomatic than diagnostic. Clash authors manifest great concern to draw lines and refuse identity negotiations with the deemed recalcitrant "other," and show very little interest in developing a nuanced, complex understanding of who that "other" actually is. Notably absent is the increasingly voluminous scholarly literature on Muslim negotiations with modernity; only a few select scholars who deal with things Islamic are deemed trustworthy. Caldwell, for example, dismisses discussion of Muslim diversity "pleasing glibness," and like other clash authors characterizes Islam as a primordial religion impervious to outside influences and change. Thus, those who seek points of contact and shared values – let alone a reflection of the self in the other – are portrayed as outlandishly naïve.

Reliance on extrapolation, with minimal context

Clash authors repeatedly employ a style of reasoning based on simple extrapolation from past trends and generalization from specific, emotionally gripping incidents. The approach treats cultural and religious entities as static vectors rather than as dynamic communities that can change in response to new circumstances and relationships, and actively selects from the most disturbing of current events to give meaning to changing demographic realities.

Superficial use of demographic data is a clear liability of the clash literature, even when the figures speak to dramatic new tendencies in European societies. Immigration rates and differences in birthrates matter, and it appears certain that Islam will henceforth (albeit not for the first time in history, given centuries of Muslim presence in Spain and in southeastern Europe) be a visible part of the European experience. The notion that this European experience will not or cannot have an impact on the way Muslims experience and express Islam, however, is as poorly founded as the notion that Muslim culture is immune to the sort of demographic transition that typically occurs in populations dynamically subsisting in industrial and postindustrial economic milieux. Anyone with close experience of young Muslim women pursuing university degrees, for example, is likely to discover that these women have professional and life aspirations that are highly similar to those of their non-Muslim counterparts. Simply put, "Islam" and "Muslims" are not categories that place human beings outside the larger continuum of human experience, and the notion that Muslims cannot adapt or will inevitably overwhelm others appears not just ill-founded but also prejudicial.

Another troubling tendency in the clash literature is its frequent exploitation of disturbing events for emotional impact. Clash authors over-select such events in their narratives and overgeneralize their representativeness, in ways that are clearly intended to arouse fear and anxiety in the reader. At the same time, they pass over incidents of violence or intimidation directed at Muslims in silence. While such selectivity and desire for emotional impact may be inevitable features of the journalistic style in which these books have been written, there is nonetheless a telling absence of humanizing portraits in the clash literature, despite the reality that "ordinary," non-threatening Muslims are much easier to encounter than extremists bent on violence or wedded to grandiose agendas. By over-selecting the negative, remaining silent about abuses committed against Muslims, and putting events and statistics in the most alarming context possible, clash authors seek to influence their audience in ways that are more alarmist than analytical.

This trend is evident in Steyn's use of data from a poll conducted by *The Times* of London. Steyn conveys that seven percent of Muslims questioned agreed that suicide bombings of civilians could be justified in certain circumstances. Steyn interprets this to mean that significant numbers of Muslims are radical extremists. However, he does not explain how many people were polled, and to what extent those polled could represent the larger European Muslim population. He also ignores other data which reveal that the percentage of people who are willing to justify intentional bombing of civilians under "some circumstances" is roughly comparable in Western and Muslim contexts. By cherry-picking facts and ignoring those that do not fit the picture, any nation or religious group can be portrayed in a dark light.

A hallmark of quality analytical literature is that it is capable of confronting problematic issues and behavioral patterns in ways that probe beneath the surface, generating insights into circumstances and motivations in a way that does not obscure common humanity or foreclose the possibility of constructive change. The clash literature falls short on these counts, by denigrating the search for drivers of extremism (an exercise that is deemed a form of capitulation), downplaying social class and social justice considerations, and ignoring the significance of prejudice, discrimination, and social exclusion. While there is no need to place all responsibility on host societies and governments or to hold immigrant communities blameless in instances where maladaptation is evident, the clash literature is deeply problematic in a host of ways: It ignores useful sociological insights, it vastly overgeneralizes about the other, it discounts the relevance of dialogical thinking, and it substitutes cultural reassertion for wide-ranging examination of policy options.

Insistence on polarization over relational engagement

Ultimately, the clash literature identifies some genuine problems with Muslim integration in the West as well as in contemporary Muslim-majority cultures, but subverts critical reflection on ways in which "the West" is either implicated in these problems or capable of positive engagement with constructive forces within Muslim communities and cultures. The worldview of clash authors is not relational, and seeks no meaningful relationship with the Muslim other. The approach is profoundly non-dialogical and polarizing, with an emphasis on winning rather than on transforming the conflict.

To an extent, the clash literature manifests continuity with Cold War narratives, albeit with a new religio-cultural twist. Like post-9/11 Europe and North America, the Cold War world was one of polarization and ideological competition, within which complex world events were often viewed through lenses of East-West competition rather than in relation to complex local circumstances and realities. Then as now, the loyalty of Europe to the Western cause was suspect in the eyes of many Cold War protagonists, and the successors of these leading Western Cold War thinkers are now among the ranks of those seeking to understand the world in light of a new polarity.

If there is to be hope of transcending this polarity and creating a world in which "Islam" and "the West" are not mutually exclusive categories, relational engagement and dialogue are indispensable. It is not enough for Western pundits to speak about or even "to" Muslims, and dysfunctional to try to resurrect a past civilization based on mythical notions of purity. New forms of engagement are needed, and Western protagonists of such engagement need not embrace "relativism" to pursue it. Indeed, interlocutors that were truly confident in such putative Western values as reason, freedom, and equality would see no need to mythologize Western history (which, after all, has been full of both contradictions and progressive struggles to overcome them) or deny the existence of Muslims whose values overlap with those held by people in the West. Insofar as the clash literature manifests a certain lack of confidence in the West's greatest virtues, particularly in the domains of self-critique, dynamic reinvention of the self, and free-spirited exploration, it offers few starting points for the needed cross-boundary engagement.

For dialogical thinkers, like Dallmayr, the clash literature is part of a larger genre and trajectory found in Western thinking even before Samuel Huntington's thesis (2002; 2014). However, in the 21st century, in particular the argument of the West "in its ultimate decline" and in "its last days" has increased exponentially, as the works noted in this chapter attest. It is interesting, as pointed out in Euben's last chapter in *Enemy in the Mirror* (1999), that there is "fundamentalist resurgence" in which the word "fundamentalism" is being used and abused by a variety of protagonists whether Islamic, Christian, atheist, secular, etc. "Islamic or Christian fundamentalisms" and "fundamentalist secularism" suggest that we are indeed living in an age of extremes. Understanding the patterns of connection within "clashing fundamentalisms" is a context that needs to be analyzed in order to better understand the global phenomenon of seemingly contradictory populist/ nationalist and religio-cultural fundamentalist movements emerging and expanding simultaneously.

Conclusion

This chapter has provided an overview and critique of a literature that is not often engaged by university-based scholars. There are reasons for this: Most of the literature is not academic in nature, ignores relevant scholarship, and traffics in oversimplifications and polarizations that few scholars embrace. Nonetheless, precisely because this literature has wide circulation and plays a powerful role in constituting political and public discourse (as evidenced by pre-emptive anti-*sharia* campaigns, right-wing populist movements, and anti-immigration policies, and the formation of anti-immigration parties in Canada, the United States, and Europe), critical examination and dialogical engagement is needed.[23]

While the term "clash literature" may seem novel or ambiguous, the term has been used here to refer to writings that articulate a number of consistent themes. First, these writings present a stark worldview in which Western liberalism is locked in a dangerous conflict with Islamic authoritarianism, with highly consequential developments currently unfolding in North America and Europe. These events put the future of the West in question, despite its unassailable moral superiority in relation to Islam and non-Western cultures. Second, clash authors maintain that this struggle is rendered all the more difficult by what they judge to be an absence of genuinely moderate, progressive, and conciliatory tendencies within the global Muslim community. Islam demands conformity, they argue, and even "moderate" Muslims identify with some of the same grievances articulated by "extremists." Third, culture-clash thinkers place a strong emphasis on threatening demographic trends associated with Muslim immigration; these trends have been made possible by (and accelerate) a loss of faith in the Judeo-Christian tradition, and make the demise of the West distinctly possible, to the extent that Europe may already be "lost" and Canada and the United States are in their decline. Fourth, clash authors seek to reinforce their arguments by claiming that resistance of Muslim immigrants to assimilation is a static and multigenerational condition. Muslims are unlike most other immigrants, and operate by values which are alien to the contemporary Western tradition. Fifth, they maintain that the West has long been in denial with respect to these growing problems, on account of pervasive political correctness and the salience of multiculturalist sensibilities. Simply put, the West is in crisis because of the disloyalty of its own intellectuals. Those responsible for economically based decisions to permit large-scale immigration in order to satisfy demands of industry for guest workers and cheap labor are not targeted with comparable accusations. Finally, clash authors propose that women's emancipation is one of the most fundamental wedge issues between Islam and the West, and needs to receive a strong focus from those seeking to stave off a Muslim takeover of Europe and push for victory in the protracted cultural war between civilizations. This last point is further explored in the next chapter by focusing on Muslim controversial public spokespersons and their best-selling books about Islam – many of which have been authored by "dissident" or "dissenting" Muslim women authors who uphold values of Western liberalism in opposition to traditional Islamic practices and positions.

Additionally, while critiques of these sweeping, pessimistic assumptions are not difficult to identify, this chapter has sought to draw particular attention to three crucial issues raised by the clash literature. First, it argued that while these writings are intensely Islamophobic and purvey hostile stereotypes, they also reveal a great deal of insecurity with respect to Western identity. The literature's deeply problematic essentializations and generalizations warrant strong criticism, but there is also a need for awareness that the popular success of this literature stems not just from prejudice and lack of knowledge but also from deep-seated anxiety and insecurity. Old visions of what Europe and "the West" should be clearly do not fit the present reality, and there is a vacuum of compelling visions for how these identity structures might evolve in the future. The clash literature seeks to fill this vacuum with disturbing, reactionary visions that conveniently stigmatize a particular identity group.

The second and third lines of critique relate to the types of argument used and to the authors' proclivity for polarizing relationships that might possibly be bridged by other means. Clash books thrive on pessimistic extrapolation of demographic trends without a deep analytical investigation of underlying factors, and rush to conclusions about entire population groups based on specific cases of delinquency and violence. Their thesis that Muslims are difficult if not impossible to assimilate closely mirrors accusations directed against Catholic immigrants to the United States during the late 19th and early 20th centuries. This pattern provides cause for reflection. Polarization and sharpening social conflict appear to be a primary goal of the genre, which actively dismisses dialogue and the value of relational engagement.

The clash literature demands a response – preferably a response that is not just a reaction or an application of pejorative labels to the authors, most of whom are doubtlessly sincere in their fear of Muslims, even when capitalizing on popular moods and anxieties for commercial gain. What is needed is a response that makes the complex nature of "Islam-West" relations more easily intelligible, and that liberates creative imagination by telling new stories. Scholars as well as journalists need to find ways to give voice to people who thrive at the intersection of cultures, who are not afraid, who honor the past but do not cling to it, and who are willing to learn and expand their sense of identity and belonging through encounters with otherness. A reaction to the clash literature that merely stigmatizes the clash theorists is a reaction that addresses symptoms but not the deeper problems. To give substance to ideas of dialogue and coexistence, authors need to dispense with simplistic dichotomies and dualisms, and with efforts to make fortresses out of Europe, North America, or any other cultural region. A scholarship that is itself dialogical and engaged might offer a stronger remedy, by surfacing latent visions, articulating "un-storied" experiences, and demonstrating that the points of intersection among cultures are sites not just of friction, but also of mutual learning, shared discovery, and common humanity.

Notes

1 Much of the material in this chapter was previously published in my article, "Pervasive Anxiety about Islam" (2013). It has since been substantially updated.
2 There are a plethora of critiques of Huntington's thesis, some including Arun Kundnani's *The Muslims are Coming!* (2014); Cemil Aydin's *The Idea of the Muslim World* (2017); Kenneth J. Long's *Contemporary Anti-Muslim Politics* (2017); and Robert Wright's article, "The Clash of Civilizations that Isn't" (2015).
3 This tone is reflected in the inflammatory language invoked in chapter titles such as "The West Loses the Will to Live" (Spencer, 2018), "'Islam Says, Kill Them': The Islamic Revolution" (Spencer, 2016), and "Shackled by Sharia" (Hirsi Ali, 2015).
4 Said (1979).
5 "The West" as defined by clash literature is implying both Europe and North America. However, some books specifically focus on Europe, with America in the background. For this chapter, it is important to note that the influence of clash literature – whether focusing on Europe and/or America – extends from North America to Europe (especially since most of the authors are originally from North America).
6 Refer to Lean (2017); Esposito & Kalin (2011); Sheehi (2011).
7 See Lockman (2009).
8 See Saunders (2012).
9 For commentary on the significance of dehumanization and enemy images within the context of identity conflict, see Montville (1993); Moses (1990); and Keen (1986).
10 As will be explored in Chapter 4, some of the Muslim dissident reformist literature which utilizes clash discursive tendencies differs on this point. Such literature has particular advocates who claim that Islam is not innately evil but that it is worth saving, and that reform is essential for any transformation to occur. Much of this literature claims to be a "wake-up" call for Muslims. One prominent example in this literature is Irshad Manji's *The Trouble with Islam* (2004).
11 See Omid Safi's blog article, "Not Conducive to the Public Good" (2013).
12 Spencer is a charismatic speaker and author who received his master's degree in Religious Studies at the University of North Carolina. He has published over 12 books on the Islamic threat to Western society, and is currently the director of *Jihad Watch*, a blog designed to monitor and report subversive Islamic theology and action. In addition, in 2009, he cofounded the American Freedom Defense Initiative which has also been called Stop Islamization of America (SIOA). (See https://www.adl.org/sites/default/files/documents/assets/pdf/civil-rights/stop-islamization-of-america-2013-1-11-v1.pdf.) Spencer has also participated in numerous seminars for American military groups (i.e., United States Central Command, United States Army Command and General Staff College, the U.S. Army's Asymmetric Warfare Group, the FBI, the Joint Terrorism Task Force, and the U.S. Intelligence community). See "About Robert Spencer," http://www.jihadwatch.org/about-robert-spencer.html.

13 Steyn is a Canadian-born writer, political commentator, and cultural critic. Steyn often writes articles for a popular Canadian news magazine, *Maclean's*. In 2007, the Canadian Islamic Congress filed human rights complaints with the Canadian Human Rights Commission against Maclean's for publishing 18 "Islamophobic" articles by Steyn. The Commission dismissed the complaints in June 2008.

14 For more about this comparison, refer to Saunders (2012).

15 Other factors in Europe's decline include the stalling of the movement toward European unity and the crisis of the welfare state, as well as a European crisis in self-confidence that is both a contributor and a result of these factors.

16 Bawer states, "Most come from poor villages in underdeveloped countries with high levels of corruption—a background that tends to breed cynicism, duplicity, and an exceptional skill at manipulating the system" (Bawer, 2009, p. 30).

17 Chapter 4 will explore more of Hirsi Ali's thought and writings.

18 William Wagner is a Baptist missionary and a professor of missions at the Golden Gate Baptist Theological Seminary in California.

19 Similarly, Hirsi Ali suggests that "the agents of dawa hide behind constitutional protections they themselves would dismantle were they in power" and argues that the "infrastructure of dawa in the U.S." needs to be dismantled (Varadarajan, 2017, p. A11).

20 Whereas most of the books cited in this chapter were published by mainstream, non-religious presses, Wagner's text was produced by a Christian publisher that is dedicated to missionary work. The mission statement of Kregel Publishers, the publisher of Wagner's text, reads, "Our mission as an evangelical Christian publisher is to develop and distribute…trusted, biblically based resources that lead individuals to know and serve Jesus Christ" (Kregel Publications, n.d., http://www.kregel.com/ME2/Default.asp.)

21 In Steyn's follow-up book, *After America* (2011), he argues that America, too, is in an inevitable rapid self-destructive decline that ultimately leads to the demise of Western civilization for the world.

22 The bifurcated view of the world as divided into *dar al-Islam* ("the abode of Islam") and *dar al-harb* ("the abode of war") was found in more conservative classical Islamic schools of legalistic thought and has been resurrected by specific contemporary Muslim revivalist thinkers like Sayyid Qutb (d. 1966). This understanding has been criticized by many contemporary reformist Muslim scholars, in particular Tariq Ramadan, who has advocated for a critique of this division in order for Muslims to fully participate in 21st century emancipatory discourses and struggles, especially when so many Muslims now live in Western pluralist societies. As Theodore Gabriel points out, most Western nations are considered *dar al-sulh* (abode of peace), where Muslims are in a minority but have religious and cultural freedoms. However, Gabriel notes that "it is difficult to say that western nations are an ideal of *dar al-sulh* since Muslims living there are often faced with problems in observing their traditions, such as in the matter of apparel, food, burial of the dead and education of children" (2005, p. 17).

23 A few examples include former President Donald Trump's (2017) Executive Order that banned travel and immigration to the United States from six Muslim-majority countries; Fidesz – Hungarian Civic Alliance in Hungary; Freedom Party in Austria; Swiss People's Party in Switzerland; Law and Justice (Prawo i Sprawiedliwość; PiS) in Poland; and League (Lega Nord) in Italy. For more about the influence of Huntington's framework on populist nationalism and anti-Muslim sentiments in Europe and the United States, refer to Jeffrey Haynes' article, "From Huntington to Trump" (2019) and Peter Mandaville's article, "Designating Muslims" (2017).

References

Aydin, C. (2017). *The idea of the Muslim world: A global intellectual history*. Harvard University Press.

Bawer, B. (2009). *Surrender: Appeasing Islam, sacrificing freedom*. Anchor Books.

Caldwell, C. (2009). *Reflections on the revolution in Europe: Immigration, Islam, and the West*. Doubleday.

Dallmayr, F. (2002). *Dialogue among civilizations: Some exemplary voices*. Palgrave Macmillan.

Dallmayr, F., Kayapinyar, M. A., & Yavlaci, I. (Eds.). (2014). *Civilizations and world order: Geopolitics and cultural differences*. Lexington Books.

Esposito, J., & Kalin, I. (Eds.). (2011). *Islamophobia: The challenge of pluralism in the 21st century*. Oxford University Press.

Euben, R. L. (1999). *Enemy in the mirror: Islamic fundamentalism and the limits of modern rationalism, a work of comparative political theory*. Princeton University Press.

Gabriel, T. (2005). Is Islam against the West? In R. Geaves, T. Gabriel, Y. Haddad, & J. I. Smith (Eds.), *Islam and the West post 9/11* (pp. 13–26). Ashgate.

Haynes, J. (2019). From Huntington to Trump: Twenty-five years of the 'Clash of Civilizations'. *The Review of Faith & International Affairs, 17*(1), 11–23.

Hirsi Ali, A. (2010). *Nomad*. Knopf Publishers.

Hirsi Ali, A. (2015). *Heretic: Why Islam needs a reformation now*. Harper.

Huntington, S. P. (1993, June 1). The clash of civilizations? *Foreign Affairs, Summer*. https://www.foreignaffairs.com/articles/united-states/1993-06-01/clash-civilizations

Ingraham, C. (2014, October 6). Ben Affleck and Bill Maher are both wrong about Islamic fundamentalism. *The Washington Post*. https://www.washingtonpost.com/news/wonk/wp/2014/10/06/ben-affleck-and-bill-maher-are-both-wrong-about-islamic-fundamentalism/

Keen, S. (1986). *Faces of the enemy: Reflections of the hostile imagination*. Harper & Row.

Kepel, G. (2008). *The war for Muslim minds: Islam and the West*. Viva Books.

Kundnani, A. (2014). *The Muslims are coming!: Islamophobia, extremism, and the domestic war on terror*. Verso.

Laqueur, W. (2013). *The last days of Europe: Epitaph for an old continent*. St. Martin's Press.

Lean, N. (2017). *The Islamophobia industry: How the right manufactures hatred of Muslims*. Pluto Books.

Lockman, Z. (2009). *Contending visions of the Middle East: The history and politics of orientalism*. Cambridge University Press.

Long, K. J. (2017). *Contemporary anti-Muslim politics: Aggressions and exclusions*. Lexington Books.

Malik, S. A. (2018). *Atheism and Islam: A contemporary discourse*. Kalam Research and Media. https://www.researchgate.net/publication/328806366_Atheism_and_Islam_A_Contemporary_Discourse

Mandaville, P. (2017). Designating Muslims: Islam in the Western policy imagination. *The Review of Faith & International Affairs, 15*(3), 54–65.

Manji, I. (2004). *The trouble with Islam today: A Muslim's call for reform in her faith*. Vintage Canada.

Montville, J. (1993). The healing function of political conflict resolution. In D. J. D. Sandole, & H. van der Merwe (Eds.), *Conflict resolution theory and practice: Integration and application* (pp. 112–127). Manchester University Press.

Moses, R. (1990). On dehumanizing the enemy. In V. D. Volkan, D. A. Julius, & J. V. Montville (Eds.), *The psychodynamics of international relationships: Volume I: Concepts and theories* (pp. 111–118). Lexington Books.

Safi, O. (2013, June 26). *"Not conducive to the public good": American Islamophobes barred from the UK.* http://omidsafi.religionnews.com/2013/06/26/not-conducive

Said, E. (1979). *Orientalism.* Vintage Books.

Saunders, D. (2012). *The myth of the Muslim tide: Do immigrants threaten the West?* Vintage Canada.

Sharify-Funk, M. (2013). Pervasive anxiety about Islam: A critical reading of contemporary 'clash' literature. *Religions, 4*(4), 443–468. https://doi.org/10.3390/rel4040443

Sheehi, S. (2011). *Islamophobia: The ideological campaign against Muslims.* Clarity Press.

Spencer, R. (2007). *Religion of peace? Why Christianity is and Islam isn't.* Simon and Schuster.

Spencer, R. (2016). *The complete infidels' guide to Iran.* Regnery Press.

Spencer, R. (2018). *The history of jihad: From Muhammad to ISIS.* Bombardier Books.

Steyn, M. (2006). *America alone: The end of the world as we know it.* Regnery Publishing.

Steyn, M. (2011). *After America: Get ready for Armageddon.* Regnery Publishing.

Thornton, B. S. (2007). *Decline and fall: Europe's slow-motion suicide.* Encounter Books.

Varadarajan, T. (2017, April 7). Ayaan Hirsi Ali, Islam's most eloquent apostate. *The Wall Street Journal.* https://www.wsj.com/articles/ayaan-hirsi-ali-islams-most-eloquent-apostate-1491590469

Wagner, W. (2012). *How Islam plans to change the world.* Kregel Publications.

Warraq, I. (1995). *Why I am not a Muslim.* Prometheus Books.

Wright, R. (2015, February 25). The clash of civilizations that isn't. *The New Yorker.* https://www.newyorker.com/news/news-desk/clash-civilizations-isnt

Chapter 4

Dissidence, Dissonance, and the Politics of Muslim Women's Emancipation

One of the central themes across the so-called clash literature, and much of the writing that has been influenced by it, is the oppression and suppression of Muslim women and the need for their liberation. As Lila Abu-Lughod observes,

> Pundits tell us that there is a clash of civilizations or cultures in our world. They tell us there is an unbridgeable chasm between the West and the 'Rest.' Muslims are presented as a special and threatening culture – the most homogenized and the most troubling of the Rest. Muslim women, in this new common sense, symbolize just how alien this culture is.
>
> (2013, p. 6)

In her book, *Do Muslim Women Need Saving?* (2013), the rhetorical question that Abu-Lughod asks challenges the prevailing notion that all Muslim women suffer from patriarchal attitudes and practices – or at least suffer more from patriarchy than non-Muslim women – and that they must be rescued.

Muslim women's emancipation has become a major literary genre in the 21st century. Personal narratives of oppression and liberation from writers such as Ayaan Hirsi Ali, Irshad Manji, Wafa Sultan, and Asra Nomani (to name just a few) are intertwined with clash literature, in ways that are suggested by the titles of their best-selling books (i.e., *Infidel, The Trouble with Islam Today, A God Who Hates, Standing Alone in Mecca*). Through an autobiographical format, authors writing within this genre provide traumatic testimonials from disaffected Muslims whose personal experiences serve to illustrate larger, more abstract arguments such as those discussed in the previous chapter. As Adam Yaghi observes,

> The astounding popularity of the testimonial autobiography – a troubling phenomenon from the perspective of several postcolonial critics – 'lies to a great extent in the ability of the Muslim [or Arab] woman author to embody the double figure of insider and victim, a key subject within Orientalist understandings of women in Muslim societies.'

DOI: 10.4324/9780429341151-5

> Testimonial works like those written by [Ayaan Hirsi] Ali, observes [Saba] Mahmood, have an 'ideological force' behind them, a force appealing to diverse readers from both the right and the left, including many feminist scholars and activists who treat them like feminist revelations.
>
> (2016, p. 87)

Cultural studies scholar Hamid Dabashi labels these writers as "native informers" (2006) whose books grab the attention of mainstream North American and European audiences by invoking themes of alarm or dissidence. Intriguingly, the authors of these books are typically women who represent themselves as people who are at odds with their faith tradition and community. Their message is one of righteous, risk-taking dissent, and the authorial image they project on the back cover is one of boldness in the face of dangerous intolerance: One woman calling for reform "from the margins," ready to "take on" fanatical jihadists or a larger, male-dominated religious establishment. However, accurate these self-portraits of defiant marginality may be (the authors' views, after all, are far from popular within Muslim religious communities), the popularity of the books attests to the fact that, at least in mainstream North American society, the authors are far from marginal.[1]

The ubiquity of these self-conscious dissident publications in mainstream American and Canadian bookstores finds a dramatic counterpoint in their virtually complete absence from shops that are oriented toward Muslim minority communities. For a variety of reasons, few Muslim book merchants would deem it appropriate to sell them, and many no doubt fear the way placing such texts on the shelves might be interpreted by their clients. The books contain generalizations about Islam and about the state of contemporary Muslim communities that have hardly been welcomed by traditional voices of authority, in North America or in the wider Muslim world. Moreover, in diaspora communities as well as in Muslim-majority countries, there is a widespread feeling that outsiders are only interested in negative perspectives on Islam, and books like Irshad Manji's *The Trouble with Islam Today* and Ayaan Hirsi Ali's *Infidel* reinforce this perception of living in the glare of intense, unfriendly scrutiny. In stating their claims provocatively, the authors of such books have aroused the ire of radicals.[2]

As we consider the simultaneous attraction and repulsion with which these books are regarded, we need to be reminded of the adage, "Fools rush in where angels fear to tread." Yet the impressive sales of these texts (which are among the best sellers on Islam in America, Canada, and many other Western contexts) and the love/hate reactions they engender are parts of a phenomenon that calls for scholarly investigation. Given the rise of intense anxiety about Islam, the success of these books is not surprising. It would appear to say something not merely about what booksellers deem worthy of promotion, but also about what the North American reading public finds plausible and engaging. The books have been written primarily for non-Muslims who adhere to mainstream Western liberal and conservative political assumptions, and their style and content respond to a market that was created in North America after the tragic events of 9/11. The genre, then, is popular because it claims to offer answers to the questions non-Muslims are asking: Why are Muslims angry at the West? Why do they reject Western solutions to political problems and resist notions such as women's liberation, LGBTQ+ rights, and freedom of choice for the individual? How do we explain phenomena such as al-Qa'ida and suicide bombing? The explanations these texts offer is straightforward, palatable to the non-academic reader, unburdened by footnotes and unfamiliar terms, politically comfortable, and easy to assimilate. Their message is one that resonates with the contemporary reader who feels at least moderately threatened by Islam, and who has come to the conclusion that there is a basic conflict between his or her values and those of most Muslims.

Sadly, the popularity of these texts comes at the expense of many other potential sources of knowledge about Islam and Muslims, many of which manifest considerably greater academic rigor and nuance. While one would expect simpler, "edgier," and more journalistic books to perform well in the aftermath of terrorist attacks and wars, the inability of a more diverse range of authors to make their voices heard creates problems for majority-minority relations in a multicultural society. To be heard and welcomed in the public sphere, Muslims in the wider North American context experience pressure to assume an adversarial posture toward the larger Muslim community, and frequently acquire credibility and even accolades[3] to the extent to which they abandon more "mainstream" minority group strategies of identity negotiation by positioning themselves as Muslim dissidents aligned with the majority culture. While self-critique is to be welcomed in any national or religious community, the enthusiasm of North Americans for Muslim dissident literature comes at a high price: The inability to more fully understand the daily concerns, "commonsense" perceptions, and existential dilemmas that accompany "being a Muslim woman in 21st century North America," and indeed to hear the claims of dissident voices in a larger context.

Following a similar structure to that used in Chapter 3, this chapter analyzes and critiques central themes articulated by leading writers in this particular literary genre, with the intention of distinguishing recurrent patterns while also mapping a spectrum of views among specific dissident authors (i.e., Ayaan Hirsi Ali, Irshad Manji, and Raheel Raza, see Table 4.1 for a summary). Attention is therefore given to both unity and diversity in style and content. Analysis begins by exploring how dissident writers portray their works as responses to terror perpetuated by Muslim extremists, and present reform within Islam as an urgent priority. The focus then turns to ways in which each dissident author develops a distinct position (and, frequently, a critical one) toward "moderate Muslims," together with an argument about how they are part of the solution or the problem when it comes to reform. This discussion of views on "moderation" is connected to a third and related topic: The manner in which dissident authors share a common emphasis on the virtues of Western liberalism and secularism, while also articulating varied positions on the prospects for Islamic reform. These positions on prospects for reform, in turn, reflect differing opinions with respect to prospects for an ultimate reconciliation between Western values and Islamic cultures, and for a desired emancipation of Muslim women. The chapter ends with a brief discussion of diverse responses to dissident writing.

Taking refuge in the West and responding to Islamic terrorism

After the tragic events of 9/11 at the beginning of the 21st century, Muslims in Canada and the United States reacted in a variety of ways. Recognizing the potentially grave implications for Muslim communities in North America as well as for international peace and security, many actively sought to bridge the gap between Muslims and non-Muslims by redoubling their engagement with interfaith dialogue and other forms of advocacy. While some reacted to heightened scrutiny of Muslim communities and institutions by retreating from the public sphere; others sought to either protect Islam from common misperceptions or to initiate new calls for change among Muslims. The dramatic rise of public interest in (and concern about) Islam brought new prominence to some Muslim commentators and spokespersons, some speaking in the name of established organizations and others acting in a freelance capacity.

Some authors writing in this context, including Nonie Darwish and Wafa Sultan, engaged in a different kind of response, reinforcing a sharp dichotomy between Islam and human rights by claiming that Islam is inherently authoritarian, violent, misogynistic and homophobic, and by focusing on extreme and violent practices such as beheading, stoning, and threats to apostates. In *Now They Call Me Infidel* (2006), Egyptian-American critic of Islam Darwish contrasts America's freedom and tolerance with the retrograde ideology of Islam, and argues against cultural relativism (Alsultany, 2013). The book description notes:

> Darwish thrives as an American citizen, a Christian, a conservative Republican, and an advocate for Israel. To many, she is now an infidel. But she is risking her comfort and her safety to reveal the many politically incorrect truths about Muslim culture that she knows firsthand.
>
> (Darwish, 2006)

In *Cruel and Usual Punishment*, Darwish equates living under *sharia* as living "in the world's largest maximum-security prison, and I for one don't want to be incarcerated again" (2008, p. x). In the pages that follow, Darwish offers an explanation of *sharia* and its impacts on individuals and society – including "the Muslim world" and "the West" (2008, p. xiii). She claims that the book is meant "not to spread hatred of a people, but to tell the truth about the wickedness of Islamic Sharia law" (Darwish, 2008, p. xiii). Darwish frames the narrative in terms of "a warning to the West" and calls to action, and notes that "the West cannot rely on Muslims to reform their religion on their own since they are themselves hostages to an ideology parading as religion" (2008, p. xxv). She continues this trajectory in *Wholly Different: Why I Chose Biblical Values Over Islamic Values* (2017), in which she argues that the tenets of Islam "are incompatible with free society" (Darwish, 2017). The book description notes that Darwish outlines "the 'seventh-century values' of Islam that religious extremists are so intent on protecting through global warfare – values that set Islam apart from the other Abrahamic religions" (Darwish, 2017). Darwish has been criticized for leveraging her insider status as an "ex-Muslim"[4] to contribute to the "shariah scare industry," which suggests that Islam is inherently opposed to the West in its imposition of religious law (Fink, 2018).

Similarly, Wafa Sultan – a Syrian-American psychiatrist and self-identified secular Muslim – has claimed that:

> The clash we are witnessing around the world is not a clash of religions, or a clash of civilizations. It is a clash between two opposites, between two eras. It is a clash between a mentality that belongs to the Middle Ages and another mentality that belongs to the 21st century... It is a clash between freedom and oppression, between democracy and dictatorship. It is a clash between human rights, on the one hand, and the violation of these rights, on the other hand. It is a clash between those who treat women like beasts, and those who treat them like human beings.
>
> (Al Jazeera TV, 2006)[5]

A *New York Times* profile of Sultan describes her as "an international sensation, hailed as a fresh voice of reason by some, and by others as a heretic and infidel who deserves to die" (Broder, 2006). While framing the clash between Islam and the West as opposing mindsets rather than a religious conflict, Sultan advances the argument that Islam is essentially oppressive while "the West" is essentially a culture of liberty. In 2009, Sultan published *A God Who Hates*, a memoir in which she argues that "any culture that hates its women can't love anything else" (Sultan, 2009) and that "the god who hates is waging a battle between modernity and barbarism, not a battle between religions" (Macmillan, 2020). Also in 2009, Sultan cofounded *Former Muslims United*, a program of the *American Freedom Defense Initiative* which seeks to "educate the American public and policymakers about the need for Muslims to repudiate the threat from authoritative Shariah to the religious safety of former Muslims" (Former Muslims United, n.d.).[6]

The following year, Sultan testified as a witness at Dutch politician Geert Wilders' trial for hate speech (for Islamophobic statements) in October 2010 and agreed with Wilders' views on Islam – featured in his film, *Fitna* (2008) – including continuities between verses in the Qur'an and actions of violent extremists (Baudet, 2011; Pipes, 2013). Sultan is also a board member of Stop Islamization of Nations (SION), which was mentioned in Chapter 3 as an international political interest group founded by Pamela Geller (described by Southern Poverty Law Center as "one of the most flamboyant anti-Muslim activists in the United States" [SPLC Southern Poverty Law Center, n.d.a]), Robert Spencer (an anti-Muslim author and blogger who insists, "despite his lack of academic training in Islam, that the religion is inherently violent and that extremists who commit acts of terror are simply following its most authentic version" [SPLC Southern Poverty Law Center, n.d.b]), and Anders Gravers Pedersen (an anti-Islam activist and chairman and founder of Stop the Islamization of Denmark).

Similar to Darwish and Sultan, many authors of "clash literature" (discussed in Chapter 3) draw heavily on the writings of or have been in conversation with Ayaan Hirsi Ali, the best-selling "ex-Muslim" dissident and controversial former Dutch parliamentarian who now resides in the United States. Hirsi Ali is the author of many popular books, including *The Caged Virgin* (2004), *Infidel* (2007), *Nomad* (2010), *Heretic* (2015), and *Prey* (2021). In autobiographical style, Hirsi Ali attributes much hardship and suffering to her fundamentalist upbringing as a Somali migrant whose family settled in Kenya. Her early Islamic education was heavily influenced by Wahhabi or puritanical forms of religious interpretation, and she extrapolates from examples derived from her own experience of conservatism within a particular branch of Muslim culture to arrive at negative conclusions concerning the whole of Islam. She describes her Dutch education in Enlightenment thinking as a liberating force in her own life, particularly after the violent incidents of September 11, 2001. Having faced deeply threatening reactions to her personal liberation from Islamic conservatism and her growing political activism, she generalizes about Muslim immigrants in Western countries and argues that they pose a grave threat to the social and political fabric of these countries. Western institutions and individuals, she asserts, need to stop supporting the preservation of foreign cultural values, particularly those derived from Muslim cultures. Instead of multiculturalism, the emphasis should be put on replacing Islamic ways of thinking and living with alternative values derived from the European Enlightenment: Democracy, individual freedom, and gender equality. Once again, "Islam and the West" are presented as antithetical wholes with diametrically opposed ideals and values. Where Islam suppresses the individual and subjugates women, the West liberates. Where Islam teaches dogmatism, authoritarianism, and ideological closure, Western rationalism promotes freedom of thought, choice, and opportunity.

The following passage from "clash" author Bruce Bawer (introduced in Chapter 3) elaborates on another perspective about Hirsi Ali's narrative approach:

> In response to the common criticism that Hirsi Ali is inappropriately disrespectful toward Muslims: "Why should anybody be expected to respect a religion that demands his or her submission, subordination, or even execution?" ... As for 'insulting'—well, exactly who is insulting who? It isn't as if European Christians and Jews are running around raping Muslim women, defacing Muslim cemeteries, shooting bullets into the facades of Muslim houses of worship, and tormenting Muslim children in school.
>
> (Bawer, 2009, p. 139)

Treating those who threatened Hirsi Ali for her advocacy against Islam and Muslims as the authentic representatives of the religion itself, Bawer does not hesitate to hold Islam responsible for the negative dynamics of Hirsi Ali's particular life experiences. Having ascribed guilt to Islam in general, Bawer then asserts the innocence of Western and specifically European parties vis-à-vis Muslims. Leaving aside the events of the former Yugoslavia during the 1990s, when behaviors such as those described by Bawer did take place, the mode of argument manifests strong elements of provocation, and can be understood to imply that Islam begets offences that are presumably alien to Christian and Jewish experiences. Insofar as historical analysis reveals that abusive behaviors in the name of Christianity and Judaism have occurred in a manner not unlike those attributed to Islam, a discerning reader could easily receive the impression that the eagerness to generalize darkly about Islam and Muslims is at least in part driven by a psychology of projection and a desire to refuse confrontation with past ghosts of the Western experience, including "religious" wars and various ways in which individual and women's rights were denied or suppressed.

This inability to articulate the complexity of the Western experience and the manner in which the story of "the West" (insofar as one can be told) is very much a struggle for "Western" solutions to "Western" problems, is intimately linked to attitudes toward Islam that some critics would describe as neocolonial. If the West represents the fulfillment of humane values, and if it is itself devoid of a shadow side, why should the West not also be the primary vehicle for saving benighted societies that lack Indigenous virtues and credible wellsprings of internal reform? Such thinking about Western superiority and the need for Western victory in a cultural war with Islam is an explicit theme in Darwish, Sultan, and Hirsi Ali's writings as well as in the clash literature more generally. Throughout, there is an equation of the West with freedom and Islam with incarceration. The following passage from Hirsi Ali illustrates this equation:

When I'm told to be careful not to impose western values on people who don't want them, I beg to differ. I was not born in the west and I did not grow up in the west. But the delight of being able once I came to the west to let my imagination run free, the pleasure of choosing whom I want to associate with, the joy of reading what I want, and the thrill of being in control of my life—in short, my freedom—is something I feel immensely as I manage to extricate myself from the shackles and obstacles that my bloodline and my religion imposed.

(2010, p. 242)

In Hirsi Ali's view, the Western story of women's emancipation through reason and education can unshackle Muslim societies from *sharia* (Islamic law), just as it liberated her own imagination (2015). She calls upon schools and universities to "openly challenge the beliefs of Muslim children and their parents" and help them to cast off Muslim "self-imposed blinkers" (2010, p. xix). The West holds an antidote to superstition, poverty, and tyranny, and should vigorously seek to win a cultural war against Islam: "There is already a clash, and we are in some sense already a war. That western civilization is superior is not simply my opinion but a reality I have experienced and continue to appreciate every day. I assume that the west will win. The question is how" (2010, p. 245). Such arguments articulate key elements of the worldview present within the dissident Muslim women and clash literature: Two civilizations are locked in struggle, one based on reason and the other rooted in religious law and stifling superstitions. The superior civilization must confidently pursue victory over the lesser civilization, but to defend its gains and to liberate those shackled by centuries of religious obscurantism.

In Canada, Pakistani-born activist and journalist Farzana Hassan (aka Farzana Hassan Shahid) has also shared her personal narrative in an effort to challenge misogyny and strive toward reforming Islam. Hassan's book, *Unveiled: A Canadian Muslim Woman's Struggle Against Misogyny, Sharia and Jihad* (2012), followed her public commentary in 2009 on proposals to ban the *burqa* and the *niqab*.[7] Speaking on behalf of the Muslim Canadian Congress, Hassan cited public safety issues, stating that, "to cover your face is to conceal your identity" (CBC News, 2009) and that "if a government claims to uphold equality between men and women, there is no reason for them to support a practice that marginalizes women" (CBC News, 2009). The book description for *Unveiled* is as follows:

The testimony of a Muslim woman's personal struggle to oppose radicalism and misogyny within her faith community. Farzana Hassan challenges the ideas that breed such pathologies among some of Islam's adherents.

She denounces not just terrorism itself, but also excuses for it. Hassan investigates specific reasons behind the prevalent anti-Western sentiment among Muslims and attempts to dispel some of their misconceptions. She also speaks out against brutal and misogynistic honour killings, and takes an honest look at political Islam and some of its pernicious symbols, such as the burka. The book is an earnest cry for reform within Islam and for all Muslims to reconcile their faith with life in the Canada of today.

(Hassan, 2012)

While Hassan calls out violence and misogyny within Islam, she differs from Sultan and Darwish in her involvement in interfaith and progressive initiatives. For example, she is a former president (2006–2010) of the Muslim Canadian Congress, an organization "that seeks to represent the Muslims in Canada who are not currently represented by another organization" and which was "the first Muslim group that has openly supported the rights of gays and lesbians" (The Muslim Canadian Congress, 2020). Hassan has also been an active participant in local interfaith dialogue initiatives and workshops on women's rights.

Additionally, in Canada, one finds Irshad Manji and Raheel Raza, two nationally recognized, self-proclaimed Muslim dissident women.[8] Manji, a journalist, activist, and former TV broadcaster for *Queer Television*, shifted toward advocacy of Islamic reform in 2003, with the publication of her top-selling and controversial book, *The Trouble with Islam*.[9] As media scholar Dilyana Mincheva points out, "regardless of whether one assesses Manji as a false expert, self-hating Muslim, and instigator, or sympathizes with her ideas of reform, her projects, activism, and public persona are indispensable to any theoretical or pragmatic speculation on the boundaries and opportunities presented by the Western-Islamic, and particularly the Canadian-Muslim, public sphere, as well as to discourses of Muslim feminism" (Mincheva, 2020, p. 43).

Raza, a journalist and proponent of interfaith dialogue, published her own views on contemporary Islam two years later in her less popular (and also less controversial) book, *Their Jihad – Not My Jihad!* (2005). Both authors have entered, albeit in different ways, into ongoing debates about "Muslimness" and Canadian identity, and have spoken with special passion on the highly charged subjects of reform, Western liberalism, and the status of Muslim women. While Manji's *The Trouble with Islam Today* largely abandons internal Islamic discursive strategies and stakes out a position in which "mainstream Canadian values" are adopted as superior normative standards – a position that has no doubt had much to do with the success of her book – Raza adopts a stance that is still controversial, yet articulated in a manner that is more consistent with internal Muslim negotiations over Islamic meaning and identity.

Similarly to other Muslim women dissident authors, Irshad Manji and Raheel Raza fall into the category of freelance Muslim commentators who have written books responding to the climate of fear and insecurity that followed the events of 9/11. Both regard themselves as protagonists in a larger struggle to reclaim Islam from jihadists or militant Muslims. In doing so, they also aspire to shed light on longstanding problems and "injustices" found in traditional Muslim societies.[10] While adopting different rhetorical styles and approaches to activism, both claim to respond to a crisis precipitated by radical Muslims through new calls for critical thinking and Islamic reform. Both insist that a time has come for Muslims to more assertively apply the principle of *ijtihad* (the traditional juristic term for "independent reasoning") and to engage the modern world with less deference to culturally and politically inflected understandings of Islamic values and traditions. Both decry what Raza (2005) describes as "the extremist voices from the pulpit," and celebrate "the freedom to logically research and interpret the Qur'an with reason and intellect" (p. 40).

In staking out these positions, Manji and Raza have clearly and unapologetically associated themselves with modernist approaches to the Islamic tradition, and with those in diaspora Muslim communities who argue that there is no necessary contradiction between being Muslim and being a Canadian or a member of another "Western" polity. They argue for delinking Islamic thought in diaspora communities from the politics and religious trends of "homeland countries," and more generally for sweeping changes in the way Muslims read and interpret their sacred texts. The problems facing Muslims, they suggest, are fundamentally epistemological and textual: New criteria for determining essential Islamic values need to be adopted, to liberate Muslims from oppressive cultural conventions and dangerous political agendas.

Though united by this call for reform, Manji and Raza differ profoundly in their understandings of what it is that must be reformed. For Raza (and indeed for most others who describe themselves as "moderate Muslims"), the basic problem is that Islam itself has been "hijacked" by radical forces. Raza, who was born and raised in Pakistan, speaks passionately about her dismay at seeing "the Islam that I love and venerate... being hijacked with the introduction of a new fundamentalism and the rise of the Taliban" (2005, p. xv). She describes her extensive public speaking in churches, schools, and community centers as "essentially damage control" (2005, p. 38) – that is, as an attempt to counter both misperceptions created by Muslim radicals and misinformation propagated by the Western media and Christian fundamentalists. After 9/11, she says, she took it upon herself to inform non-Muslims about authentic Islam by "teaching Islam 101" (2005, p. 38). She describes her new vocation in the following terms:

Muslims have been stripped naked by the likes of Christian fundamentalists Jerry Falwell and Pat Robertson and political interviewer Oriana Fallaci. Even some local Muslims made a name for themselves by pointing out the trouble with Islam. In this atmosphere rampant with distrust and fear, people became confused. As a Muslim involved in doing damage control, it was time to go back to the books and read, which is the first message of the Qur'an.

(2005, p. 60)

In an interview with journalist and television producer Christine Douglass-Williams, Raza speaks about how her work as a reformer was inspired by Muslim women authors, including Amina Wadud,[11] who gave her hope that there are "options of other ways it [the Qur'an] could be translated and interpreted to be more compassionate, humane, and merciful" (2017, p. 43). She contrasts moderate Muslims with Islamists, whose "goal is to enforce Sharia law globally and take women back to the Dark Ages. Essentially, they believe that the only good Muslim is a seventh-century Muslim" (Douglass-Williams, 2017, p. 43). For Raza, Islam itself is *not* implicated in terrorism, political violence, or intolerant thinking. Islam has been misunderstood and misinterpreted by Muslims and non-Muslims; a reformed understanding of Islam needs to "come from within" (Douglass-Williams, 2017, p. 47) to achieve reconciliation between Muslims and the West. When asked about the ultimate goal of reformists, Raza responded as follows:

To live the spiritual message of our faith and to bring about the change within the faith. For us, Canada is where we are, and we try to create an atmosphere where our children and grandchildren can grow up to be caring, respectful Muslims, but at the same time believe in the separation of mosque and state, where they can live as Western Muslims and feel proud of their identity. I want my children and grandchildren to be able to stand up proud and say that they are Canadian Muslims and have respect for everyone else. For me personally, being a reformer also means gender equality, including in places of worship... A second important goal of reformers is the relationship and respect for people of other faiths. We live in a pluralistic society. You want to celebrate pluralism and differences. It's a simple ethos. Equal rights and respect for those of other faiths are a problem for Islamists. In fact, the sooner women shut up, the better it is for them".

(Douglass-Williams, 2017, p. 53)

Counting herself among "moderate Muslims" as a self-identified "feminist liberal Muslim" (Real Time with Bill Maher, 2015), journalist and cofounder of the *Muslim Reform Movement* Asra Nomani notes that those who have joined the Islamic feminist movement since the 1990s "are not anti-sharia (Islamic law) or anti-Islam" (2005).[12] Rather, she and others who identify with this movement "use the fundamentals of Islamic thinking – the Koran, the Sunnah, or traditions and sayings of the prophet Muhammad, and *ijtihad*, or independent reasoning – to challenge the ways in which Islam has been distorted by sharia rulings issued mostly by ultraconservative men" (2005). And yet, Nomani publicly stated that she voted for Donald J. Trump in the 2016 U.S. presidential election, despite Trump's Islamophobic, misogynistic, and anti-immigration remarks during – and prior to – the campaign (2016).[13] She argued that the history of civil rights in the United States "will never allow the fear-mongering that has been attached to [then-] candidate Trump's rhetoric to come to fruition" (2016) and that her main concerns were "the influence of theocratic Muslim dictatorships, including Qatar and Saudi Arabia, in a Hillary Clinton America" (2016). Since this opinion piece was published, Nomani has protested former President Barack Obama's first visit to a mosque in 2016 for being a "tacit acceptance of a form of gender apartheid" (Bridge Initiative Team, 2018), criticized the Women's March for "apologetics, this standing shoulder-to-shoulder with Muslims that are on the far right of the Westboro Baptist Church" (Real Time with Bill Maher, Feb. 2017, quoted in Bridge Initiative Team, 2018), and has advocated for safe-guarding "against fundamentalist Muslim terrorists, for the sake of human rights and women's rights, L.G.B.T.Q. rights and other basic principles of human dignity" (Hirsi Ali & Nomani, 2017).

In a panel presentation at the 2019 Steamboat Institute Freedom Conference, Nomani speaks about standing up to the interpretation of Islam that justified killing journalist Daniel Pearl in 2002 in Karachi, Pakistan (Steamboat Institute Freedom Conference, 2019). She notes that was how the *Muslim Reform Movement* was born, "to try to put forward an interpretation of Islam that believes in peace, women's rights, and another really important principle of secular governance" (Steamboat Institute Freedom Conference, 2019). Nomani goes on to outline her analysis of how "the ideology of political Islam" has become embedded into American politics, as follows:

> First the Saudis, and now the government of Qatar and also now the current government of Turkey have funded Muslim organizations in the United States that believe in this Islamism, which is the ideology of political Islam, the idea of Muslim supremacy. And these are organizations… like, the Council on American-Islamic Relations, and activists like an activist from Brooklyn named Linda Sarsour [2017 Women's March national co-chair]. These individuals have now taken the ideology of Islamism and put it forward in America as one of their agenda items. And what comes with that? What's really important to any of you that care about pluralism is, anti-Semitism, a very clear agenda to destroy the state of Israel. […] Now, with the rise of [U.S. Representative] Rashida Tlaib and [U.S. Representative] Ilhan Omar as spokeswomen for this lobby, we see really clearly, we've seen just in this past week, their propaganda tour cancelled by the Prime Minister of Israel. Because he knew that in

their agenda is destruction of Israel. And so that's the alarm bells that we want to raise… They have inserted themselves into the Democratic Party platform, they have decided that liberal America and the left is the way that they are going to enter into American politics.

(Steamboat Institute Freedom Conference, 2019)

Later in the discussion, Nomani claims that the *Muslim Reform Movement* is offering:

A vision for an interpretation of Islam that is in the history of Islam – it was called the *Mu'tazilites* – they were living in Iraq during the 10th–12th centuries and they believed in critical thinking. They believed in this critical principle of education system in America, they believed in rational thought. And just like philosophical movements in history have been crushed and then reborn, they were crushed. And that was when the gates of *ijtihad*, or critical thinking, were closed. And what we're trying to do is burst it open. […] It's only in this country that offers so many freedoms, that we're able to do this with relative safety and security.

(Steamboat Institute Freedom Conference, 2019)

Nomani urges the conference delegates to:

Please look at Islam not as a monolithic interpretation, but one that has a continuum. And we're not trying to do anything except to bring principles with which Islam was born that are the most progressive and able to live in the 21st century.

(Steamboat Institute Freedom Conference, 2019)

In an appearance on WHUT/Howard University Television's *The Mimi Geerges Show*, Nomani speaks about an internal conflict about women's rights within Islam (Geerges, 2016). She states:

Men have tried to take control and power in the communities throughout all of society. And in our Muslim communities, unfortunately, they have so much of the power. And so that tension exists and they use religion. They use our faith of Islam to maintain their power and control. And we – the bad girls of Islam – are fighting back.

(Geerges, 2016)

Nomani asserts that Muslim feminists share the belief with all feminists in "the equality of all people" (Geerges, 2016). This aspect of Nomani's activism is reflected in a variety of Muslim women in North America who are creating gender-inclusive mosques which is explored in the Chapter 5 of this book. Nomani goes on to speak about her experience of entering through the main doors and praying in the central hall of her mosque in Morgantown, West Virginia,[14] and states:

> I have never left those main halls, because we have a right to the front rows, we have a right to the pulpit. And it's not just a matter of real estate. It's a matter of presence. You know, it's a matter of this idea of Islamic feminism, this idea that we are equal in our practice.
>
> (Geerges, 2016)

On the topic of the *Muslim Reform Movement*, Nomani claims:

> We would not have to reform anything if we did not have this ideology of Salafi-ism [*sic*], exported to the world by the governments of Qatar and Saudi Arabia for the last 40 years. The Islam that I learned as a little girl, and that my parents have practiced, is a religion of women's rights, peace, and secular governance. This political Islam is what we are trying to challenge. And that is really the bottom line. But it's something that needs to be challenged. They have so much power, they have money – as we know. And we, as Muslims, and the world as a community, have suffered for the last four decades because of this extremist ideology. And I say to the world, you know, "Wake up to this! Join us," because more blood will spill as long as we stay silent. We have to have the moral courage to stand up.
>
> (Geerges, 2016)

Nomani's activism reflects the nuance and range of political opinions held by individuals who self-identify as "moderate Muslims" which will be discussed later in this chapter.

In comparison to Nomani, Manji (2005) criticizes those who argue that Islam itself is "innocent" with respect to contemporary violence, and rejects the notion that the Qur'an provides an adequate response to the messages of radicals. In her view, Islam is not purely a religion of peace and tolerance; neither Islam nor "moderate Muslims" should be insulated from the harsh questioning of those who have been alarmed by recent developments. Muslims, she suggests, are complicit in the events of 9/11 insofar as they refuse to adopt a critical view of their religion.

> With morose faces, we [Muslims] said that our faith had been "hijacked." … As if our religion was an innocent bystander in the violence perpetrated by Muslims. Hijacked. An emotionally charged word that acquits mainstream Muslims of the responsibility to be self-critical.
>
> (Manji, 2005, pp. 46–47)[15]

For Manji, Islam is emphatically not an ideal system of values, and contains within itself contradictions that permitted the events of 9/11.

Though Manji professes to be a Muslim, Islam itself – and not Muslims alone – is the target of her criticisms and the object of her calls for change. While Manji's earlier work focuses on her own experiences and identifying problems with Islam, her works after *The Trouble with Islam Today* focus on reforming Islam and transcending labels in a divided time. As Christine Douglass-Williams observes, in *Allah, Liberty and Love* (2011), Manji:

> Rebukes 'moderate' Muslims as being part of the problem for not advocating reform, stating that Muslims must reinterpret the troubling passages of their scriptures 'just as Christians and Jews' have done. She rails against the widespread fear that Muslims have of speaking out, and condemns the tolerance of what she refers to as intolerable customs like female genital mutilation, honor killings, and stonings, decrying moderates for putting 'awkward Koranic verses in context.' Manji refers disparagingly to well-known writer and renowned Swiss-French academic Tariq Ramadan, who is often referred to as a 'moderate,' to highlight her disdain for the term.
>
> (2017, pp. 164–165)

In her 2011 book, Manji advocates for practicing *ijtihad* – "beyond religious authorities and outside the boundaries of established interpretations" (Mincheva, 2020, p. 53) – to reinterpret the Qur'an, and argues that valuable change needs to come from within Islam, rather than being imposed by external sources. As Mincheva describes, Manji calls "for radical openness, freedom, and solidarity with other human beings, regardless of whether they identify as Muslims, based on a moral *Islamic* imperative rooted in individual agency and reason" (2020, p. 53). Mincheva goes on to describe Manji's arguments as follows:

> For Manji, the whole concept of Allah becomes meaningful only if human things and actions can be imbricated in life-affirming and infinitely inclusive conversation about what submission to Him entails. Otherwise, Allah is a meaningless absolute that requires blind and repetitive following, devoid of moral agency; the mute and distant authority of Allah and anyone who claims to be His ambassador on Earth becomes a breeding ground for fundamentalism.
>
> (2020, p. 53)

The question of reform

Though Muslim dissident authors appear to agree on many substantive issues connected to responding to terror, the contrast between reforming Islamic *interpretation and practice* and challenging foundational Islamic *beliefs and doctrines* constitutes a major difference in their respective forms of advocacy. For example, Raza's condemnation of Muslim militants and, even more, her decision to lead a mixed gender Friday prayer service in Toronto, have subjected her to harsh criticism from radical and conservative thinkers. However, her basic style of argumentation (affirming that Islam, authentically understood, has the solutions wayward Muslims need) is compatible with the language of faith utilized by most observant Muslims. Though Raza (2005) may argue that "Today, the Muslim world stays dangerously silent," she insists that the problem is Muslims and not Islam (p. 39). On the other hand, Manji's approach in *The Trouble with Islam Today* directly challenges the faith that observant Muslims place in the essential goodness, sacred meaning, and spiritual truth of their religious tradition. For Manji, the approach of moderate Muslims (Raza is indirectly included in this) who base their calls for reform on the assumption that it is Muslims rather than Islam that is the root of the problem, is lacking in the level of honesty necessary to affect real change (2007, p. A15). She argues that Islam is not the divinely inspired "straight path" sought by Muslims in their daily prayers and life aspirations; it is an inherently contradictory set of injunctions and proscriptions that bears the marks of its human founders (Manji, 2007, pp. 49–50). "Far from being perfect," Manji states, "the Quran is so profoundly at war with itself…" (Manji, 2005, pp. 49–50). Though Manji alleges that there are "good" as well as "bad" statements in Islamic texts, her writing devotes greater attention to the latter, and exhibits reticence with respect to the reasons why the author continues to describe herself as Muslim. Many Muslim readers have found this stance, which deconstructs Islamic doctrines and texts with the intent of revealing incoherence rather than consistency, alienating and threatening to their core identity at a time of profound existential vulnerability.

In *Allah, Liberty and Love* (2011) and in her public commentary since its publication, Manji acknowledges the plurality and multivocality of Islam – including its extremes. Rather than focusing on violent extremism or "moderate Muslims," Manji emphasizes the capacity of "*ijtihad* – Islam's own tradition of dissenting, reasoning and reinterpreting" (2011, p. xiv) "to change the world for good" (2011, p. xiv). As Mincheva observes, Manji's messages:

> Are simple and unifying: everyone deserves dignity; abuse against women and gender minorities does not need epistemological, cultural, or religious yardsticks for measurement and punishment; all women and minorities who are victims of abuse deserve equal attention, regardless of race, religion, class, education, or geographical location; even if some crimes against Muslim women or gender minorities are viewed as legitimate by clerics and religious authorities, this does not mean that Islam – understood as civilizational and spiritual praxis and, fundamentally, as the testimony of one's individual consciousness before the One and Only God – should

be tarnished. Most importantly, Manji's message asserts that Islam is plural and plurivocal, and while it houses extremes (like every universal religion), it also contains multiple voices who position themselves, at the risk of facing vitriolic attacks by conservatives and liberals alike, in vehement resistance to these extremes. She claims that these dispersed people are not "community representatives" and do not stand for some kind of manufactured diversity with political stakes; instead, they represent the extraordinary amalgamation of Muslim identities, a true plurality, made visible by digital communication (to those prepared to break the boundaries of their "filter bubbles"), which cannot be reduced to the binary spectra of liberal versus conservative, Western versus Islamic, or free versus subjugated... Even on the most heated and divisive topics, Manji tells us that Muslim responses are multiple, variegated, and unexpected.

(2020, pp. 49–50)

In light of this plurality across Muslim communities and individuals, Manji's reformist message is informed by an effort to reconcile faith and reason through *ijtihad*, or independent reasoning. She suggests that transformation is possible through individual encounters – "with scripture or with the Other (understood broadly as all kinds of uncomfortable difference existing in the world)" (Mincheva, 2020, p. 53). As Mincheva observes:

> Manji offers the perspective of "a life beyond categories" and, therefore, a project of reform beyond the traditional restraints of political and social identities. Her personal and political choices attempt to embody this life in and with contradictions. In a sense, her media presence – which is global and traverses the left, right, and radical spectra – also speaks to this.
>
> (2020, p. 54)

The implications of these divergent approaches to Islamic reform become especially apparent on the "religion of peace" issue. Raza asserts that Islam is fundamentally a religion of peace that has been misinterpreted and abused by Muslim radicals. Though those who speak out against extremists are few, most Muslims are able to recognize the basic priority Islam gives to peace over war:

> What needs to be done? The solution, I believe, lies with the silent majority in Islam who need to speak up and ensure the hateful rhetoric and actions of people like Osama bin Laden and his supporters die before they take root. They need to ensure the pulpit of a mosque is not used to spew hate, and, most of all, they need to empower other Muslims to take action against injustice, intolerance and violence wherever it is happening.... We must reiterate that Islam was and should remain a message

of peace and love. The few of us who speak out will face resistance and criticism. But maybe what we need right now is a renaissance or revival in Islam to clean out the extremist elements that have muddied our clean image. For this to happen, we have to first accept that the enemy is not outside, but within us.

(Raza, 2005, p. 28)

Unlike Manji, Raza reads passages of the Qur'an that relate to conflict contextually, as do many Christians and Jews dealing with conflict verses in their own scriptures. She rejects traditional Western stereotypes about Islam "as a religion of force and violence" and proposes that, "tolerance is the cornerstone of Islam and has emerged out of the very nature and history of Islam" (Raza, 2005, p. 30). Problems in Islamic practice relate to religious interpretation – which is not absolute – rather than in the religious texts Muslims must strive to understand.

Manji offers a perspective that is more in line with traditional "Western"[16] perceptions of Islam. She rejects the "religion of peace" argument as an "emotionally comforting" fallacy: "While I would have loved to believe this account of things, the more I read and reflected, the less sense it made" (Manji, 2005, p. 49). Believing that Islam is a religion of peace, she argues, absolves Muslims of responsibility for thinking critically about their tradition. In making this argument, she does not qualify her position by proposing that the inherent peacefulness of other religious traditions might also be questioned, or by cautioning against a return to religious polemics attributing violence to "the Other."

For Manji, as the title of her first edition, *The Trouble with Islam*, implies, there is something inherently flawed in Islam and, in turn, in Muslims. Manji makes no attempt to correct traditional misperceptions or stereotypes, nor does she allow for the possibility that problematic historical and political relations between Western and Muslim-majority countries can be invoked as contributing causes of religious militancy. The "trouble" is inherent to Islam and is not circumstantial.

Critics of Manji have argued that her approach is lacking in balance and attention to the larger context of Islamic-Western relations. There is no mention or disclaimer that a larger history is present in the contemporary struggles. Manji is silent with respect to contemporary scholars (such as Karen Armstrong, Richard Bulliet, Norman Daniel, and María Rosa Menocal) who argue that, in historical terms, Islam and Muslims have been predominantly perceived in the Judeo-Christian West as outsiders – i.e., that Islam has been unjustly treated as an "exception" to humane or progressive trends in world civilization, and that Islamic civilizations' many contributions to world civilization have too seldom been acknowledged. It is therefore not surprising that some Muslim and non-Muslim scholars regard Manji's treatment of Islam as more reminiscent of the Orientalist tradition than of recent scholarship in North American universities. Although Khaled Abou El Fadl, Professor of Islamic Studies at UCLA (whom Manji mentions in her book), does not refer to Manji directly, he appears to offer an implied reference in his foreword to Amina Wadud's *Inside the Gender Jihad* (2006), by stating:

> [U]nlike so much of the sensationalistic and at times Islamophobic, writings that are published these days, this is not a book about the trouble with Islam, what went wrong with Islam, why Islam is a problem, why Islam is some type of implicitly failed religion.
>
> (p. ix)

What sets Manji apart from so many other self-proclaimed Islamic reformists is her insistence on bluntly and directly challenging core Islamic beliefs, and her dismissal of those who have staked out more modest reform programs rooted in historical Muslim reform and renewal movements. In her manner of arguing against the absolutizing of essential Islamic precepts or of declaring that Islam cannot be regarded as "a wholly original way of life," Manji insists on rupture with the past rather than continuity, and favors individualism rather than what she describes as a "herd" mentality. The following quotations are illustrative:

> ...[We must] openly question the perfection of the Quran so that the stampede to reach a correct conclusion about what it "really" says will slow down and, over time, become an exercise in literacy instead of literalism. At this stage, reform isn't about telling ordinary Muslims what not to think, but about giving Islam's billion devotees permission to think.
>
> (Manji, 2005, p. 40)

> The Quran's perfection is, ultimately, suspect...What if the Quran isn't perfect? What if it's not a completely God-authored book? What if it's riddled with human biases?
>
> (Manji, 2005, p. 50)

> The very act of questioning the Quran is a central piece of the reform puzzle because it signals a breach with the herd.
>
> (Manji, 2005, p. 52)

As will be explored in the next chapter, where Raza and most other Islamic feminists advocate change through rereading sacred texts and acknowledging the relativity of human interpretations, Manji argues that the solution lies in a more secular and skeptical attitude toward sacred texts. Where Raza (2005) argues that the central challenge is "to separate culture from religion; truth and justice from propaganda, and the ritual from the spiritual" (p. xv), Manji rejects the notion that Islamic reform can come from a renewal of internal Islamic spiritual resources and opts for a direct confrontation with religious certitudes.[17]

Moderate Muslims: Problem or solution?

The nature of each writer's reform project determines her attitude toward ideas of moderation in Islam. Raza (2005) chooses to label herself as a "pluralist practicing Muslim and a caring Canadian" (p. 35) and as a "moderate Muslim" (p. 50). In the process, she seeks to distinguish herself from "immoderate" (i.e., radical, extremist, or fundamentalist) Muslims who in her view are seeking to hijack Islam and silence a less politically driven majority. "Moderate Muslims like me," she states, "…want to differentiate our faith from extremist Muslims' twisted ideologies are facing increasing resistance" (p. 50).

The appeal of this "moderate" label – and its utility in a Western context, may seem obvious in an era of elevated security concerns, in which members of the majority culture tend to be curious about who their Muslim allies may be and anxious about the intensity of patriotism or extent of acculturation among Muslim citizens. It should come as no surprise, then, that designations such as "moderate Muslim" have become commonplace.

Predictably, many Muslims feel frustrated or ambivalent about these labels. While the connotation of being "against violence" has its appeal, there is an additional undesirable implication: That violence committed by Muslims takes place for primarily ideological (as opposed to political, economic, or historical) reasons. As some scholars have observed, labeling Muslims as either "moderate" or "immoderate" tends to silence a majority of Muslim voices, reinforcing problematic "good Muslim" versus "bad Muslim" dichotomies (refer to, e.g., Mamdani 2005). In the Summer 2005 special volume of *The American Journal of Islamic and Social Sciences* that was dedicated to "Debating Moderate Islam," Asma Barlas (2005), a prominent Islamic feminist, offers a sharp critique:

> The official view of Islam as a pair of good and evil twins conjoined at the hip performs two crucial political functions. On the one hand, by portraying "militant Islam" as the real threat to global security, Washington is able to deflect critiques of the U.S.'s role in underwriting injustice and oppression on a global scale. On the other hand, by shifting the burden of "defeat[ing] and eradicat[ing] militant Islam" onto "moderate Islam," the U.S. is absolved of the responsibility to rethink its own injurious policies.
> (p. 161)

For Barlas, the project of supporting "moderate Muslims" comes at a high cost for both non-Muslims and Muslims. Non-Muslims misread the sources of Muslim resentment, while genuine Muslim voices go unheard.

According to Barlas and other critics, terms such as "moderate Muslim" provide little insight into the actual beliefs and policies of those who bear the label, and are primarily used in a strategic manner. At the same time, the "moderate Muslim" label implies (however subtly) that most Muslims are *not* moderate:

> If calling oneself a moderate at a time when there is such pressure to "toe the official line" can thus "easily become too much a badge of mindless loyalty," refusing to call oneself a moderate can just as easily become a sign of disloyalty. Either way, the state's advocacy of "moderate Islam" is a kiss of death for Muslim critics abroad, wary of the US's agendas, and of a non-Muslim critics at home who are convinced that a moderate Muslim is merely a militant in denial or in disguise.
>
> (Barlas, 2005, p. 162)

As a quick Internet search can reveal, there is a diverse range of Muslims who are being labeled "moderate."[18] Though few would dispute Raza's moderate credentials, it is possible for a Muslim to be regarded as "moderate" by some commentators and as "radical" by others. This raises many questions: Is a consensus definition of "moderation" possible? Is moderation the hallmark of a particular epistemological or interpretive tendency, or can it be found among diverse varieties of Muslims – not only among "ex-Muslims," Muslim secularists, and reformists, but also among traditionalists and revivalists? Raza suggests that most Muslims are moderate yet passive, but does not draw attention to problems inherent in the "moderate"/"extremist" binary.

In comparison, Hirsi Ali discounts the notion of Muslim moderation, focusing particularly on what she sees as the inherent contradictions of this position. Because Islam, in her view, is scripturally wired for immoderate beliefs, an authentic Muslim cannot truly be "moderate" or "modern." Writing as if a large number of moderate, educated, and religiously dedicated interpreters of Islam did not exist, Hirsi Ali proposes that Muslim insistence on basic articles of faith such as the inspired nature of the Qur'an and "unquestioning reverence" for the Prophet Muhammad (2015) precludes intelligent reflection on the meaning of scripture for today:

> A moderate Muslim does not question Muhammad's actions or reject or revise parts of the Quran. A moderate Muslim may not practice Islam in the way that a fundamentalist Muslim does—veiling, for example, or refusing to shake a woman's hand—but both the fundamentalists and the so-called moderates agree on the authenticity and truthfulness and the value of Muslim scripture.
>
> (p. 195)

In making this argument, Hirsi Ali chooses to ignore the vast differences in position taken by Muslims of differing ideological and interpretive dispositions, and demonstrates a lack of awareness that even so-called fundamentalists *interpret* their religious sources.

Interestingly enough, Manji rejects use of the "moderate Muslim" label, but for reasons that differ profoundly from those cited above. Aligning herself more closely with Western critics of Islam, Manji creates a more sweeping and deeply polarizing distinction between "good Muslims" and "bad Muslims" by suggesting that so-called "moderates" are in effect apologists for Islamic extremism: They provide cover for their more radical coreligionists by insisting on superficial rather than penetrating and thoroughgoing reforms. For her, moderates contribute to the risk of failing to address real sources of problems within the Muslim community such as violence, because while denouncing violence committed in the name of Islam today, they deny that Islam today has anything to do with it. To distinguish herself from moderates, Manji (2005) elects to define herself as a "modern Muslim" (p. 24) and, more pointedly, as a "Muslim Refusenik" (p. 3). With the latter label, Manji evokes the ideological competition of the Cold War era, and the legacy of Soviet Jews whose "persistent refusal to comply with the [Soviet Union's] mechanisms of mind-control and soullessness helped end a totalitarian system" (p. 3). Thus, does she portray herself as an agent of liberation in a new Cold War between the West and a presumably "totalitarian" Islamic system.

Virtues of Western liberalism and secularism

The concept of reform presupposes not only "something that is wrong" and needs to be changed, but also "something that would be better" as a normative standard to guide aspirations. Most "dissent" authors, like Hirsi Ali, Manji, and Raza, agree that the transformation of Muslims is inextricably connected to the many values of Western liberalism and secularism. They differ, however, in their manner of approaching what they regard as the virtues of liberalism and secularism. For Raza, essential Islamic and Western values are compatible, so the task of reforming Muslims does not require fundamental changes in Islam. For Manji, there are basic contradictions between Islamic and Western values, and the task of Islamic reformation requires a transformative Westernization of religious culture. In contrast, Hirsi Ali argues that since Islam is directly responsible for radicalism and terrorism (2010, pp. 138–141) including but not limited to domestic physical abuse of women (2010, p. 135), honor killings (2010, p. 129), and women being forced into marriages that disadvantage them while benefitting men (2010, p. 163), it is not worth reform. Rather, to Hirsi Ali, if Muslims developed a better understanding of Islam it would lead them to reconcile with the West, yet only because they would be compelled to turn away from Islam, and likely turn toward Christianity (2010, pp. 239–240).

In *The Trouble with Islam Today*, Manji upholds "the West" as a haven for ideal modern values such as critical thinking, individual freedom, and democracy. These values, she suggests, are largely alien to the Muslim experience, but nonetheless ought to be embraced and emulated. Reflecting on her cultural formation in Canada, Manji makes repeated references to the Western virtues and goes so far as to entitle her final chapter, "Thank God for the West." The following quotations are exemplary:

> ...I lived in a part of the world that permitted me to explore. Thanks to the freedoms afforded me in the West—to think, search, speak, exchange, discuss, challenge, be challenged, and rethink—I was poised to judge my religion in a light that I couldn't have possibly conceived in the parochial Muslim microcosm of the madressa.
>
> (Manji, 2005, p. 21)

> But it wasn't Islam that fostered my belief in the dignity of every individual. It was the democratic environment.
>
> (Manji, 2005, p. 6)

> I look back now and thank God I wound up in a world where the Quran didn't have to be my first and only book, as if it's the lone richness that life offers to believers.
>
> (Manji, 2005, p. 6)

> Lord, I loved this society. I loved that it seemed perpetually unfinished, the final answers not yet known—if ever they would be. I loved that, in a world under constant renovation, the contributions of individuals mattered.
>
> (Manji, 2005, p. 10)

Manji highlights the virtues of secularism over not only religiously directed politics, but also religion itself. At a Detroit screening of her documentary film for PBS, *Faith Without Fear* (McLeod, 2007), she responded to a question about Islam and its compatibility with secularism by stating, "There are very few times when I feel comfortable saying that something is superior to something else. I feel very comfortable saying that secularism is superior to religion on its own because secularism makes room for religion."[19]

Manji's (2005) discourse attributes almost providential significance to Western values and includes direct challenges to Western multiculturalists (pp. 220–221) and peace activists (p. 214) who demonstrate excessive tolerance toward Islam and Muslims. The Western value of individuality must not be compromised in efforts to reform and liberalize "tribal" or "desert" Islam (p. 33).

For Manji, the resources to transform the Islamic world are readily available in the Western world. In contrast, most of the Muslim world (with the possible exception of Turkey) is mired in traditions linked to desert Arab tribalism. Although Manji briefly mentions some Muslim reformists outside of the West (including Zainah Anwar, a Malaysian feminist who founded the *Sisters in Islam* civil society organization based in Kuala Lumpur, Malaysia), her predominant emphasis is on the need for reform to come from Muslims in the West and from Western policies that support objectives such as the liberation and economic empowerment of women. Muslims in the West, she states, are ideal for reforming Islam since they "have the luxury of exercising civil liberties, especially free expression, to change tribal tendencies" (Manji, 2005, p. 207). She cites the *Progressive Muslim Union of North America* (PMU), a former network of Muslim thinkers and activists, as evidence that "the freedoms of the West can impel a new generation of Muslims to revive ijtihad, Islam's lost tradition of creative thinking" (p. 175).[20]

Although Raza also upholds values that are commonly regarded as "Western," the stated intent of her writing is to defend what she understands as true Islamic values from Muslim distortions (political violence, oppression of women) and Western misunderstandings. She credits her Western experience with deepening and broadening her faith through interfaith dialogue and advocacy, but unlike Manji she hesitates to evoke an attitude of cultural triumphalism in which the West assumes a virtually providential role vis-à-vis contemporary Islam. The West can support Islamic reformation by providing a context in which Muslims recognize their own universal values, but it does not assume the role of mentor. The fundamental distinction is not between Islam and the West, but rather between authentic values and their abuse or politicization. Raza also practices what some scholars call "multiple critique" by arguing that responsibility for introspection does not lie with Muslims alone. Though she does not delve deeply into the complexities of North American and Western policies toward Muslim countries, she does encourage Westerners to reconsider their attitudes toward Islam, particularly those conveyed by the media. "Thanks to Western media's irresponsible use of jingo-ism instead of journalism," Raza (2005) states, "Muslims today have been made synonymous with terrorism, fundamentalism and militancy" (p. 43).

While Raza protests Western stereotypes of Muslims, she also calls upon Muslims to move beyond their love/hate relationship with the West, and especially the tendency to use the West as a scapegoat. It is unfair, she suggests, for Muslims in Pakistan and other countries to evade responsibility for their own internal problems by blaming them on America or the West. She also claims that many Muslims observe double standards, criticizing the West one moment and then pursuing a Western dream by eating at McDonald's or vacationing in Florida (Raza, 2005, p. 36).

Where Manji argues that Western and especially North American democracies exhibit too much tolerance toward Muslim minorities, Raza exhibits more sympathy toward her coreligionists even as she calls upon them to become more integrated with the majority culture. She notes that Western Muslims "are under massive pressure since 9/11 and have faced severe backlash" (Raza, 2005, p. 60), and calls for interfaith solidarity against phenomena such as hate speech and vandalism, whoever their source or target may be (2005, pp. 60–61). Nonetheless, "fitting in the mainstream," as Raza states, has become increasingly important for Muslim Canadians. (One argument Raza makes is while the *hijab* is perfectly acceptable, the *niqab* – a garment that completely covers the woman's face – is inappropriate in the Canadian context. Moreover, Muslims should not accept extremism in their own community: "In Canada, we must take back the mosques to ensure the voices of reasonable Muslim men and women are heard over the stringent calls for a physical *jihad*" (p. 61).[21]

Overall, these authors demonstrate positive regard for North American models of secularity, and articulate arguments that are compatible with what some writers describe as a Judeo-Christian-Secular synthesis. Hirsi Ali and Manji portray contemporary Islamic culture as antithetical to this synthesis, while Raza represents Islam as a system of values that is compatible with it.[22] Where Manji's approach frames Western superiority in the domain of values as an established fact that should be confronted with "honesty," Raza rejects such comparisons while remaining staunch in what she regards as widespread abuses of Islam. While both Manji and Raza highlight contradictions in Islamic societies, neither grants weight nor legitimacy to Islamic counter-critiques of Western contradictions (e.g., excesses of consumerism, commercial objectification of women as sex objects, foreign policy double standards, social fragmentation, environmentally unsustainable practices, unfair management of the global economy). Manji and Hirsi Ali go much farther in denying the value of engaging and listening to mainstream Muslim voices; neither author emphasizes the importance of gaining a more nuanced understanding of Muslims' diverse perceptions concerning the West. Manji (2005) is especially curt in dismissing Muslim critiques: "Liberal Muslims have to get vocal about this fact: Washington is the unrealized hope, not the lead criminal" (p. 145). Muslims, her argument suggests, have so many internal problems that their critiques of others need not be taken seriously. Whatever historical contributions they may have made to Western civilization, these contributions are largely irrelevant in the present context.

Pivoting away from the emphasis of her earlier work on leveraging Western liberal values and freedoms to reform Islam, Manji's (2019) book, *Don't Label Me* – framed as a conversation between Manji and her late, beloved dog

– advocates for a departure from dogmatically invoking labels to pit groups against each other. Reflecting on the ways in which her own work has been perceived by different audiences, Manji states:

> There are some conservatives whose bias is to bomb Muslims into oblivion. They interpret my 'Muslim' label to mean that I'm a stealth jihadist. Then there are particular atheists who take it on faith that as a Muslim, I'm a dupe of superstitious cave dwellers. Either way, I'm not an individual in my own right. I'm an involuntary avatar of other people's projections.
>
> (2019, p. 20)

She also encourages the reader to engage meaningfully with their "Other," following Martin Buber's claim that the "most liberating relationships [are] 'I–Thou' rather than 'I–It'" (2019, p. 16) since they presume that the other person is "multifaceted" and not perceived as a mere inconvenience (2019, p. 16). While issues of justice, diversity, and identifying as a queer, reform-minded Muslim woman remain part of Manji's work, her 2019 book is less about a call to solve problems with Islam than it is an invitation to practice dialogue regardless of political, sexual, and religious orientation. It is important to point out that although Manji's focus changes in her later works, she does not revoke her former book, *The Trouble with Islam Today* (2005) which received more public attention than her later works. It was a #1 Canadian bestseller and *The New York Times* bestseller and was published internationally in over 30 languages.

Women's emancipation as a focal point

Both Manji and Raza view women's emancipation as an issue that is inseparably linked to Islamic reform and the liberalization of Muslim culture. For both writers, the strengthening of women's rights is regarded not merely as an outcome of reform, but also as a catalyst. Hirsi Ali, often selected by other clash authors as the most authoritative voice on the oppression of Muslim women, represents the plight of women under Islam in starkly negative terms. Her portrait offers minimal nuance, and takes no note of variation in Muslim women's experiences in accordance with interpretive beliefs, geography, culture, or social class. "The will of little girls," she states, "is stifled by Islam":

> [B]y the time they menstruate they are rendered voiceless... they are reared to become submissive robots who serve in the house as cleaners and cooks... they are required to comply with their father's choice of mate and after the wedding their lives are devoted to the sexual pleasures

of their husband and to a life of child-bearing... their education is often cut short when they are still young girls, and thus as women they are wholly unable to prepare their own children to become successful citizens in modern, Western societies. Their daughters repeat the same pattern.

(Hirsi Ali, 2010, pp. xvi–xvii)

Nowhere in this account can one find acknowledgment of facts which do not fit stereotypes, such as the dramatic growth of women's presence at university campuses (where they sometimes outnumber Muslim men) and in variety of professions. Hirsi Ali's characterization is entirely consistent with Robert Spencer's hostile representation of Islam as a faith that in its immutable essence promotes gender inequality and violence toward women through genital mutilation, honor killings, stoning adulteresses, and holding women responsible for being raped (Spencer 2007). Neither author seeks to educate the reader about the non-universal character of such practices, nor about Muslim voices who argue against them on an Islamic basis.[23]

As will be discussed in Chapter 5, reasonable arguments can be made that traditional forms of Muslim patriarchy pose barriers to the advancement of Muslim women and to the successful integration of Muslim communities within Western societies. Hirsi Ali underscores this issue, albeit in a manner that equates the essence of Islam with specific historical practices and interpretations, and presents religion as an overwhelmingly negative factor:

I believe that the subjection of women within Islam is the biggest obstacle to the integration and progress of Muslim communities in the West. It is a subjection committed by the closest of kin in the most intimate place, the home, and it is sanctioned by the greatest figure in the imagination of Muslims: Allah himself.

(2010, p. 160)

As a formerly Muslim informant testifying to her own experience of oppression by family members in the name of religion, Hirsi Ali has produced a raw account that has a powerful impact on North American and European readers. Most Islamic feminists, however, would object strongly to her rhetorical equation of cultural pathology with the essence of a religion, articulated in a manner that seems intended to provoke outsiders to fight for the souls of Muslim women. Hirsi Ali argues that Western feminists (not Islamic feminists) should take on the plight of Muslim women and make it their own cause. There are three goals they must aspire to: Ensuring that Muslim girls are free to complete their education; helping them to gain ownership over their own bodies and sexuality; and making sure that Muslim women have the opportunity to enter the workforce and stay in it, without restraints. Western feminists might also be at the forefront of a campaign to educate Muslim men on the importance of Muslim women's emancipation (2010, p. xix).

Although it may be an exaggeration to describe this approach to Islam and Muslims as "kill the Muslim, save the woman," most writers of Western-sourced clash literature, like Hirsi Ali, regard fighting to liberate Muslim women as a critical front in the culture war between Islam and the West. They are profoundly impatient with "mainstream" voices of reform and moderation within Muslim communities, and give disproportionate attention to individuals who have written off Islamic reform movements and denounced Muslim culture categorically. The predominant tendency is to use the "status of women" issue as a key talking point in generalized critiques of Islam, with the goal of demonstrating the superiority of contemporary Western norms.

In comparison, one of Raza's (2005) chapters bears the title, "To Change the Image of Muslims, Let's Begin with the Women" (p. 76). Once again, Raza articulates criticism of Western stereotypes (2005, p. 68), while also calling for honesty about challenges and problems facing Muslim women. Raza believes that it is necessary to educate non-Muslims about the diverse realities experienced by Muslim women, while continuing to engage in advocacy for those women who must wrestle with cultural norms that permit honor killings, domestic violence, inequitable inheritance, and obstacles to divorce. With women's rights as with liberalism, Raza asserts that there is no inherent contradiction between her positions and the essential values of her faith:

> ...I was battling a series of questions from a journalist about how I could profess to be Muslim and a feminist! To her, this was contradictory and in order to answer her query satisfactorily, I had to go through practically the entire history of Islam and explain a simple fact that many people forget, even when they study Islam: Islam was sent as a system of social justice and to free women from infanticide, slavery, oppression and bondage... In theory Islam gives women the basic rights to live, work, marry, vote, have freedom and justice based on the Qur'an. How these rights are being practiced today in culturally male-dominated societies is something the entire community must face and address.
>
> (2005, p. 76)

As an activist, Raza admits to facing a "catch-22" scenario: Talking about problems facing women tends to reinforce Western stereotypes in the West and provide fuel for anti-Islam rhetoric. Yet allowing one's agenda to be determined by the possibility of distortions would mean becoming silent about issues that genuinely matter.

Manji's discourse on women's emancipation does not exhibit a similar concern about Western stereotypes. "Muslims," she states categorically, "exhibit a knack for degrading women and religious minorities" (Manji, 2005, p. 176).

Table 4.1 Comparison of three prominent "dissident" authors and some of their key perspectives[25]

	Raheel Raza	Irshad Manji	Ayaan Hirsi Ali
Self-description	• "Moderate Muslim" • "Pluralist practicing Muslim and a caring Canadian"	• "Modern Muslim" • "Muslim Refusenik"	• "Ex-Muslim" • "Infidel"
Response to terrorism	• Islam itself is not implicated in terrorism, political violence, or intolerant thinking. • Bases her activism mainly within an existing framework of internal Muslim negotiations over Islamic meaning and identity, yet is still controversial for pushing the traditional boundaries. • Calls for reform in Islamic interpretation and practice.	• Islam is not "innocent" with respect to contemporary violence, and the Qur'an does not provide an adequate response to the message of radicals. In arguing their innocence (Islam and the Qur'an), mainstream Muslims are acquitted of the responsibility of being self-critical. • Largely abandons internal Islamic discursive strategies and stakes out a position in which "mainstream Canadian values" are adopted as normative standards while criticizing both Islam and Muslims. • Calls for reform in Islamic beliefs and doctrines.	• Islam is directly responsible for radicalism and terrorism (138–142), including suicide bombing (191); domestic physical abuse of women (135); honor killings (129); women being regarded as having little intrinsic worth (137); women being forced into marriages that disadvantage them while benefitting men (163); widespread unhealthy Muslim attitudes toward sexuality (155–157); a widespread inclination toward violence among Muslims (191); anti-Semitism (197); unstable families due to polygamy (26). • Has called for a genuinely intolerant Western stance toward Islam and has argued that Islam cannot be reformed and reconciled with Western values.

(Continued)

Table 4.1 Comparison of three prominent "dissident" authors and some of their key perspectives (Continued)

	Raheel Raza	Irshad Manji	Ayaan Hirsi Ali
Essentials for reform	• Muslims must engage in *ijtihad* in their engagement with the modern world. Textual interpretation is problematic (not Islamic texts themselves); difficult passages are to be read contextually. Advocates change for reform through rereading Islamic texts and acknowledging the relativity of human interpretations.	• Muslims must engage in *ijtihad* in their engagement with the modern world. Muslims must be allowed to question the Qur'an, even to the point of questioning its assumed perfection: "The very act of questioning the Qur'an is a central piece of the reform puzzle because it signals a breach with the herd" (52). Parts of Islamic texts are problematic. Rejects the argument that Qur'anic verses that relate to conflict are meant to be read contextually.	• Muslims must embark on "a campaign of enlightenment" in their engagement with the modern world (205–217). *Ijtihad* will play a part in this, yet *ijtihad* will not produce the results necessary for their successful integration into the modern world so long as they are unwilling to reject altogether troublesome parts of Islamic scriptures (196). An honest reading of them will inevitably lead one to realize that some Qur'anic passages as well as some of Muhammad's actions were cruel and inhumane (195–196). Furthermore, Muslims must approach independent investigation of religious texts using the tools of the Enlightenment, including critical reasoning; employing facts instead of faith; evidence instead of tradition; and humanly constructed standards of morality" (206).
Islam: A religion of peace?	• Islam is a religion of peace that has been "hijacked" by radical forces. • "Tolerance is the cornerstone of Islam and has emerged out of the very nature of the history of Islam" (172).	• Islam is not purely a religion of peace and tolerance and thus should not be insulated from the harsh questioning of those who have been alarmed by recent developments. The argument that Islam is a religion of peace is "emotionally comforting" but false: "While I would have loved to believe this account of things, the more I read and reflected, the less sense it made" (49).	• Islam is not a religion of peace. In contrast to modern Christianity: "Christianity of love and tolerance remains one of the West's most powerful antidotes to the Islam of hate and intolerance" (xx).

(Continued)

Table 4.1 Comparison of three prominent "dissident" authors and some of their key perspectives (Continued)

	Raheel Raza	Irshad Manji	Ayaan Hirsi Ali
Opinion of "moderate Muslims"	• Raza describes herself as a "moderate Muslim."	• Moderate Muslims are apologists for Islamic extremism. Their belief that it is Muslims rather than Islam that is the root of the problem is lacking in the level of honesty necessary to affect real change. All Muslims are complicit in the events of 9/11 insofar as they refuse to adopt a critical view of their religion.	• "Moderate" Muslims not really moderate because they are unwilling to reject altogether troublesome parts of Islamic scripture (196), and because they purposely engage in double-speak in order to gloss over cruel aspects of the faith (196). Western theologians/moderate Muslims suffer from "cognitive dissonance" and are "trapped in confusion" (197).
Positioning in relation to Western liberalism and secularism	• Essential Western and Islamic values are compatible; thus no fundamental changes are needed in Islam. The West can support Islam by providing a context in which Muslims can recognize their own universal values but this does not mean that Western values are superior to Islamic ones. • Credits her Western experience with deepening and broadening her faith through interfaith dialogue and advocacy.	• There are basic contradictions between Islamic and Western values, thus reformation requires Westernization of Islamic culture. The West is a haven for ideal modern values including critical thinking, individual freedom, and democracy. Secularism is superior to religion because it makes room for religion (and not simply religiously directed politics). • Credits her Western experience with allowing her the freedom to explore, challenge, and judge her faith.	• There is an inherent clash between the values of Western and Islamic civilizations. "The culture of the Western Enlightenment is better" (213). Western cultures celebrate femininity and considers women to be masters of their own lives, while Islamic cultures mutilate girls' genitals; confine them behind walls; veil, flog, and stone them; allow men to have an advantage over them by marrying four wives at once and by denying them alimony (212–213). • Credits her Western experience with enabling her to "escape the world of dogma and oppression," and to enter "the sunlight of independence and free ideas" (129).

(Continued)

Table 4.1 Comparison of three prominent "dissident" authors and some of their key perspectives (*Continued*)

	Raheel Raza	Irshad Manji	Ayaan Hirsi Ali
On Muslims living in the West	• Sympathetic toward, yet firm in her criticism of, Muslims in the West. Some foreign cultural trends among Muslims not appropriate in Canada, such as the wearing of the *niqab*. Calls on Muslims to move beyond their love/hate relationship with the West and to use the West as a scapegoat for problems in Muslim countries.	• Western and especially North American democracies exhibit too much tolerance toward Muslim minorities.	• Western institutions and individuals need to stop supporting the preservation of foreign cultural values within their lands, particularly those derived from Muslims cultures. They are a threat to democracy, individual freedom, and gender equality.
Women's emancipation	• Educate non-Muslims about the diverse realities experienced by Muslim women, while continuing to engage in advocacy for those women who must wrestle with challenging cultural norms.	• Places women's empowerment at the top of her list of prescriptions for Islamic reform, as a means of overcoming traditional male dominance in the economic as well as religious domains.	• The subjection of women within Islam is the biggest obstacle to the integration and progress of Muslim communities in the West (160).

Placing particular emphasis on her negative personal experiences with Muslim men, especially her father (2005, p. 10), Manji places women's empowerment at the top of her list of prescriptions for Islamic reform, as a means of overcoming traditional male dominance in the economic as well as religious domains:

> The road forward, it seems to me, must try to tackle three challenges at the same time: first, to revitalize Muslim economies by engaging the talents of women; second, to give the desert a run for its money by unleashing varied interpretations of Islam; and third, to work with the West, not against it... My tentative conclusion: God-conscious, female fueled capitalism might be the way to start Islam's liberal reformation.
>
> (2005, pp. 175–176)

Manji refers to her program as "Operation Ijtihad" (a title of her seventh chapter in *The Trouble with Islam Today*), and makes it clear that her primary intended audience is Western. "In each case," she states, "what we're undermining is hoary tribalism" (Manji, 2005, p. 175). Unlike Raza, she makes no effort to inform the reader about profound differences between the life circumstances experienced by Muslim women. Manji's critics have objected to this implied equation of rural Saudi Arabia with the streets of West Beirut, and to what they see as an equally problematic silence concerning the progress achieved by Muslim women in recent decades.[24]

Responses to "dissident" authors

Controversies surrounding the brisk sale of dissident texts on Islam reveal a great deal about identity negotiation between "majority-culture" North Americans and the Muslim minority community, as well as within the Muslim minority community itself.[26] Whereas many non-Muslims feel that by reading these books they have been liberated from "political correctness," excessive politeness, and other niceties, a solid majority of Muslims regard the same books as fuel for an oppressive environment of fear, misunderstanding, and Islamophobia. The same authors who may be regarded as heroes and exemplars of moral courage by the majority community are regarded as purveyors of hurtful stereotypes by members of a Muslim diaspora community who feel burdened by the intense scrutiny that accompanies the transformation of their religion into a "security threat." Books which strike so many non-Muslim readers as "the truth about Islam" evoke exactly the opposite reaction among so many Muslims.

In the majority-culture, popular Muslim reactions to dissident texts would seem to confirm many of the accusations they contain. Reports of death threats against authors are profoundly disturbing, and emotional denunciations of the authors incline many spectators to wonder if uncomfortable truths are being spoken.[27] The popularity of the authors among readers from the majority culture would appear to depend in no small part on the unpopularity of the writers' arguments among members of their "root" communities. Books such as *The Trouble with Islam Today* are read by many North Americans as timely reminders against excessive multicultural tolerance, and as affirmations of a need to reassert a more uniform approach to Western culture, identity, and values. The implication is that Canadian, American, or European identities need to be renegotiated in favor of a past Anglo-Saxon/French/Western synthesis, with stronger pressure for immigrant communities to abandon the values, loyalties, and traditions of their countries of origin insofar as they diverge from authentic North American norms.

This notion that the majority-culture has been too accommodating diverges dramatically from commonplace perceptions among members of the Muslim minority community, who tend to read the message of the dissident texts differently. These texts' defiant calls for reform appear to have little appeal not only among "extreme" Muslims, but also among the many Muslims in America, Canada, and beyond who genuinely wish for changes in their tradition. The messages of defiant reformers sell to non-Muslims far better than to Muslims, in no small part because these messages appear to have been crafted with non-Muslim or secular audiences in mind. Among those who feel that Islam has been misunderstood and subjected to unfair attacks, there is great discomfort with the manner in which many authors of the bestselling books about Islam have utilized their lack of "good standing" within the Muslim community as a selling point, and have marketed books with a noticeable absence of back-cover blurbs by Muslim scholars. For example, scholars, such Leila Ahmed, Saba Mahmood, Lila Abu-Lughod, and Hamid Dabashi, have voiced their concern for the impact of dissident writings on Muslim women in particular and predominantly Muslim countries in general. In *A Quiet Revolution* (2011), Ahmed offers a critique of dissident writings that underscores the usefulness of the genre among those seeking to propagate neo-Orientalism and justify military conflict:

> Such [dissident] writers are invaluable to the neoconservatives… because they can deliver the message of women's oppression in Islam in 'authentic Muslim women's voice,' a message that fosters feelings of hostility toward Islam and Muslim men under the guise of concern for Muslim women, feelings that translate into support for war in Muslim countries as legitimate and morally justified.
>
> (p. 226)

Sa'diyya Shaikh, proponent of the movement for Islamic feminism which will be discussed in Chapter 5, agrees with this assessment, and observes that dissident authors such as Manji and Hirsi Ali explicitly support military interventions in Muslim-majority countries while being lauded as champions of feminism:

> ...[They] have explicitly supported American-led military interventions in Afghanistan and Iraq as an effective form of resistance to fundamentalist Islam... Ironically, in the American and European media that seethes with moral outrage at the reported experiences of women like Hirsi Ali and Manji in Muslim contexts, there is little mainstream critical coverage of the destruction, damage, and death of Muslim women, men, and children at the hands of occupying U.S.-led armies in these same countries. Some of these native informers have been hailed by American and European feminists as courageous feminists. Hirsi Ali received the Simone de Beauvoir Prize for Women's Freedom in 2008, while Irshad Manji was named as 'Feminist for the 21st Century' by *Ms. Magazine.* Among many of their Western feminist supporters, there is little critical attention directed at these women's intersecting and compromised political locations... Their testimonials filled with sweeping, generalized, and essentialist statements about Islam and Muslim societies echo orientalist stereotypes of an unchanging monolithic religion unable to transcend medieval norms. There is no recognition of the internal pluralism and myriad forms of lived contemporary Islam as well as the rich internal contestations of gender ethics in the Muslim world.
>
> (2018)

For scholarly critics of dissident authors, geographical location and readership are central concerns; the extent to which dissident discourses can be instrumentalized for imperialist or liberal hegemonic purposes invalidates the claims made by their authors, making them unworthy of further closer scrutiny. In the process, however, distinctions and transformations among these authors are not typically acknowledged. Instead there is a homogenization of the dissident discourse and of its liberal context. While supporting Western attitudes of ideological closure (vis-à-vis Islam and Muslims) is arguably a valid line of critique, those who dismiss certain Muslim discourses outright on account of their potential for ideological cooptation are not necessarily immune to the perception of fostering intellectual closure themselves. For example, a great many readers of "dissident Muslim women" texts are most likely not supportive of war and occupation, and would likely wonder about possible connections between the critical discourse they are reading and the "contestations of gender ethics" evoked by Shaikh.

Conclusion

Dissident female writers, such as Hirsi Ali, Manji, and Raza, have become increasingly influential sources of information about Islam and Muslims for the lay reader in North America and Europe, and (in the case of Hirsi Ali and Manji) beyond. These authors write in a highly accessible and conversational style, offering critiques that make some references to academic literature while ultimately deriving their legitimacy from personal narratives and lived experiences. Their approaches are centered on issues that intrigue the mainstream reading public, and book sales (especially for Hirsi Ali and Manji) appear to indicate that a large number of readers find "Muslim dissident" literature appealing.

While the narratives of fraught journeys evoked by dissident writers should not be negated as inadmissible on political grounds alone, some critics legitimately note continuity with colonial motifs, and observe that their arguments are constructed in ways that may fail to win the confidence of most Muslim readers in Western as well as Muslim-majority countries. Such criticisms appear especially applicable to Hirsi Ali and Manji, who have achieved the greatest prominence as a result of the controversies their books have generated, and who have framed the best-selling status of their books as a sign of progress. More cautious Muslim reformists and women's advocates who now go to great lengths to differentiate themselves from these dissident authors may beg to differ. By dismissing as inappropriate or ill-founded virtually all Muslim complaints vis-à-vis the West and upholding the West as a model for sweeping changes in Islamic religious and gender cultures, many dissident authors are constructing arguments which have little traction among all but the most secular of Muslims. In contrast, other dissident writings, though not necessarily easy reading for many Muslims, are nonetheless couched in a language of faith that establishes a connection of sympathy with coreligionists.

Among various dissident writers, Hirsi Ali and Manji's styles and market successes have ensured stronger political criticism, particularly among those who fault them for failing to practice multiple critiques. Whatever merit there may be in some of their criticisms of contemporary Muslim practices, why do they dismiss peace activists and encourage Western readers to resist multicultural accommodation of differences? Is it truly inappropriate to discuss lingering residues of the colonial era or the impact of power imbalances on Muslim behavior? The fact that these women need bodyguards lends credibility to their allegations about close-minded and unreasonable opponents, but political critics are arguably correct to point out larger implications of their cultural and religious arguments.

Other lines of critique should also be noted. Those who assume a postmodernist stance may find that, when written in a "Western" (i.e., predominantly non-Muslim) context, books in the dissident Muslim genre tend to say as much about the author's immediate personal, social, cultural, and political context as they say about the Muslim realities to which they refer. Islamic scholars are likely to take another tack, focusing on the journalistic and unsystematic style of both Hirsi Ali and Manji, and on the need for deeper engagement with historical texts and precedents. None of the dissident authors, for example, take the time to explain to the reader the juridical roots of *ijtihad*, a concept that is central to their reformist arguments and repeatedly invoked. Even a brief discussion of past usage of this concept in juristic reasoning would provide valuable context for considering ways in which the principle might be expanded and applied more vigorously within contemporary Muslim communities.

At a time of profound international and intercultural tension, unprecedented numbers of people are seeking quick answers about Islam. One place in which quick answers can be found is the dissident Muslim literature. The genre is by no means monolithic, as these comparisons of Hirsi Ali, Manji, and Raza have demonstrated. There is a range of responses within dissident writings.

Reading from dissident Muslim women writers is a reminder that we are indeed living in interesting times. Let us hope that, in the decades to come, today's heated controversies begin giving way to more enlightening negotiations while providing an intriguing window into the politics of Muslim identity in North America and beyond. Such writings ultimately (at least for this author), generate more questions than answers: To what extent must the cause of reform in the Muslim world be directly linked to the values associated with Western liberalism and secularism? Are dissident writers wise to invoke Western standards as guiding principles for the renegotiation of Islamic identity and norms, or would they be well-advised to imagine "Islamic futures" that would represent less of a rupture with internal Islamic resources, values, and traditions? Is the contemporary encounter of Western liberalism and Islam making each tradition more rigid and exclusive, or is there potential for bridge-building, mutual accommodation, and more consciously pluralistic forms of social identity? And, lastly, are not Muslims constantly rereading their texts to live in the contexts of today? This last question brings us to the focus of the next chapter, which explores the intersections among Muslim women in North America, Qur'anic interpretation, religious authoritative leadership, and gendered sacred space.

Notes

1 Many of these titles (i.e., *The Trouble with Islam* and *Infidel*) have been on the best-seller lists in North America.

2 As stated in various interviews, several of these authors have received death threats. One author, Raheel Raza, claims on her website to be the sixth name on a "World's Most Hated Muslims" list (www.raheelraza.com).

3 Irshad Manji has held various honorary positions, as stated on her former website, www.muslim-refusenik.com. Here is a list of some of these positions: Senior Fellow with the European Foundation for Democracy; Visiting Fellow at Yale University; Journalist-in-Residence at the University of Toronto; The World Economic Forum has selected her as a Young Global Leader; *Ms. Magazine* has named her a Feminist for the 21st century; The Jakarta Post in Indonesia identifies her as one of three Muslim women creating positive change in Islam today; the Government of Canada claims that "she is on a journey around the world to reconcile Islam and freedom".

4 In Germany, a group of secularists from Turkish, Iranian, and Arabic backgrounds established the *Central Committee for Ex-Muslims* in 2004 as a form of protest against being automatically identified as Muslim by the German government. This committee was also formed in opposition to the *Central Committee of Muslims*, which is Germany's most prominent Muslim organization. For more information about this organization, refer to Saunders (2007). Following a trend from Europe, in 2013, *Ex-Muslims of North America* was founded to "stand for the rights of those who leave Islam" and promote secular values. See website: https://exmuslims.org.

5 Writing about this appearance, Nomani states: "Sultan blames Islam; I blame Muslims. But we both believe the Muslim world is in the Dark Ages" (2006).

6 As mentioned in Chapter 3, the American Freedom Defense Initiative, led by Pamela Geller, was listed as an active anti-Muslim group in Southern Poverty Law Center's "Extremist Files" database (Yan, 2015).

7 Other books by Hassan are *The Case Against Jihad* (2018) and *Islam, Women and the Challenges of Today* (2006).

8 See my chapter, "Marketing Islamic Reform" in Jasmin Zine's edited volume, *Islam in the Hinterlands* (2012), in which I initially started to compare themes found in Manji and Raza's writings. The author is grateful to Jasmin for all of her support and encouragement over the years and for the opportunity to publish with her.

9 The latest edition of Manji's book was published with the new title, *The Trouble with Islam Today*. As noted in the Afterword of her 2005 edition, Manji was approached by a variety of Muslims who encouraged her to change her title to reflect the idea that the trouble is not with Islam but with Muslims. In response, Manji comments that her critics have a point; however, she states, "…calling this book, *The Trouble with Muslims*, as a lot of my critics have proposed, would invite another distraction: the charge – however politically motivated – that I'm attacking an identifiable group of people. Great for sales; not for sparking sincere conversations" (2005, p. 241). Her compromise would be to change the title of her (2003) book from *The Trouble with Islam* to *The Trouble with Islam Today*. This change in title implicitly acknowledges the possibility that Islam previously had no trouble. But from the content, Manji argues there were problems with Islam even before "today".

10 In *Their Jihad – Not My Jihad!* (2005), Raza introduces the problems and "injustices" which concern her about Muslims: fundamentalism and the rise of militant Islamic groups including the Taliban; widespread injustices against women; and the challenges of separating culture from religion, truth and justice from propaganda, and rituals from the spiritual. Raza founded *Muslims Facing Tomorrow*, an organization whose mission is to "reclaim Islam for, as the word itself means, securing Peace for all people, and to oppose extremism, fanaticism and violence in the name of religion" (Muslims Facing Tomorrow, n.d.). Manji, in her book *The Trouble with Islam Today* (2005), and in a documentary entitled, *Faith Without Fear* (McLeod, 2007), critiques a variety of problems and "injustices" in Muslim-majority countries, such as the forcing of the *burqa* upon women in Yemen, the widespread phenomenon of fanaticism which led Mohammed Bouyeri to murder filmmaker Theo van Gogh, and the suppression of independent thought regarding religious matters in any non-Western country where Muslims live. For more examples, refer to *Faith Without Fear* (McLeod, 2007).

11 Refer to Chapter 5 for more about Wadud and her impact on female leadership in 21st century North American Islam.

12 For more information about the *Muslim Reform Movement*, refer to this Factsheet by Bridge Initiative Team at Georgetown University: https://bridge.georgetown.edu/research/factsheet-muslim-reform-movement/

13 Nomani's endorsement of Trump is, perhaps, unsurprising, given the blurred line between progressive and right-wing activists over a "shared concern for Muslim women" (Abu-Lughod, 2013, p. 7). By focusing on blatantly violent practices such as female genital cutting, forced veiling, and honor crime (Abu-Lughod, 2013, pp. 7–8), what these two seemingly contradictory groups share is an emphasis on "the common Western story of the hapless Muslim woman oppressed by her culture" (Abu-Lughod, 2013, p. 9), while neglecting the variety and complexity of experiences which Muslim women live, in various places. While progressive and right-wing activists arguably have different values and objectives – for example, using this story to mobilize efforts for reproductive and legal rights for women vs. rationalizing foreign military interventions – they share references to victimized Muslim women as a way to advance their arguments.

14 Nomani produced a documentary, *The Mosque in Morgantown* (2006), which explores the various challenges she faced at her local mosque in West Virginia. Refer to https://www.pbs.org/weta/crossroads/about/show_mosque.html.

15 Manji and Dajani discuss the difference between "moderate Islam" and "reformist Islam" in her presentation at the Washington Institute for Near East Policy (2015). To open this presentation, Manji shares a video produced for *The Guardian*, in which she notes that moderate Muslims "exhibit all of the traits of orthodoxy, including dogma and fear. And what they're most afraid of is busting out of group identity" (Maynard & Gallagher, 2012). In contrast, Manji self-identifies as a "reformist," which she defines as "somebody who recognizes that the Qur'an contains three times as many verses calling on Muslims to engage in critical thinking rather than blind submission" (Maynard & Gallagher, 2012). Manji argues that rather than seeking moderate Muslims, "what we ought to be seeking and supporting are reformists" (2015).

16 While acknowledging the limitations to using such terms as "the West" and "Western," I have tried to use them to illustrate the perspectives taken by Manji and Raza. That being said, these labels ultimately tend to mask reality as much as they reveal it.

17 Many wonder why Manji continues to label herself a Muslim if she is hanging onto Islam "by her fingernails," as she declares in the first lines of her (2005) book. Hirsi Ali states, "I could not believe she [Manji] was not an atheist" (Gewen, 2008, p. 3).

18 After the tragic events of September 11, 2001, there were numerous articles, reports, and initiatives supporting the project of "moderate Islam," all of which share a common objective: preventing terrorism by Muslim extremists. Other examples of supporting a "moderate Islam" agenda are found in mainstream American institutions like the RAND Corporation's project and subsequent report, "Civil Democratic Islam: Partners, Resources, and Strategies" (refer to Haddad, 2004). The Carnegie Council on Ethics and International Affairs also sponsored a program entitled, "The War for Muslim Minds" (2004), in which Gilles Kepel, a French Arabist, argued with Ian Buruma, author of books dealing with radical Islam, that moderate Muslims (especially those living in the Muslim diaspora in Europe) may be more powerful than previously perceived. There are also Muslim organizations, like the Center for the Study of Islam and Democracy (CSID), which advocate the project of "moderate/liberal" Muslims. However, as pointed out by Radwan Masmoudi (Executive Director of CSID), to be labeled "moderate Muslim" may benefit a Muslim in a Western context (i.e., moral support as well as funding from Western political institutions) and simultaneously delegitimize a Muslim in an Islamic context (i.e., all your projects are seen as Western conspiracies). For more, refer to Masmoudi (2003; 2004).

19 Refer to the "Special Features" section in *Faith Without Fear* (McLeod, 2007).

20 PMU was a liberal Muslim organization that comprised mostly of North American academicians, founded in 2004 and disbanded in 2006 due to internal conflict, especially over the women-led Muslim prayer by Amina Wadud in 2005 (which will be discussed in Chapter 5).

21 For more about the "niqab paradox," refer to Todd (2016). As Douglas Todd points out:

> A postelection profile in *Toronto Life* concluded: 'The media loved [Zunera] Ishaq. She positioned herself as a valiant voice for all Muslim women… (saying) she was not oppressed, that religious freedom was paramount and that the sudden focus on her niqab was nothing but dirty politicking.' How did it come to pass that the so-called 'liberal' media, and prominent Canadian feminists, championed the 29-year-old suburban Toronto woman who insisted on wearing in a civil ceremony one of the world's most provoking symbols of patriarchy?
>
> (Todd, 2016)

For more on the debates about and politics of veiling in North America, refer to Chapter 6 of this book.

22 Both use modern Muslims to illustrate their points of critique. One shared resource mentioned by both authors is Khaled Abou El Fadl, who is the Omar and Azmeralda Alfi Distinguished Professor of Law at UCLA. He is the author of several books, including *Reasoning with God* (2014), *The Great Theft* (2005), and *Speaking in God's Name* (2001).

23 Still, as Jonathan Kay observes, Hirsi Ali:

> has toned down her message somewhat in recent years. In 2007, she infamously called the Islamic faith 'a destructive, nihilistic cult of death.' These days, she is careful to avoid that sort of sweeping statement. In my interview with her, she also is careful to distinguish herself from anti-immigrant firebrands such as the Netherlands's Geert Wilders, who wants to ban the construction of mosques. 'You just can't do that in a liberal society,' she says.
>
> (2015)

Tunku Varadarajan adds that in contrast with her declaration that Islam is incapable of reform, Hirsi Ali now believes that Islam can and must be reformed, "and that it can be reformed only by Muslims themselves – by those whom she calls 'Mecca Muslims.' These are the faithful who prefer the gentler version of Islam that she says was 'originally promoted by Muhammad' before 622. That was the year he migrated to Medina and the religion took a militant and unlovely ideological turn" (2017).

24 While Muslim women do indeed face many difficulties that are increasingly unfamiliar to the average middle class North American woman, as stated by many scholars of Muslim societies, in most Muslim countries progress can be seen in a variety of areas, some being: the majority of university students are now women, the increase of more female Muslim political and religious leaders, and Muslim women's diverse participation in social and political movements.

25 The following books were consulted to develop this table: Raheel Raza's *Their Jihad – Not My Jihad!* (2005), Irshad Manji's *The Trouble with Islam Today* (2005), and Ayaan Hirsi Ali's *Nomad* (2010).

26 Speaking of a "majority-culture" in North America and a singular "Muslim minority community" is potentially misleading. Even less diverse societies than America and Canada are far from monolithic, and as discussed in Chapter 1, Muslims in

North America are sufficiently diverse that some would deny the existence of a coherent "Muslim minority community." Notions of a "majority-culture" and a "Muslim minority community" do, however, have sufficient symbolic resonance within America and Canada as distinct wholes and among Muslims to merit the use of this terminology, as a point of departure for more nuanced discussion of identity politics.

27 Hirsi Ali's book, *Prey* (2021), appears to follow a similar rhetorical strategy to her earlier works, such as *Heretic* (2015), by presenting statistics, criminal cases, and personal testimony that draw a connection between an increase in sexual violence and the arrival of young men who have migrated from Muslim-majority countries. According to Hirsi Ali, these incidents of sexual harassment and assault by young Muslim men are informed by "the roots of sexual violence in the Muslim world from institutionalized polygamy to the lack of legal and religious protections for women" (HarperCollins Publishers, n.d.). Critics have noted a lack of evidence for Hirsi Ali's claim that "70% of global violence in the world today – Muslims are responsible" (The Daily Show, 2015, quoted in Bridge Initiative Team, 2017). Still, it is worth noting that the tone of *Heretic* is slightly more tempered than Hirsi Ali's earlier books in that it advocates for reforming Islam rather than entirely suppressing it (Pulcini, 2017, p. 200). However, like Manji, Hirshi Ali has not revoked any of her previous works.

References

Abou El Fadl, K. (2001). *Speaking in God's name: Islamic law, authority and women.* Oneworld Publications.

Abou El Fadl, K. (2005). *The great theft: Wrestling Islam from the extremists.* Harper Collins.

Abou El Fadl, K. (2006). Foreword. In A. Wadud (Ed.), *Inside the gender jihad: Women's reform in Islam* (pp. vii–xiv). Oneworld Academic.

Abou El Fadl, K. (2014). *Reasoning with God: Reclaiming Shari'ah in the modern age.* Rowman and Littlefield.

Abu-Lughod, L. (2013). *Do Muslim women need saving?* Harvard University Press.

Ahmed, L. (2011). *A quiet revolution: The veil's resurgence from the Middle East to America.* Yale University Press.

Al Jazeera TV. (2006, February 21). Interview with Wafa Sultan. Distributed by the Middle East Media Research Institute (Memri). Retrieved from https://www.youtube.com/watch?v=UFLc5IX8x6k

Alsultany, E. (2013). Arabs and Muslims in the media after 9/11: Representational strategies for a "postrace" era. *American Quarterly, 65*(1), 161–169.

Barlas, A. (2005). The excesses of moderation. *The American Journal of Islamic and Social Sciences, 22*(3), 158–165.

Baudet, T. (2011, January 19). Thou shalt not offend Islam: A firsthand account of the Dutch trial of Geert Wilders. *City Journal.* https://www.city-journal.org/html/thou-shalt-not-offend-islam-10804.html

Bawer, B. (2009). *Surrender: Appeasing Islam, sacrificing freedom.* Anchor Books.

Bridge Initiative Team. (2017). Factsheet: Ayaan Hirsi Ali. https://bridge.georgetown.edu/research/factsheet-ayaan-hirsi-ali/

Bridge Initiative Team. (2018). Factsheet: Asra Nomani. https://bridge.georgetown.edu/research/factsheet-asra-nomani-2/

Broder, J. M. (2006, March 11). For Muslim who says violence destroys Islam, violent threats. *The New York Times.* https://www.nytimes.com/2006/03/11/world/middleeast/for-muslim-who-says-violence-destroys-islam-violent.html?searchResultPosition=1

CBC News. (2009, October 8). Muslim group calls for burka ban. https://www.cbc.ca/news/canada/muslim-group-calls-for-burka-ban-1.863810

Dabashi, H. (2006, June 1–7). Native informers and the making of the American empire. *Al-Ahram Weekly, 797.* https://web.archive.org/web/20060603021934/http://weekly.ahram.org.eg/2006/797/special.htm

Darwish, N. (2006). *Now they call me infidel: Why I renounced jihad for America, Israel, and the war on terror.* Sentinel.

Darwish, N. (2008). *Cruel and usual punishment: The terrifying global implications of Islamic law.* Thomas Nelson Publishers.

Darwish, N. (2017). *Wholly different: Why I chose Biblical values over Islamic values.* Regnery Publishing Inc.

Douglass-Williams, C. (2017). *The challenge of modernizing Islam: Reformers speak out and the obstacles they face.* Encounter Books.

Fink, S. (2018). The Shariah scare industry and the clash of temporalities. *Journal of Islamic and Middle Eastern Multidisciplinary Studies, 5*(1), 1–19. https://doi.org/10.17077/2168-538X.1092

Former Muslims United. (n.d.). *About us.* http://formermuslimsunited.org/about/

Geerges, M. (2016, October 28). Are Islam and feminism compatible – liberal, Muslim feminist Asra Nomani. *The Mimi Geerges Show.* WHUT/Howard University Television. Retrieved from https://www.youtube.com/watch?v=lNA2JFpspJw&list=UUXxguhsAm62mptyjGxEB84A&index=15

Gewen, B. (2008, April 27). Muslim rebel sisters: At odds with Islam and each other. *The New York Times,* 3.

Haddad, Y. (2004). The quest for a 'moderate Islam'. *Al-Hewar Magazine, 115*(2), 8–12.

HarperCollins Publishers. (n.d.). *About – Prey: Immigration, Islam, and the Erosion of Women's Rights.* https://www.harpercollins.com/products/prey-ayaan-hirsi-ali?variant=32126595203106

Hassan, F. (2006). *Islam, women and the challenges of today: Modernist insights & feminist perspectives.* White Knight Books.

Hassan, F. (2012). *Unveiled: A Canadian Muslim woman's struggle against misogyny, sharia and jihad.* Freedom Press.

Hassan, F. (2018). *The case against jihad.* Mantua Books Ltd.

Hirsi Ali, A. (2004). *The caged virgin: An emancipation proclamation for women and Islam.* Atria Paperback.

Hirsi Ali, A. (2007). *Infidel: My life.* Free Press.

Hirsi Ali, A. (2010). *Nomad: From Islam to America – A personal journey through the clash of civilizations.* Free Press.

Hirsi Ali, A. (2015). *Heretic: Why Islam needs a reformation now.* Harper.

Hirsi Ali, A. (2021). *Prey: Immigration, Islam and the erosion of women's rights.* Harper.

Hirsi Ali, A., & Nomani, A. Q. (2017, June 23). Ayaan Hirsi Ali and Asra Q. Nomani respond to readers. *The New York Times.* https://www.nytimes.com/2017/06/23/opinion/ayaan-hirsi-ali-and-asra-q-nomani-respond-to-readers.html

Kay, J. (2015, May 14). Ayaan Hirsi Ali's decades-long – perhaps generations-long – Islamic reform project. *National Post.* https://nationalpost.com/opinion/jonathan-kay-ayaan-hirsi-alis-decades-long-perhaps-generations-long-islamic-reform-project

Macmillan. (2020). *A God who hates: The courageous woman who inflamed the Muslim world speaks out against the evils of Islam* by Wafa Sultan. https://us.macmillan.com/books/9781429984539

Mahmood, S. (2011). Religion, feminism and empire: The new ambassadors of Islamophobia. In L. Martin Alcoff, & J. D. Caputo (Eds.), *Feminism, sexuality and the return of religion* (pp. 77–102). Indiana University Press.

Mamdani, M. (2005). *Good Muslim, bad Muslim: America, the cold war and the roots of terror.* Harmony Publishers.

Manji, I. (2003). *The trouble with Islam: A wake-up call for honesty and change.* Random House of Canada.

Manji, I. (2005). *The trouble with Islam today.* Random House of Canada.

Manji, I. (2007, July 4). Moderate Muslims must do more than preach moderation. *The Globe and Mail*, p. A15.

Manji, I. (2011). *Allah, liberty and love: A path to reconciliation.* Free Press.

Manji, I. (2019). *Don't label me: How to do diversity without inflaming the culture wars.* St. Martin's Press.

Manji, I., & Dajani, M. S. (2015, December 16). Is there a 'moderate' Islam? Policy Forum. The Washington Institute for Near East Policy. Washington, D.C. https://www.washingtoninstitute.org/policy-analysis/view/is-there-a-moderate-islam

Masmoudi, R. (2003). The silenced majority. *Journal of Democracy, 14*(2), 40–44.

Masmoudi, R. (2004, October 26). Why the U.S. should engage moderate Muslims everywhere. *The Daily Star*, n.p.

Maynard, P., & Gallagher, A. (2012, March 12). Irshad Manji: 'I'm not a moderate Muslim, I'm a reformer' – video. *The Guardian.* https://www.theguardian.com/commentisfree/video/2012/mar/12/irshad-manji-muslim-video?CMP=twt_fd

McLeod, I. (Director). (2007). *Faith without fear: Irshad Manji's quest* [Film]. National Film Board of Canada.

Mincheva, D. (2020). Reform and utopia in Canadian Islamic feminism: The contradictory project of Irshad Manji. In L. Zisman Newman (Ed.), *Women and popular culture in Canada* (pp. 42–60). Women's Press.

Muslims Facing Tomorrow. (n.d.). https://muslimsfacingtomorrow.com/

Nomani, A. (2005). *Standing alone in Mecca: An American woman's struggle for the soul of Islam.* HarperSanFrancisco.

Nomani, A. (2006). *The Mosque in Morgantown.* PBS.org. https://www.pbs.org/weta/crossroads/about/show_mosque.html

Nomani, A. Q. (2006, April 30). Wafa Sultan. *Time.* Retrieved from https://web.archive.org/web/20080214075735/http://www.time.com/time/magazine/article/0,9171,1187385,00.html

Nomani, A. Q. (2016, November 10). I'm a Muslim, a woman and an immigrant. I voted for Trump. *The Washington Post.* https://www.washingtonpost.com/news/global-opinions/wp/2016/11/10/im-a-muslim-a-woman-and-an-immigrant-i-voted-for-trump/?arc404=true

Pipes, D. (2013, May 13). Islam and its infidels: How extremists distorted a religion of millions. *The Washington Times.* https://www.washingtontimes.com/news/2013/may/13/islam-and-its-infidels/

Pulcini, T. (2017). Cyber-apostasy: Its repercussions on Islam and interfaith relations. *Journal of Contemporary Religion, 32*(2), 189–203.

Raza, R. (2005). *Their jihad – Not my jihad!: A Muslim Canadian woman speaks out.* Basileia Books.

Raza, R. (n.d.). *Raheel Raza.* www.raheelraza.com

Real Time with Bill Maher. (2015, November 13). *Asra Nomani Interview.* Retrieved from https://www.youtube.com/watch?v=yWNv97yq4Fc&list=PLU2oQmnTNoY O466pihYf0-VjGifqrkHnE&index=1072

Saunders, D. (2007, March 10). Muslims find their voice outside religion: Secular movement stirring controversy across Europe. *The Globe and Mail.* A01 and A20.

Shaikh, S. (2018). Explorations in Islamic feminist epistemology. Article at *Humanities Futures*, Franklin Humanities Institute, Duke University. https://humanitiesfutures. org/papers/explorations-islamic-feminist-epistemology/

Sharify-Funk, M. (2012). Marketing Islamic reform: Dissidence and dissonance in a Canadian context. In J. Zine (Ed.), *Islam in the hinterlands: A Canadian Muslim studies anthology* (pp. 137–160). University of British Columbia Press.

Spencer, R. (2007). *Religion of peace? Why Christianity is and Islam isn't.* Simon and Schuster.

SPLC Southern Poverty Law Center. (n.d.a). *Pamela Geller.* https://www.splcenter.org/ fighting-hate/extremist-files/individual/pamela-geller

SPLC Southern Poverty Law Center. (n.d.b). *Robert Spencer.* https://www.splcenter.org/ fighting-hate/extremist-files/individual/robert-spencer

Steamboat Institute Freedom Conference. (2019, August 23). *Combating Anti-Semitism and Muslim Supremacy.* Panel presentation with Asra Nomani and Sara Carter. Steamboat, CO. https://www.c-span.org/video/?463337-5/combating-anti-semitism-muslim-supremacy

Sultan, W. (2009). *A God who hates.* St. Martin's Press.

The Muslim Canadian Congress. (2020). *The Muslim Canadian Congress.* https://www. muslimcanadiancongress.org/

Todd, D. (2016, September 24). The paradoxical world of Zunera Ishaq (Part 1). *Vancouver Sun.* https://vancouversun.com/opinion/columnists/douglas-todd-niqabs-and-the-paradoxical-world-of-zunera-ishaq

Wilders, G., & Pimpernel, S. (Writers). (2008). *Fitna* [Film]. LiveLeak.

Yaghi, A. (2016). Popular testimonial literature by American cultural conservatives of Arab or Muslim descent: Narrating the self, translating (an)Other. *Middle East Critique,* 25(1), 83–98. https://doi.org/10.1080/19436149.2015.1107996

Yan, H. (2015, May 4). Garland shooting: What is the American Freedom Defense Initiative? *CNN.* https://www.cnn.com/2015/05/04/us/what-is-american-freedom-defense-initiative/index.html

Chapter 5

Muslim Women Prayer Leadership and Gendered Sacred Space

As mentioned in the previous chapter, some dissident female Muslim writers, like Raheel Raza and Asra Nomani, emphasize that Islamic texts (such as the Qur'an) are not the problem when it comes to challenges facing Muslim women in North America. Rather, these sacred texts need to be reread from a feminist perspective to acknowledge the relativity of human interpretations. Such a perspective seeks the enablement or empowerment of Muslim women; the foundation of this "empowerment" is a call for *women* to return to and *interpret* the primary Islamic textual sources (the Qur'an and Hadith collections) as well as subsequent sources (i.e., *Usul al-Fiqh* – the intellectual and scientific structure of *shariah*, Islamic law) from their own perspectives. By claiming the right to interpret texts, Islamic feminists in North America are challenging existing hermeneutical understandings (intellectually and through practice) of Islamic history, authority, social structures, and gender relationships.

Although Islamic feminist critique was prevalent before the 21st century – as seen in the works of pioneering scholars, such as Leila Ahmed (1992; 2011, Fatima Mernissi (1991; 1993; 1996), Azizah El-Hibri (1982; 1997)[1] – within the past several decades, feminist Qur'anic interpretation has been increasingly recognized as a "movement," both among its protagonists and opponents (Hidayatullah, 2014, p. 1; Wadud, 2020, p. 34). Some scholars, like Yvonne Haddad (2009), claim that this movement or phenomenon is a response to the condemnation of terrorist ideology that exploded in North America post-9/11, which ultimately fostered a new impetus to review Islamic theological discourse. Other scholars, within the movement, like to clarify that feminist Qur'anic interpretation is not a product of Western liberation (which can easily feed into cultural triumphalism and "savior narratives") (Hammer, 2020, p. 3) or a response to the "modern 'crisis' of Islamic authority" (Hidayatullah, 2014, p. 2). Rather, most would agree with Jerusha Tanner Rhodes that it is a "response not only to patriarchal and androcentric interpretations and practices within the tradition but also to hegemonic and patriarchal discourse that emanate from outside the tradition" (Rhodes, 2020, p. 17). Amina Wadud, one of the movement's main advocates and a

DOI: 10.4324/9780429341151-6

former professor of Islamic Studies at Virginia Commonwealth University, defines the movement's purpose as a "gender jihad" which she describes as:

> A struggle to establish gender justice in Muslim thought and practice. At its simplest level, gender justice is gender mainstreaming—the inclusion of women in *all* aspects of Muslim practice, performance, policy construction, and in both political and religious leadership.
>
> (Wadud, 2006, p. 10)

In her definition, Wadud emphasizes an egalitarian approach to being a Muslim woman in all walks of life. In particular, she stresses the importance of "critical interrogation of Islamic canonical sources" in order to challenge gender biases and ultimately, "to reconstruct Islam from its own principles" (Wadud, 2020, p. 43). Wadud's "gender jihad" and the climate of reform would instigate many to address gender religious roles and inspire many to practice their own forms of gender justice which would manifest in a variety of ways – from feminist hermeneutical dialogue circles to the initiatives of diverse Muslim women prayer leaders and the creation of egalitarian congregational spaces and events.

This chapter explores the dynamics of gender justice in the Islamic feminist movement and its critics as connected to women prayer leaders and gender-inclusive mosques in North America. In particular, it attends to Islamic feminist understandings of basic textual debates and the conception of Muslim women's needs in prayer leadership and gendered sacred space. Throughout, this chapter attempts to clarify a central paradox of the Islamic feminist movement: That it is *both* a highly contingent response to specific cultural and political circumstances *and* a manifestation of long-term negotiations within the larger Muslim community that favor the opening of new spaces for women within religious and social life.

Negotiating diverse identity, Islam, and feminism

Many commentators on feminist Qur'anic hermeneutics and activism, as these practices are expressed by Muslim women prayer leaders (*imamahs*)[2] and within gender-inclusive as well as women-only mosques, have been tempted to represent them as either the leading edge of "gender *jihad*" within the global Muslim community, or as the latest politically motivated attempt to "Americanize" Islam (Haddad, 2009; Hammer, 2009). In fact, it is all the above and more. In particular, it is one manifestation of longstanding, ongoing, and complex negotiations over gender norms within an inescapably diverse and indeed pluralistic "imagined community" of global Islam and the North American context. Within this setting, what transpires for Muslims in one world region (like North America) is indeed consequential for Muslims in other regions, and vice versa, yet only insofar as geographically distant developments acquire meaning within localized negotiations concerning Islamic religious texts and the genuine aspirations of Muslim women.

It is a widespread practice for religious and cultural communities to continually renegotiate identity and internal norms in relation to "core" or sacred texts, ranging from holy books to constitutional documents. These negotiations do not take place in a vacuum, however. Rather, they are conducted in relation not only to changing historical circumstances and conditions of daily life, but also to comparisons with significant "others" whom in-group members recognize as manifesting either positive or negative contrasts with themselves. Interpretation of Islam in North America, for example, is responsive to concrete life circumstances experienced by Muslim minority groups as well as to ongoing efforts to define the internal norms of these groups in relation to the lifeways of other social and cultural communities. Both the agenda and outcomes of dialogue and contestation over the meaning of holy books and authoritative documents are profoundly impacted by the relevance of particular arguments to "on the ground" circumstances, specific social ecologies, the priorities of locally rooted activist movements, and awareness of "attractive" or "repulsive" examples set by other communities.

The multiple levels of negotiation over identity and socioreligious norms are complex, but can be represented schematically and ideal-typically by three concentric circles. The innermost circle, representing the central reference point for in-group negotiations over social norms, is the *text*, understood to include not only foundational documents but also prevailing religious cultures and interpretative syntheses. The next circle, significantly constituted by negotiation of norms derived from foundational and authoritative sources, is the *local context* – a given set of social relations, coextensive with political and economic systems that derive legitimacy and meaning in no small part from appeals to the founding documents and ideas within the innermost circle. A third circle, *intergroup context*, highlights the importance of comparison groups (positive/attractive as well as negative/repellent) in shaping the outcomes of internal conversations about identity and social norms (see Figure 5.1).[3]

In this chapter, the innermost circle (*text*) refers to both religious and secular sources of textual authority that shape Muslim deliberations concerning the meaning of Islamic identity and its implications for roles women are expected to play (or not play) in society. Whereas the core texts are largely the same in most Muslim social contexts – including the Qur'an and the Sunnah (the authoritative example of the Prophet Muhammad) – the more "secular" constitutional documents (ranging from the American Bill of Rights to the Canadian Charter of Rights) vary considerably, as do localized dynamics of contestation between various currents of religious orthodoxy and dissent. The primary questions shaping negotiations over identity and norms at this level include: What do the texts say about women and gender relations? Which texts, passages, or interpretations take priority, and why? How are

Text:
What do texts
say about
women?

Local Context:
What do
Muslim women
locally want and
need?

Intergroup
Context:
Whose agenda
is being served?

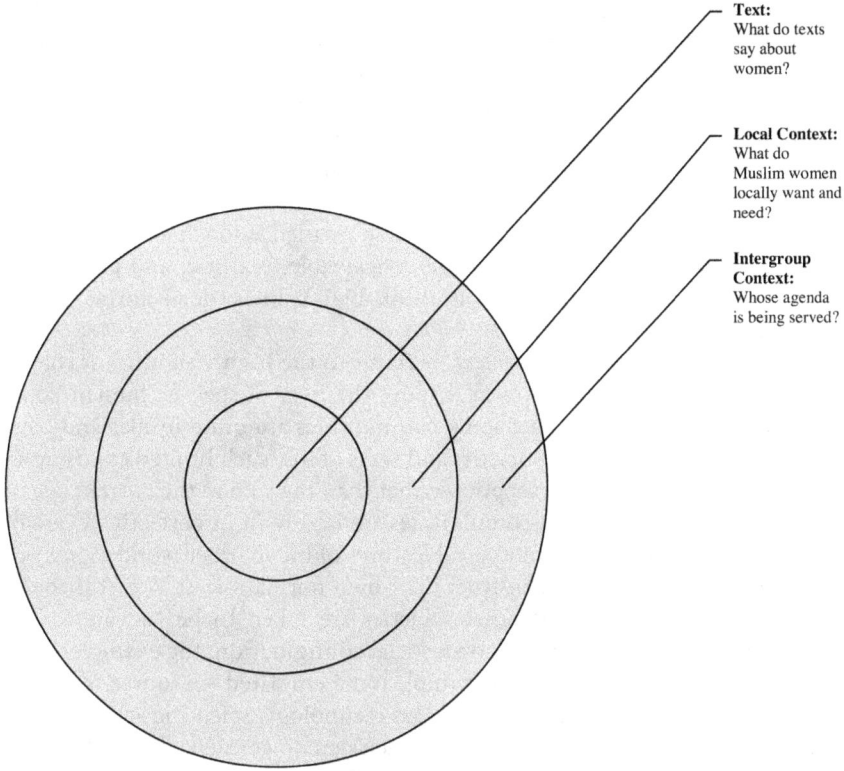

Figure 5.1 Three levels of identity negotiation: Text, local context, and intergroup context.

Diagram by the author.

Muslim women to conduct themselves if they wish to live within the values embedded in the text?

The second circle (*local context*) refers to a specific regional context of communal life – in this book, the North American Muslim experience broadly construed, as a context for living Islam among many other contexts. From an analytical perspective, this circle brings another dimension of identity negotiations into focus; negotiations concerning the "fit" between prevailing orthodoxies (religious as well as political) and the conditions of daily life. These "conditions of daily life" include a wide range of factors, including the accessibility and content of formal education, economic and social circumstances, standard modes of sharing or dividing labor between genders, openness of various avenues for professional advancement, and opportunities for political participation. With respect to Muslim women, local contexts vary profoundly throughout the many regions in which Muslim communities are situated. In North America, conditions of daily life present Muslim women with a far different set of options and constraints than those experienced by Muslim women living in contexts shaped by greater economic scarcity[4] and sociopolitical traditionalism. Nonetheless, overarching questions can be identified; Muslim women around the world are continually engaging in negotiations over localized questions such as, What does it mean to be a Muslim woman within this localized context? What do Muslim women want and need? To what are Muslim women entitled, and what are their obligations? What sorts of aspirations are conceivable, realistic, and potentially legitimate? What is thinkable or unthinkable? Which social norms appear questionable or unquestionable?

The third circle, *intergroup context*, pertains to the highly significant role of social and cultural comparison in shaping the lives of specific human communities. While it is true that some communities are quite insular and have limited knowledge of other societies and ways of life, such limited exposure to the ways of "others" is the exception rather than the rule in the current age of globalization. Most cultural communities are highly (if imperfectly) aware of at least the more basic or stereotypical features of life in other world regions or cultural communities, and construct their own norms at least in part through comparison and contrast. If other societies are taken to be "advanced" or "progressive" in relation to one's own social configuration, the example set by these other societies becomes an example to be emulated – a source of attraction, at least in some key domains such as technology, scientific achievement, political management, education, or women's empowerment. If, on the other hand, another society or cultural group is deemed to exhibit negative traits (e.g., cultural "decadence") or a tendency to dominate or exclude other communities, various aspects of that social experience become repellent rather than attractive, leading to conscious efforts to define the "self" through opposition to the problematic "other." With respect to ongoing Muslim conversations concerning the relationship between Islam and other "civilizational" entities and identities – especially that of the "West" – longstanding political conflicts have often served to limit the extent to which emulation is regarded permissible/desirable and have increased the frequency with which "Western" social and cultural patterns are deemed threatening. As a result, identity negotiation for Muslim women often takes place in a context in which the following questions feature quite prominently: How culturally and religiously *authentic* is the proposed change in the status or social role of Muslim women? Is this in harmony with "pure" Islamic teachings, or an attempt to please "the West"? If this change is desired by outsiders, is there a hidden agenda? Will addressing this issue lead to greater communal strength or disunity in the face of external pressures? Will it increase the level of respect for Islam in the world, or is it a form of cultural and religious surrender?

This "three-level identity negotiation" framework illuminates the complexity of the issues at stake, while also helping to explain why the women prayer leadership and gender-inclusive as well as women-led mosques have increasingly emerged in a North American setting. The framework enhances insight not only into the *textual* strategies associated with highly publicized woman-led prayer events but also into the *local contexts* within which it has emerged and into the global *intergroup* dynamics of identity politics that shape the way in which arguments for reform are received.

Textually derived authority (and authority to interpret texts)

Significantly, although the recent activism for woman-led congregational prayer in North America has potential recourse to authoritative secular discourses in which gender equality is normative, the predominant mode of debate is theological. Protagonists of change seek to derive their authority to interpret religious texts from the texts themselves, and embrace hermeneutic strategies employed by other members of a growing international "Islamic feminist" movement that is "spiritually and intellectually rooted in the faith" (Haddad, 2009). Within the 21st century the Islamic feminist movement has evolved, as Wadud explains, into different generations of Islamic feminists:

> Using gender as an analytical lens, we re-examine the underlying assumptions in patriarchal interpretations of the sacred texts and devise more egalitarian conclusions. Among the more well-known Islamic feminist thinkers in the West are its first-generation: scholars like Fatima Mernissi, Rifaat Hassan, and Leila Ahmed; the second generation: Kecia Ali, Sa'diyya Shaykh, Asma Barlas; a whole new generation, including Jerusha Lamptey and Aishah Hidayyatullah. Their scholarship has led the way in challenging entrenched and persistent double standards in all aspects of women's lives.
>
> (2019)

Over the years, there has been some debate over semantics. For example, some of the "whole new generation" prefer utilizing the concept of "Muslima theology" to describe their new interpretive efforts, while Wadud, whose works influenced this generation, openly criticizes the usage of this label for being "redundant and elitist" and "lacks epistemological coherence relative to the history of Muslim women's movements" (Wadud, 2020, p. 42).

Additionally, the debate over "Muslima theology" is similar to the differences of opinion over "Islamic feminism" versus "Muslim feminism." Just as there are many different "feminisms" and "waves of feminism," so too are there many different Muslim feminisms and many different scholars who have developed theories about feminism in Islam (Badran, 2009; Karam, 1998; Moghadam, 2005). Among these scholars, Azza Karam complexified the subject of Islamic feminism by developing certain categories for types of feminism articulated by Muslim women (i.e., Islamist feminism,[5] secular feminism,[6] and Muslim feminism).

According to Karam, North American women-prayer leaders fit into the category of "Muslim feminists" since they are individuals who "use Islamic sources, like the Qur'an and the Sunnah (the Prophet's actions and sayings), but their aim is to show that the discourse of equality between men and women *is* valid, within Islam" (1998, p. 11). Many Muslim feminists also deliberately try to reconcile "Western" human rights discourses with sociopolitical and cultural realities influenced by Islamic norms and values. As a consequence, these Muslim individuals do not have a problem with being labeled "feminist" since the term itself implies their main activist objectives.

In contrast, Wadud argues that "Muslim feminist" is too broad a category by connoting a variety of perspectives whereas "Islamic feminist" intentionally means the participation "in the rigorous intellectual process of critical interrogation of Islamic canonical sources to discern the basis of their gender bias and then reconstruct Islam from its own principles" (Wadud, 2020, p. 43). For this chapter, the label of "Islamic feminist" will be used due to the impact that Wadud has had on the overall movement.

Social dynamics and the importance of local context: One Ummah, diverse Muslims

Although positions on the issue cannot be neatly classified in accordance with geography, local contexts nonetheless have a profound impact on whether and how women-led prayer and gender-inclusive mosques are attempted, and whether protagonists of reform regard the issue as worthy of attention relative to other possible priorities. Some scholarly observers, for example, have noted similarities between the Islamic feminist movement and the actions of women in other North American religious groups, such as Catholic women who have been fighting for the right to priestly ordainment since the early 1970s (Ligier, 1978, p. 5), and Jewish American women, among whom seek the right to be appointed to senior rabbinic positions within Conservative, Reform, and Reconstructivist congregations.[7] Given these similar experiences within other North American religious communities, it would appear plausible that developments for women within a shared North American social and cultural space have encouraged women in all three of these Abrahamic traditions to seek advancement within the domain of religion, in ways that coreligionists have not uniformly sought.

However, it is important to recognize that Muslim women prayer leadership is not a new phenomenon within specific Muslim minority communities found in North America. *Shaykhas*, or women religious leaders, are found within certain Sufi Muslim communities, each having a diversity of roles from leading daily prayers and *dhikr* sessions[8] to guiding their students. Some examples of Sufi female leaders in North America are: Shaykha Fariha,

Head of the Nur-Ashki Jerrahi Sufi order and Masjid al-Farah in New York City; Camille Adams Helminski, Co-Director of the Threshold Society (a branch of the Mevlevi Sufi order, based in California); and Devi Tide, Head and Vice-President of the Sufi Healing Order of North America and the Emeritus Secretary General of the Sufi Order International.[9]

Additionally, in the Ismaili Shia Muslim community both women and men share a variety of leadership responsibilities including leading daily as well as other special prayer gatherings. Sahir Dewji, an Ismaili scholar based in Ottawa, described these responsibilities:

> The current and forty-ninth Imam of the Ismaili Shia Muslim community, Karim Aga Khan IV, is deeply concerned with equitable practices and issues of gender. Both women and men are able to lead the daily obligatory prayer (du'a) at places of worship (jama'atkhana). Women are also able to hold positions of leadership associated with the jama'atkhana as well as the various subbranches that fall within the wider Ismaili institutional structure. With respect to the former, the daily religious affairs of the community (jama'at) are administered in each jama'atkhana by a group of two men and two women appointed by the Imam on a two to three year-term basis. As religious heads, these men and women are charged with the responsibility to oversee religious and social ceremonies (i.e.: daily prayers; birth, marriage and death rites etc...). The jama'atkhanas across Canada fall under larger institutional umbrella that is governed by a national council and its counterparts in different regions, known as local councils. These are setup to offer a number of community services (i.e.: education, youth development, sports, economic and social welfare, health etc.) for the jama'at. Within this institutional matrix, women have and continue to be appointed to the different governing boards. Both women and men are also able to volunteer their time and skills to carry out the mandates of the boards which contribute to religious, cultural, and social wellbeing of the Ismaili community and beyond.
>
> The active role and participation Ismaili women play is a result of the Ismaili community's ethos that is driven by the Aga Khan IV's interpretation of Islam and quest for equitable reform. Important as this may be, one cannot ignore the socio-cultural systems that shape Ismaili women's experiences and therefore delineating the boundaries of women's participation both in their civic and religio-cultural spheres.[10]

Within the scholarship of women-prayer leadership and gender-inclusive mosques, it is interesting to note how there is an emphasis on the Sunni sectarian experience and an absence of a comparative study with Muslim minority communities like Sufi and Ismaili Shia congregations. These differences in gender dynamics raise several questions: Why is there a blindspot to Muslim minorities who have established woman-led prayer practices and traditions?

Why has highly publicized Sunni women prayer leadership been emphasized more than other Muslim women who have led prayers in North America? What is it about certain prayer leadership (like Wadud's 2005 prayer in New York City which will be discussed shortly) precipitated such an intense, global reaction and contradictory positions? Why has the influence of Sufi thought and practice on Wadud and other women prayer leaders not been acknowledged in discussions about these highly publicized prayer events?

For some North American Muslims, whether male or female, the idea of women prayer leaders and gender-inclusive mosques is often seen as "a bridge too far" or as an issue that does more to polarize Muslims than to generate advancements for women. Hadia Mubarak speaks for many in stating, "[W]hether I stand behind, in front of or next to the men of my mosque while praying is not my measure of female empowerment or progress" (2009). For Mubarak, "real" indicators of equality and empowerment would include women's representation on mosque boards, provision of adequate and equal space to pray in mosques, extension of invitations to women speakers by Muslim community organizations, and empowerment of women to make choices that concern their own life journeys and well-being (2009). Mubarak is not alone in questioning the relevance of the debate to "on the ground" issues facing Muslim women in many if not most social contexts, and in suggesting that other issues deserve higher priority and are more likely to yield real results.

Ingrid Mattson, the first woman, first person born in North America, and first convert to lead (from 2006–2010) the Islamic Society of North America (ISNA), the largest Muslim advocacy organization in North America, wrote a similar argument like Mubarak in June 2005.[11] In Mattson's article, she too describes how there is too much emphasis devoted to the women becoming imamahs and not enough introspection about the variety of roles that Muslim women could play in relation to the imam and the mosque community (2005). Natana DeLong-Bas notes that although Mattson maintains the need for more leadership positions, she still "supports male privilege in leading prayers, based on her understanding of the Sunnah (Muhammad's example)" (2020). However, it is important to note that Mattson also describes the significance of understanding the tradition in Islam of "women's mosques" like in China and India and how these mosques and their understandings of leadership may offer answers to the controversial *imamah* questions. As will be discussed later in this chapter, the form and function of women's mosques became and are becoming a "middle-way" between the patriarchal extreme of not addressing women's mosque needs to the feminist extreme of completely changing mosque cultures.

Intergroup politics and polarization

Within many if not most Muslim communities, the fact that many woman-led prayer events and gender-inclusive mosques have arisen in North American and especially American contexts raises profound questions about its legitimacy, while also evoking concerns about a hidden agenda pertaining to intergroup politics. As Yvonne Haddad, Juliane Hammer, and others have noted, historical Islamic-Western relations and current hostilities have a profound impact on how such a movement is perceived. Such authors cite the centuries-long preoccupation of Western governments and Christian missionaries with "liberating" Muslim women – a theme that has been used to justify military campaigns in Afghanistan and Iraq, and which casts suspicion on the motives of North American Muslim women involved in the gender *jihad*. Noting the profoundly defensive tone of many detractors, Haddad observes that Muslim advocates for the liberalization of traditions pertaining to women largely stand accused of "being complicit in Western efforts to undermine Islam" (Haddad, 2009).

Current dynamics in US-Islamic relations place pressure on American Muslims to differentiate themselves from practices of Muslims overseas, while also putting North American Muslim women involved in the struggle to reform/liberalize Islamic traditions in a highly disadvantageous position. This includes women who advocate for woman-led congregational prayer and gender-inclusive mosques as well as specific scholars who seek to reform the role of women in Islam, such as Amina Wadud, Asma Barlas, Riffat Hassan, Nimat Hafez Barazanji, Kecia Ali, and Juliane Hammer, just to name a few. The fact that the protagonists of gender justice are successful professionals within North American institutions and that their professional statures have been instrumental within their campaigns for reform within Islam also puts them at a disadvantaged position in terms of their views gaining or establishing legitimacy within the larger, transnational Muslim community. Perspectives on Islamic belief and practice that can be characterized as "American" or "Western" innovations face serious obstacles to popular acceptance in most of the world's Muslim societies, and also meet resistance at a grassroots level in North America.

Despite these constraints, the ideas advanced by the Islamic feminist movement are not without consequence. The heated response to women prayer leadership reveals not only high-stakes intercultural politics, but also an awareness of potential implications concerning the nature of religious authority and the power of religious beliefs to influence broader social norms. While the Islamic feminist movement phenomenon is best analyzed within its North American context and should not be sensationalized as having an agenda to expand into the global Muslim community, it is nonetheless a significant development in the ongoing negotiations within and among Muslim communities over text, local context, and relations with the larger world.

The agenda of gender justice and Muslim women prayer leadership

As previously mentioned, although women prayer leadership is not a new phenomenon within specific Muslim minority communities, Hammer argues that highly publicized and debated Muslim woman-led prayer events are "part of a larger trajectory of events, debates, and developments, focus[ing] and chang[ing] existing intra-Muslim discussions and reflections on issues ranging from women's interpretation of the Qur'an, leadership, mosque space, and religious authority to gender activism and media representations" (2012, p. 1). Hammer adds that such prayer events "should be read as an embodiment of a *tafsir* (Qur'anic exegesis) of gender justice, which is at the center of women's interpretations of the Qur'an" (2012, p. 10) and at the heart of what Amina Wadud calls the "gender jihad".

Amina Wadud's "gender-jihad"

Amina Wadud, who has led many controversial gender-inclusive or "mixed-gender" congregations, is probably the most influential figure in the Islamic feminist movement.[12] Wadud self-identifies as an "Islamic feminist" (Wadud, 2010; 2020) who is "pro-faith" and "pro-feminist" (Wadud, 2008). She acknowledges that her personal positioning as a woman of the West, born and raised in Maryland, USA, has profound consequences and that her decision to embrace Islam in the 1970s was influenced by her experiences as an African-American woman (Wadud, 2002, p. 201), particularly encounters within contexts of racism. She credits her consciousness about issues of social justice not only to her rereading of the Qur'an but also to the American Civil Rights Movement (Wadud, 2020, p. 35). In addition, she remarks on the significance of her conversion being concurrent with the heightened ethos of idealism engendered by the second wave feminist movement (Wadud, 2002, p. 201).

Wadud's concern with social and gender justice led her to embark on independent research on the Qur'anic position on women in 1986 (Wadud, 1999, p. ix), after having been struck by the discrepancies between what she had been told Islam guarantees women – namely care, protection, and adoration for women at large – and the reality of Muslim women having to accept "second-class status vis-à-vis other women worldwide, as well as Muslim men in their own families and communities" (Wadud, 2006, p. 59). The confirmation of women's equality that resulted from her studies led to the publication of her first book in 1992, *Qur'an and Woman* (Wadud, 1999, p. x), which proved to be groundbreaking for its innovative approach to understanding the question of women in Islam. It examined the question of women solely from the Qur'anic perspective (to the exclusion of Hadith literature), and relied on methods of sociohistorical contextual and syntactical analysis to draw alternative meanings from Qur'anic passages.

In contrast to dissident authors like Manji (as discussed in the previous chapter), Wadud's "new *ijtihad* approach" (Wadud, 2000) advocates for empowering women through the continual interpretation of the Qur'an and applying this rereading to reform authority and gendered space. In Gisela Webb's book, *Windows of Faith* (2000), Wadud describes how "alternative

Qur'anic exegesis" resembles "other alternative interpretations of the primary sources of Islam" by emphasizing "both Islamic legitimacy and agency" (Wadud, 2000, pp. 3–4). She notes that "although the sanctity of the primary sources is maintained, the hermeneutics of those sources – how they are understood, interpreted, and then applied – reflect new levels of understanding and human participation" (Wadud, 2000, pp. 3–4). Wadud identifies three major contradictory strategies to interpreting the Qur'an: Namely, two that are neotraditionalist (one of which is conservative, and the other which is reactionary), and one that is secular (Wadud, 2000, pp. 5–8).

According to Wadud, the neotraditionalist strategy continues from traditional approaches in upholding the:

> ...pristine honor attributed to women as articulated within classical texts such as al-Ghazzali's book on marriage and sexuality. Traditionally, a woman was dependent upon a male member of society, usually her father or husband, for establishing her legitimacy and maintaining her social honor... In both of the neotraditionalist strategies, the Muslim woman is perceived only in terms relative to the man's home: a pious or recalcitrant wife, mother, daughter, or homemaker... Both... might be considered responses to the misrepresentation of Muslim women and Islam throughout the colonial period. This misrepresentation continues to be projected by Western academia and popular media... [and] asserts or implies that Islam itself oppresses women.
>
> (2000, pp. 5–6)

She adds that within this neotraditionalist strategy, the conservative approach emphasizes:

> A symbolic return to the Madinan model... Women may be heavily veiled... [and are] rarely called upon to perform competitive public duties such as wage-earning employment outside the home. In some cases, the women in the groups who adhere to this perspective may also fall below the national trends toward higher education because educational institutions themselves are viewed as vehicles of corrupt Western or un-Islamic values.
>
> (Wadud, 2000, pp. 6–7)

In comparison, the reactionary approach within the neotraditionalist strategy responds to a "double bind" or contradiction of women accessing and receiving increased higher education and professional training, and making more public contributions, yet having continued responsibilities for domestic labor and childcare (Wadud, 2000, p. 7).

The other strategy to Qur'anic interpretation that Wadud describes – the secularist strategy – opposes Islamic spirituality in discussions of women's rights, in favor of approaches that are "pro-Western, pro-modern, and anti-tradition, even though they fail to distinguish between lived Islam, the intellectual legacy of the Muslims, and Islam as a reflection of the primary sources" (Wadud, 2000, p. 8).

While there have been examples of female scholars of Qur'an and Hadith throughout history, Wadud notes the absence of women's voices in commentaries:

> The gap that results from the voicelessness of women in *tafsir*, a major Islamic intellectual discipline, cannot be closed with the mere rhetoric of equality in Islam. Closing this gap will be a major contribution to the current debates over the status of women in Islam.
>
> (2000, p. 13)

To work toward addressing this absence, Wadud calls for the need to continually interpret scripture, and to strive for gender justice. She argues that "for Islam to remain vital and dynamic, the Qur'an must be continually interpreted and reinterpreted" (Wadud, 2000, p. 13). Wadud adds that "it would also expand the perception of the role of women, which could lead to the implementation of a social system with genuine justice and equity between the women and men" (2000, p. 14). She also states that this interpretative process needs to be one that intentionally includes "female perspectives on these sources and that validates female experiences" (2000, p. 20). Wadud also reminds readers of the Qur'an's core message of leading humans to create and maintain "a just and moral social order" (2000, p. 15): "the Qur'an provides the guidance. Muslim males and females are individually and collectively held accountable for following that guidance and establishing a just and moral social order" (Wadud, 2000, p. 21).

As Wadud explains in her book, *Inside the Gender Jihad*, the "tawhidic paradigm" is crucial to her understanding of Islam's intention for women as affirming their full humanity (Wadud, 2006, p. 24). This concept represents a contemporary formulation of the Qur'anic concept of "*tawhid*," denoting the oneness of God, in which a radical vision of equality among all human beings, under one God, is articulated. It confronts the matter of linguistic ambiguity in terms of the phrase (often repeated by Muslim men in an attempt to surreptitiously maintain privilege over women), "women and men are equal" in Islam. The *tawhidic* paradigm does this by pointing out that as long as men's and women's positions are not interchangeable, there is neither the potential for reciprocity nor actual equality (Wadud, 2006, p. 26).

Consistent with her belief that women's use of Islamic primary sources is a "fundamental strategy for empowerment" (Wadud, 2006, p. 9), Wadud utilizes Qur'anic notions of equality as a basis for developing symmetrical and reciprocal relations between men and women in all areas of society – including in the familial, political, and spiritual realms. As such, the explicit expression of female inclusiveness inherent in delivering *khutbahs* (Friday sermons) and/or leading prayer for gender-inclusive congregations is justified by the *tawhidic* paradigm. It is also important that she emphasizes the fact that there are no prohibitions stated *against* women fulfilling such roles in Islam's primary sources. She explains:

> If human beings really are horizontally equal, independent, and mutually co-dependent, each has the same potential for performing any social, religious, political, or economic task. The cultural and historical precedent of exclusive male leadership in the role of religious ritual is not a requirement. Although it has served as a convenience which later became legally inscribed, it was merely customary and should not be prescribed as religious mandate. Women's *tawhidic* humanity allows them to function in all roles for which they develop the prerequisite qualifications.
>
> (Wadud, 2006, pp. 168–169)

Elsewhere, Wadud has compared the "gender asymmetry" – the denial of women's equal access to religious roles and responsibilities by elevating men – to the most serious offence in Islamic law: Attributing partners to God (*shirk*). She has therefore called the logic that supports such asymmetry "satanic" (Wadud, 2008, p. 437).

"The Wadud prayer" and its impact

As Wadud's activism for women prayer leadership attests, her conception of living gender justice and embracing the *tawhidic* paradigm consists not only of rereading texts but also of engaging the context in a manner that reflects her interpretive stance. Although her first highly publicized and debated woman-led prayer event was in 1994 at a mosque in Cape Town, South Africa, where her delivery of the sermon for Friday prayer proved quite controversial,[13] it was the event of March 18th, 2005, at the Synod House of the Cathedral of St. John the Divine in New York City,[14] which sparked a global firestorm of controversy and incited "heated exchanges all over the Muslim and non-Muslim world" (Wadud, 2006, p. vii). The ensuing debates addressed not only the immediate issue at hand – the prospect of a woman imamah – but also a plethora of contradictory views concerning women's places within mosques. The event drew a massive media presence, and video footage shows Muslim detractors, both male and female, raucously hurling insults at Wadud and the prayer's participants from behind the barbed wire fence surrounding the church, declaring the illegitimacy of both the act and Wadud's Muslim-ness.[15]

"The Wadud Prayer" – as Ahmed Elewa and Laury Silvers (2011) call it – was organized by the *Progressive Muslim Union of North America* (PMU) in conjunction with Asra Nomani (Wadud, 2006, p. 248), an American Muslim dissident author (previously mentioned in Chapter 4) and women's rights activist who organized the Muslim Women's Freedom Tour that year, and was sponsored by the *MuslimWakeUp* website (Hammer, 2012; Wing, 2005). The motivation behind the event, according to members of the PMU, was not to impose this particular style of prayer on the rest of the Muslim community, but "to insist that a wide spectrum of interpretations be respected and discussed" (Wing, 2005). Saleemah Abdul-Ghafur, a participant in Nomani's Freedom Tour who also joined in organizing the event and was editor of *Living Islam Out Loud* (2005), stated that the prayer served as an act that would symbolically reclaim "the egalitarian roots of Islam" (Hammer, 2009, p. 94).

Although Wadud's role as Friday prayer leader was by far the most contentious characteristic of the event, this service departed from tradition in several more respects. Worshippers were organized in prayer rows in which men and women were either totally intermixed or which consisted of partly men and partly women, rather than in a traditional formation that placed women in rows behind men or in a separate space altogether. In addition, some of the women in attendance, including key organizer Asra Nomani and Suehyla El-Attar, who filled the traditionally male role of *muezzin*, were not wearing head coverings (Hammer, 2009, pp. 93, 95). Such details defied many traditional understandings of ritual requirements of Muslim Friday prayer, which include guidelines as to the size of the congregation, dress code, prerequisite expectations of the imam and muezzin, the number of prayer cycles, and other details.

As an immediate response to "the Wadud Prayer," Muftis, sheikhs, imams, scholars, and other authoritative spokespersons from Muslim organizations from as far as Qatar, Egypt, and Spain quickly made their positions on women-led prayers publicly known.[16] In the two weeks following the prayer, Wadud reported that she received about 50 requests for interviews on a daily basis – none of which she accepted (Wadud, 2006, p. 248). In addition to bringing contemporary Muslim gender issues into the spotlight, much of the opposition directly assaulted Wadud's character and pronounced disparaging conclusions regarding her motivations.[17] For instance, two days before the anticipated prayer service, one leading international Islamic scholar based in Qatar, Yusuf al-Qaradawi, warned American Muslims against answering Wadud's "stirring call" in an "Islam Online" posting (Al Qaradawi, 2005).[18] In its aftermath, Al Qaradawi dedicated an hour-long episode of his twice-weekly Al-Jazeera television program to arguing that women-led, mixed-gender prayer is Islamically unacceptable and (in Khaled Abou El Fadl's words) "attacking" Wadud's character (Wadud, 2006, p. vii). In North America, prominent spokesmen for authoritative councils, including the Islamic Council of Imams Canada (ICIC) and the Islamic Society of North America ISNA, opposed Wadud's actions by promulgating the widely held belief – which Wadud and her supporters refute – that there is no historical precedent for a woman leading men in prayer (Scrivener, 2004, p. A8). At the same time, Gamal al-Banna, an Egyptian Islamic scholar and younger brother of Hassan al-Banna, the founder of the Muslim Brotherhood, voiced a defense of women's right to lead congregational prayer (Stackman, 2006), and was reported to have written a book arguing that Wadud's act is well supported within Islamic sources (Abou El Fadl in Wadud, 2006, p. vii).

The impact of Wadud's prayer leadership – as seen in March 2005 and later prayer services she offered in Spain and Britain in October 2005 and October 2008, respectively – is evident not only in the magnitude of reaction that these events provoked, but also in the fact that as a result of it, more North American Muslim women were prompted to unconventionally lead mixed-gender public prayers (yet not all Friday prayers) themselves.[19] The women, who include both North American-born converts to Islam and North American immigrants from Muslim families who identify proudly with their American or Canadian identities, share loose connections to one another through their advocacy for Islamic reform in general, and collectively identify with each other in their promotion of women-led prayer. The women are connected professionally to North American institutions mainly within academia and journalism, both highly public professions in which values such as liberalism and gender equality are promoted.

Some examples in the United States since the Wadud Prayer, include Asra Nomani organized the Muslim Women's Freedom Tour in which she too led mixed-gender Islamic prayer. On March 23, 2005, while on a visit to Brandeis University in Boston to promote her second book, *Standing Alone in Mecca*, Nomani presided over two 'asr (afternoon) prayer services: One at the university's Women's Studies Research Centre and another outside of three on-site chapels.[20] Additionally, as part of the Muslim Women's Freedom Tour, Nomani instigated a mixed-gender Friday prayer service in Boston led by Nakia Jackson, a writer, women's rights activist, and African-American convert to Islam, on March 25, 2005. Jackson would also lead Eid prayers in 2006 and 2007 (Fawcett, 2013). Nomani also promoted a mixed-gender Friday prayer service in Toronto led by Raheel Raza (who was previously mentioned in Chapter 4) in April of 2005 and then in 2010 became the "first woman to lead Friday prayer in UK" in Oxford (Taylor, 2010). In 2012, *Muslims for Progressive Values* at the Los Angeles Unity Mosque had Jamila Ezzani, lead a mixed-gender group in the Eid al-Fitr prayers (Fawcett, 2013).

In Canada, before the Wadud Prayer, Maryam Mirza broke tradition in 2004 at the United Muslim Association mosque in Etobicoke by leading the second part of an Eid al-Fitr service (Scrivener, 2004, pp. A3, A8) and in the same year Yasmin Shadeer led the night 'Isha prayer to a mixed-gender congregation. Then in addition to Raza's 2005 service, Pamela K. Taylor, a writer and Euro-Canadian convert to Islam who was a founding member and co-chair of the *Progressive Muslim Union of North America*, delivered a Friday sermon in Toronto on July 1, 2005, which was supported by the Muslim Canadian Congress and the United Muslim Association.

Taylor would also be "the first Muslim woman to lead a Grand Mufti in prayer" on February 19, 2006 when the former Grand Mufti of Marseilles, Sohaib ben Cheikh, invited Taylor to lead a public prayer while he was visiting Toronto (Elewa & Silvers, 2011, p. 151). Nevin Reda, Associate Professor of Qur'anic Hermeneutics at University of Toronto, supported the Wadud Prayer by writing an essay entitled, "What Would the Prophet Do?" which was published on *MuslimWakeUp* website in March 2005. In it, Reda argued that the Prophet Muhammad "not only permitted women-led mixed-gender prayer, but also ordered a woman in his community to perform it" (p. 152).

In response to Reda, Zaid Shakir, cofounder of Zaytuna College (the first accredited Muslim college in the United States), pointed out that the "female-led *Jumu'ah* prayer is a *Fitnah* [civil discord] for many Muslims" which has created "deep divisions, bitter contestation, and outright enmity" (Shakir, 2008. He then argued how traditional Sunni legalistic schools of thought do not condone a woman to lead mixed-gender, public congregational prayer, even as he also acknowledged that "there are many issues in our community involving the neglect, oppression, and in some instances, the degradation of our women" (Shakir, 20085). It is interesting to point out that Hamza Yusuf, also a cofounder of Zaytuna College, came forward with similar arguments in 2007 before offering a more nuanced position in 2010 at a "Rethinking Islamic Reform" conference. In the latter pronouncement, Yusuf did not contradict Shakir but instead emphasized that Islamic tradition is "vast" and "largely unread." Further reading, he proposed, will unearth new examples with the potential to enhance understandings of women's prayer leadership. As one such example, Yusuf cited Imam Tabari, who "considered it permissible for women to lead the prayer if they were more qualified than men – to lead men in prayer." He also mentioned how "Ibn Taymiyyah himself permitted women to lead men in prayer if they were illiterate and she was literate. He just said that she should lead from back because she might distract the men if she was leading from the front." Yusuf also stressed how it will take "very, very highly qualified people" to take on the task of reading and finding exceptions to the rule (Yusuf, 2010).

The use of traditional Islamic concepts such as *fitnah* (civil discord) and *bid'a* ("dangerous" innovation) demonstrates the serious concerns that the prospect of women's prayer leadership evokes for many Muslims and Muslim scholars. From their perspective, events that feature women leading mixed-gender prayer services are dividing the Muslim community, deviating from the sanctioned Islamic law, and elevating the presumably Westernized ideals of women who want liberation over the preservation of unifying traditions that safeguard the greater good of all Muslims. In addition – and particularly for traditional, conservative Islamic scholars – the idea of women leading men in communal prayers often evokes fears of a direct threat to traditional gender roles, which emphasize male/female complementarity and prioritize modesty over public engagement as a virtue for women. In traditional understandings, women who become highly engaged in public affairs are liable to become vulnerable to the depredations of men from beyond the protective enclosure of the extended family and household. Furthermore, the female form cannot help but evoke male desire. Within the context of a prayer service, the presence of a female leader is therefore likely to distract men from the purposes of prayer, due to the sensuality inherent in a women's bodily presence and even in her voice.

Although discourse on such topics is likely to be tempered in a North American setting – Yusuf and Shakir, for example, focus on legal precedents rather than claims about intrinsic differences between men and women and the dangers of distraction from prayer – belief in the importance of gender differences is strongly held in more traditional Muslim cultural contexts. Thus, it is not surprising that North American interpreters who aspire to position themselves as relatively progressive may nonetheless feel pressure to downplay the significance of any potential traditional precedents and scriptural arguments for female-led prayers. Alignment with the cause of female-led prayer, after all, would be likely to produce a rupture with mainstream religious thought leaders in traditional Muslim "homelands."

In this regard it is worth noting that, in both North American and global settings, differences between Islamic and Western secular/progressive gender norms play a significant role in the construction of Muslim identity. Beliefs about the need for clear gender distinctions and gender roles are closely linked to convictions about regulating or sublimating human sexuality, maintaining traditional family structures, and cultivating an experience of public life in which sexual themes and images are peripheral rather than central. Though not always expressed, there is a fear that embracing Western cultural norms, as manifest in interchangeable male/female roles and a full mixing of the sexes, could rapidly deprive Muslim identity and culture of its distinctiveness, authenticity, and even spiritual integrity. From this standpoint, discussions of gender equity and complementarity are welcome and critiques of patriarchal excesses are similarly permissible. Arguments that appear to eclipse presumably inherent Islamic/Western as well as male/female differences, however, are more sensitive and have the potential to evoke a pointed response.

Gender-inclusive and women-only mosques in Canada and the United States

Together with other highly publicized women-led prayer events in the beginning of the 21st century, the Wadud Prayer ultimately accomplished the objective of instigating a much wider debate about the place of women in spaces of Muslim prayer as well as in prayer leadership. Significantly, these events also created the opportunity for a variety of Muslim scholars and communities to revisit and explore the needs and potential contributions of Muslim women, especially within the mosque cultures of North America. Consequently, a development of diverse gendered sacred spaces started to emerge from gender-inclusive or mixed-gender mosques to more "women-friendly" mosques to "women-only" mosques in Canada and the United States.

Most of these communities are seeking to promote different perspectives on religious authority by creating a cooperative atmosphere in which all qualified congregants have an opportunity to lead. To this end, they are seeking to remove traditional barriers to women's leadership while also opening up mosque spaces in ways that are intentionally gender inclusive – with inclusion understood in ways that range from the dedication of special mosques primarily for women, to the provision of gender-mixed worship spaces for men and women, to the active inclusion for sexual minorities. In the process, these new mosque communities are challenging patriarchal cultural norms by reconceptualizing gendered sacred space in terms of social needs rather than traditional requirements. Notably, these developments have led both to greater diversity among mosque cultures and also to a greater disparity among these cultures.

Many of the women who have been involved in the highly publicized women's prayer events in Canada and the United States have also been heavily involved in reconstructing gender-inclusive or mixed-gender mosques. For example, Laury Silvers,[21] in addition to her scholarship and activism on women-led prayer, also cofounded (with El-Farouk Khaki and Troy Jackson) the Toronto Unity Mosque (el-Tawhid Juma Circle), one of the first gender-inclusive and LGBTQ+ affirming mosques in North America, and served as an imam and khatib there (HuffPost News, 2020a). As its website explains, the el-Tawhid Juma Circle is "a compassionate focused, inclusive, Islamic mosque space. We are an LGBTQ+ affirming, Gender Equal, Place of Healing and Learning" (El-Tawhid Juma Circle Unity Mosques, n.d.). The el-Tawhid Juma Circle was established in May 2009:

> [...] with the intention of creating an inclusive tawhidic Muslim identified prayer space where diversity and inclusivity are celebrated and not just given lip service: where the inherent dignity of every human being regardless of gender, gender identity, sexual orientation, race, linguistic group, dis/ability, religion or class is recognized as Allah-given as underscored in the Qur'anic declaration that Allah is closer to each one of us than our own jugular vein, without distinction.
>
> El-Tawhid Juma Circle is Human Positive in that its foundation is that all humans are equal agents of Allah in all aspects of ritual practice. Since May 2009, the Toronto Unity Mosque has been meeting every Friday for congregational prayer. Our service exemplifies the notion of shared authority as jamaat members take turns in giving the call to prayer, delivering the sermon and leading the prayer. Our service is accessible by skype as some of our members are isolated due to health, geography or conscience.

Our mosques are places of ritual and spiritual healing for everyone – regardless of whether they identify as Muslim or not. Since May 2009, eTJC has inspired, resourced and/or helped establish 9 similar communities in North America.

(El-Tawhid Juma Circle Unity Mosques, n.d.)

As of 2021, in connection to Toronto Unity Mosque, a variety of Unity mosques have emerged across Canada from the west in Vancouver and Calgary to the east in Montreal and Halifax. These mosques in their names and mission statements reflect Wadud's "tawhidic paradigm" and have become safe spaces away from sexism, homo- and transphobia, racism, ethnocentricism, and Islamophobia.

In comparison, similar objectives are found at Masjid al-Rabia in Chicago which became "the first trans-led, women-centered, and LGBTQ+ affirming mosque in North America" in 2018 (Masjid al-Rabia). Mahdia Lynn, the cofounder of the mosque, describes how the mosque was named after the early female Muslim mystic, Rabia al-Basri (d. 801) who was known for holding "a torch in one hand and a bucket of water in the other. When townspeople asked her why, she said she wanted to burn down heaven with the torch and put out hellfire with the water so that people could worship without fear of punishment or desire for reward, for the sake of God alone" (Husain, 2019). This message of resisting the desire for reward and the fear of punishment is what Lynn describes as "the story [which] defines the space" of Masjid al-Rabia. In taking this stance, the founders of Masjid al-Rabia have simultaneously laid claim to the legacy of an iconoclastic early Muslim saint – a woman whose firm resolve and spiritual stature made her the subject of frequent and favorable comparisons to the less enlightened male religious leaders in her milieu – and also staked out a counternarrative to religious discourses that members of sexual minority communities have experienced as punitive in nature. In a broader religious culture that has generally equated membership in a gender minority community with willful sexual license, forgetfulness of God, and the likelihood of punishment in the afterlife, the story of Rabia as a paragon of worshiping God for love's sake alone offers a striking counterpoint.

Although "tawhidic" spaces like the Unity mosques and Masjid al-Rabia are still controversial, the emergence of spiritual homes for "the marginalized" in Islam[22] raises larger questions about the intersectionality of gender, sexuality, authority, and the sacred. These 21st-century prayer spaces have become solutions for some and challenges for others. For example, some mainstream Muslim advocacy organizations (ISNA, CAIR-Canada, Islamic Circle of North America, Muslim Alliance of North America, Muslim Association of Canada, MSA-National) have responded to the debates about women's position in the mosque by forming a coalition to promote and distribute a booklet, "'Women-Friendly' Mosques and Community Centers:

Working to Reclaim Our Heritage." Muslim scholars like Ingrid Mattson and Zaid Shakir (who both were vocal and wrote responses that did not support women leading mixed-gender prayer congregations) were consulted for this booklet, which offered a call to action for masjid leaders to grant women more access and participation in North American mosques. In it, there is discussion about the alienation of women from masjid culture, in light of gender discrimination as reflected in the lack of "dignified accommodations," an affirmation women's right to access the main prayer hall and not be segregated to separate, isolated spaces where they are neither seen nor heard.[23] Additionally, the booklet supports women's right to educational and administrative opportunities (e.g., women representatives on governing boards and in community programs). In contrast to the messages of the gender-inclusive mosques, this booklet specifically states, "we do not advocate that women lead a mixed gender congregation in prayer at a masjid," rather women are encouraged "[to] pray in congregation with a woman leader when they gather as an all-female group." This position reflects the majority of traditional legal opinions which were voiced during the highly publicized women-led prayer events.

A recent increase in the number of "women-only mosques" appears to be a direct result of the debate sparked by assertions of women's prayer leadership and the consequent debates between traditionally conservative mosques and alternative gender-inclusive mosques. One example is the Women's Mosque of Canada, cofounded by Farheen Khan, as a pop-up gathering of Muslim women and allies who held their inaugural Friday prayer congregation at Trinity-St. Paul's United Church in Toronto, Ontario, in the spring of 2019 (Elghawaby, 2019). According to Khan, the Women's Mosque of Canada "is an attempt to engage women, like myself, to reconnect with their religion in a space with other women" (Khan, 2019).[24] The Women's Mosque of Canada offers prayer and Friday congregations, study circles, support, and resources for women of all faiths and values (Women's Mosque of Canada, 2019b). Its website describes a commitment to "raising the status of Women in our Faith and in our Communities" in a number of different ways:

- by offering a "safe space, for women by women, where women can connect with our Creator Allah SWT, each other and heal;"
- by advocating for "the rights of women both within the faith and in broader society;"
- by supporting women who are "impacted by violence and/or abuse (in all its forms) by offering spiritual care;"
- by fostering "spiritual and religious learning from a gendered lens;" and
- by focusing on "the love and compassion of the Lord" (Women's Mosque of Canada, 2019a).

The website describes its values and history as follows:

> The concern for the traditionalists was the lack of precedence for such a space to exist for women only. For the progressives, the need for a sacred space was more of a question versus, the need for an inclusive Islam which involved a deeper dive into the sacred scriptures from a lens of diversity and inclusion more broadly.
>
> The Women's Mosque of Canada is founded primarily to ensure that women within Islam and in broader society have equal rights. We stand against all forms of violence and oppression against women including Sexual Assault, Trafficking, Domestic Violence, Gendered Islamophobia, Forced Marriage, Polygamy, FGM and more.
>
> To date the Women's Mosque gatherings have been attended by a number of community leaders and dignitaries including the Honourable Governor General of Ontario Elizabeth Dowdeswell.
>
> (Women's Mosque of Canada, 2019c)

As this statement suggests, "women-only" mosques can offer a "middle-way" between the traditionalists and the progressives in which they are not challenging either position. Rather, they are promoting female leadership and security in general. As reflected in its website, the main motivations for establishing a women's mosque are as follows:

- We don't see ourselves in the faith institutions as playing an active role within the mosques.
- We are not able to address gatherings and speak on topics relevant to women.
- We are told that being leaders in our faith is not the role of women.
- And in fact, we are discouraged from coming to the mosque and engaging in faith-based leadership.

> These statements are completely contradictory to the role that Muslim women played in Islam in its formative years and for many years subsequent to that.
>
> (Women's Mosque of Canada, 2019b)

Similar to the argument made by supporters of mixed-gender congregations, Khan too cites historical precedents and notes that "we aspire to be like the great heroines of the past, such as Sayeda Khadija, one of the most influential women in Mecca at the time of the Prophet Muhammad, and Hazrat Ayesha, a top scholar and thought leader of her time" (Khan, 2019).

In the United States, M. Hasna Maznavi founded in 2015 the Women's Mosque of America, the first all-female mosque in that country.[25] Maznavi, who is a "comedy writer and director committed to changing the way Muslims are represented in mainstream American media" (HuffPost News, 2020b), reflects on how:

> Building a mosque was my childhood dream and prayer; it's something I've been collecting ideas and planning for my entire life. But the inspiration for establishing a women's mosque came in recent years, after learning about the thousands of Muslim women scholars and leaders who were actively engaged in the formation and spread of Islam; spending a year studying under an inspiring Shaykha at a Muslim women's college; and reading the riveting book *Destiny Disrupted* [by Tamim Ansary, 2009], which revealed the fascinating – and surprisingly arbitrary – history behind the formation of *shariah* (religious law).
>
> (Maznavi, 2015)

The Women's Mosque of America opened in 2015 at the multifaith Pico Union Project building in downtown Los Angeles, California, as "a non-denominational mosque [that] welcomes women of any faith who may be curious to learn about Islam and encourages visitors to come as they are" (Hammer, 2015; Tan, 2015). It provides women-led Friday jummah services for women and children once per month, and "programming, events, and classes open to both men and women that aim to increase community access to female Muslim scholars and female perspectives on Islamic knowledge and spirituality" (The Women's Mosque of America, 2020). According to Maznavi and Women's Mosque co-president Sana Muttalib, "the space isn't meant as an alternative to local mosques but as a complementary place where women can begin to feel empowered" (Tan, 2015). Sheema Khan notes that the Women's Mosque of America "is a natural outgrowth of the lack of meaningful inclusion of women in many mosques across North America" (Khan, 2015). She adds that a 2013 report on a 2011 survey of American mosques conducted by a coalition of national Muslim organizations and Hartford Institute for Religion Research (ISNA, 2013) found that:

- [...] on average, just 18 per cent of congregants attending Friday prayers were women. The report points to imported Muslim cultural practices that discourage female attendance as one source of the poor numbers;
- Two-thirds of mosques were using dividers (or separate rooms) to demarcate women's prayer spaces in 2011, an increase from 50 per cent in 1994;
- While 71 per cent of mosques had some sort of women's programs, only 4 per cent indicated that these were top priority;
- The proportion of mosques that allow women to serve on boards was up significantly, from 69 per cent in 2000 to 87 per cent in 2011. However, 83 per cent of Salafi mosques barred female board members, whereas

Shia and African-American mosques place few or no such gender restrictions. Roughly 60 per cent of mosques had female board members serving in the period between 2006 and 2011 (Khan, 2015).

The combination of a women's mosque and a gender-inclusive space is Qal'bu Maryam Women's Mosque in Berkeley, California. Established in 2017 by Rabi'a Keeble,[26] the mosque is "a sacred space run by and for Muslim women" (Qal'bu Maryam Women's Justice Center, n.d.) but also is a space "for all Muslims, men and women, and for those curious to learn about the religion in a relaxed, supportive environment" (Escobar, 2017). According to the mosque's website, gender and social justice are main objectives connected to worship:

> At Qal'bu Maryam we believe that worship is based on what issues from the heart, more so than the mouth. We will adhere to Islamic norms and conduct for prayer. However, sticking with a social justice model, we will not give preferential treatment to men in seating, teaching, or in any other way. All engagement will flow from individual desire to be part of a community and to learn and contribute. We will lift up our Islamic matriarchs, and teach about their contributions to Islam, as well as contemporary Muslim women who are scholars and leaders in the world. We will also teach women those skills to conduct Jumu'ah prayer wherever they are and whenever it's needed. We believe that women are not a threat to males in prayer, nor are males a threat to women. In our everyday lives we mix with the opposite sex, even at the holiest of shrines to Islam, at the Kaaba men and women mingle as they pray and supplicate. The idea of separating men and women is an innovation created by men putting women in a subservient role and space. We do not believe women's bodies are dirty, a threat, or somehow supernaturally able to have an affect [sic] on man that would call for absolute segregation.
>
> (Qal'bu Maryam Women's Justice Center, n.d.)

Keeble named the mosque "'Qal'bu Maryam,' which translates from Arabic to 'the heart of Mary' – to honor the mother of Jesus Christ (whom Muslims know as Isa), as an 'elevated, formidable' woman in the Quran" (Escobar, 2017). Rather than having an imam, women lay leaders "rotate in leading the prayers and the talks" (Fernandez, 2017) and women "lead the call to prayer each week" (Ravani, 2017). In addition to Friday jummah, Qal'bu Maryam Women's Mosque offers Islamic education "for the progressive Muslim and non-Muslim student" (Qal'bu Maryam Women's Justice Center, n.d.). The mosque also "supports a network of other inclusive mosques and Muslim organizations around the world, including the Musawah gender equality movement and the Women's Mosque of America. Spiritual advisors and teachers at the mosque include rabbis, theology students, and Islamic and Quranic scholars" (Escobar, 2017).

As Keeble pointed out in 2017, the mosque offers a response not only to less inclusive strands of Muslim religious life, but also offers an answer to those who would stereotype Muslims and Islam more generally:

> Given the atmosphere we live in right now – the Muslim ban, our president [former President Trump] whipping up a fervor or hatred against Muslims because they've been framed as terrorists – maybe we can reframe (Islam) a little bit through a women's mosque, (as) a gentle, more accepting, inclusive religion.
>
> (Ravani, 2017)

While it remains true that gender-inclusive and women-led mosques are new phenomena in the North American landscape, and as such spaces with which many religiously observant Muslims do not identify, Keeble's point about their role in reframing Islam nonetheless appears to have merit. The North American Muslim community is far more internally diverse and differentiated than popular stereotypes allow, and includes both individuals who are comfortable in traditional mosque spaces and those who – while still identifying as Muslim – have not found a spiritual home in such spaces. Rather than just a development on the margins of North American Islam, intentionally inclusive mosque spaces may well reflect a growing and consequential trend.

Conclusion

As the phenomenon of women-led prayer and gender-inclusive mosque spaces in North America suggests, feminist Qur'anic interpretation has developed into a significant movement over the last several decades. Due to highly publicized events, this movement has sparked heated debates among various interested pundits – Muslim as well as non-Muslim – projecting their hopes and fears for the future of Islam. Advocates embrace and affirm the goal of reforming Islam in the direction of gender justice and inclusiveness, and speculate that the actions of emboldened North American Muslims could prefigure a dramatic transformation of patriarchal religious traditions throughout the globe. Detractors, in contrast, discount the female prayer leaders as brazen interlopers who are in some sense part of a broader assault on authentic Islamic traditions.

The tensions and contradictions between these stances are real and enduring. While the critics' views may not reflect the totality of Islamic history and traditions, their concerns do express a deep discomfort among many contemporary Muslims with what they experience as Western pressure to embrace an ethos of gender non-differentiation and sexual freedom that they consider alien to the values and worldview of Islam. From this standpoint, the move to elevate women and create new prayer spaces is at least potentially a serious threat to institutions of traditional Islamic culture and to a communitarian ethos that often places women and men in different social spheres. The protagonists of change, on the other hand, consider the traditionalist and conservative revivalist stances themselves to be inauthentic – that is, contrary to liberating scriptural truths concerning the spiritual equality of men and women, and incompatible with a standard of personal faithfulness to God that is more important than many traditional forms and authoritative rulings. To the claim that their position is purely "Western" in inspiration, advocates of women's prayer leadership and of new prayer spaces argue that the call for change is global in nature and not limited to North America.

In fairness to the advocates of change, the reality of the Islamic feminist movement defies simple generalizations and is not contained geographically within North America alone. Although its main protagonists are centered in a cultural region where women's religious leadership is an increasingly mainstream reality, it is nonetheless rooted in contemporary transnational debates about textual interpretation. Though to some extent motivated by the events and aftermath of 9/11, women prayer leaders, such as Amina Wadud, are neither participants in a "conspiracy against Islam" nor likely "game changers" in the "War on Terror." They are, rather, educated and professional North American women seeking avenues for participation in public religious life that are consistent with the ways in which they have come to read their texts and practice personal faith. Their ideas appeal to some but by no means all women of comparable cultural and social background, in no small part because they attempt to find areas of common ground between Islamic values and the broader North American cultural ethos. They have responded to macro-level intergroup dynamics between "Islam and the West" by underscoring their participation in both communities, albeit in a manner that is more likely to be warmly received in Western contexts than in traditional Islamic communities.

Although inspired in significant ways by transnational Islamic feminist networks and conversations, the impetus behind the women-led prayer movement can be understood more clearly when it is analyzed in intersectional as well as contextual terms. In this respect, the experiences and outlook of the movement's leading figure, Amina Wadud, are instructive. Neither a defender of U.S. foreign policy choices nor a person who would be inclined to feel like a comfortable insider in traditional Islamic contexts, Wadud's journey into Islam was defined by her status as an African-American and as a woman – both identities which align with major contemporary movements for equality and change. In embracing Islam as an American convert, she added another potential source of social exclusion to her U.S. cultural profile, and entered into a community which was not fully prepared to embrace her distinctive perspective, concerns, and activist identity. Wadud notes that her experiences as an African-American woman have played a profound role in her intellectual and activist journey. It appears that her experiences have sensitized her particularly to scriptural reference points within Islam that prioritize active justice-seeking, the value of equality, and the pursuit of reform through the nonviolent assertion of faith principles. Additionally, although Wadud is cognizant of larger dynamics of cultural politics associated with longstanding Islamic-Western and Muslim-American tensions, her status as Muslim 'convert' may well have restricted her sense of a need to "stand in solidarity" with other Muslims in a conformist manner. Instead, her distinctive background and positionality have inclined her to challenge tradition through independent textual interpretation that addresses issues affecting the quality of life of women and other groups who experience social exclusion. While her social and gender identities did not predetermine her intellectual conclusions with respect to Qur'anic interpretation, these identities did arguably make the search for expanded interpretative possibilities more existentially urgent to Wadud than to American Muslims who were born into the faith.

The broader appeal of the gender-inclusive and women-only mosques phenomenon – though still far from mainstream in the larger North American Muslim community – can also be understood intersectionally. As this chapter's brief review of new, non-traditional prayer spaces and communities suggests, there appears to be a growing constituency of North American Muslim or "Islam-identified" individuals who do not feel at home in traditional mosque communities, and who are seeking actively inclusive and pluralistic spaces that express alignment with progressive values and changing social norms. In a social milieu that has been profoundly impacted by movements that highlight gender-based violence (e.g., Me Too), LGBTQ+ rights, and the oppression of minority communities (e.g., Black Lives Matter), the creation of new prayer spaces offers the promise of a place that is safe for people whose experiences and identities cannot be fully expressed within traditional communal settings, and whose spiritual needs align with humanistic, poetic, and mystical currents of Islamic expression much more than with norms underpinned by traditional jurisprudence. In the new spaces where women play important roles, people seeking new forms of inclusive spiritual companionship can literally as well as figuratively "take off their veils."

As intriguing and significant as these new developments may be, a majority of observant North American Muslims still seek community, authenticity, and inclusion within more traditional spaces, and through more widely embraced forms. Among the more significant of these common forms – itself a symbol that means profoundly different things to different constituencies – is the Muslim veil. The next chapter explores a variety of controversies in America and Canada surrounding both the *hijab* and its more uncommon and conservative cousin, the Muslim face veil or *niqab*.

Notes

1 For more about these pioneering scholars, see my chapter, "Trends and Transformations in Contemporary Islamic Hermeneutics" in *Encountering the Transnational* (2008, pp. 23–59).

2 *Imamah* is the feminine form of the Arabic term, *imam*, which literally means "in front of". In the Sunni Islamic context, it also is the title for an individual who is in front of and leads congregational prayer.

3 Initial ideas for Figure 5.1 and the three levels of identity negotiation started to be developed in a coauthored article with Munira Kassam Haddad entitled, "Where Do Women 'Stand' in Islam?" (2012), *Feminist Review*, vol. 102, 1: pp. 41–61. Copyright © 2012 Sage Publishing. doi.org/10.1057/fr.2012.10.

4 Although economic conditions faced by North American Muslim women are, in general, more favorable than those experienced by Muslim women in many other contexts, there are many North American Muslim women who experience economic adversity and social marginalization.

5 According to Karam, Islamist feminists are individuals who "are aware of a particular oppression of women, *and* they actively seek to rectify this oppression by recourse to Islamic principles" (1998, p. 9). Many of the individuals placed in this category have a problem with the label of "feminist" and construe the term as being "disrespectful to religion" (1998, p. 10). Additionally, Karam's definition of Islamist feminists also stipulates that their idealized condition for Islamic societies is a state of "complementary roles." In other words, they favor a "compartmentalized cooperation" in which men and women have distinctive, separated duties in society but a unified purpose of preserving moral and social order. In this worldview, equity is preferred over equality.

6 In contrast to Islamist feminism, secular feminists, according to Karam, firmly believe in "grounding their discourse outside the realm of any religion… and placing it instead, within the international human rights discourse" (1998, p. 13). Religion is understood as private and should not enter the realm of women's empowerment and emancipation. Such an understanding of religion allows for the focus on a "secular bypass" of the religious authoritative sphere in order to gain reform for women's position and status in society through the state.

7 According to Silverstein (2013), 1200 women rabbis have been ordained globally since 1972. See also the Jewish Women's Archive encyclopedia article by Goldman (2021) particularly the section on "Achieving Religious Leadership".

8 *Dhikr* is an important practice for Sufi Muslims which literally means "remembrance." The Qur'an commands Muslims to perform *dhikrullah*, the "remembrance of the one God," and Sufis in particular seek to integrate the remembrance of God with each moment of life. Different Sufi orders developed their own unique ritual practices to remember God, usually involving the collective chanting of some of God's Names mentioned in the Qur'an.

9 For more on these women and others, see my chapter "'Women of Light': Contemporary Female Sufi Leaders" in *Contemporary Sufism* (2018).

10 See Dewji, 2018.

11 Mattson is also the London and Windsor Community Chair in Islamic Studies at Huron University College at Western University and a Senior Fellow of the Royal Aal al-Bayt Institute for Islamic Thought in Amman, Jordan (Ingrid Mattson, 2020). In her previous role as Professor of Islamic Studies at Hartford Seminary in Connecticut, she developed and directed the first accredited graduate program for Muslim chaplains in the United States (Ingrid Mattson, 2020). Mattson's writing has focused on Qur'anic interpretation, Islamic theological ethics, interfaith relations, and gender and leadership in contemporary Muslim communities (Ingrid

Mattson, 2020; HuffPost News, 2020a). Mattson has served as a member of the Interfaith Taskforce of the White House Office of Faith-based and Neighborhood Partnerships, the Council of Global Leaders of the Council of 100 (C100) of the World Economic Forum, and the Leadership Group of the U.S.-Muslim Engagement Project (USME) (Ingrid Mattson, 2020).

12 Scholars, such as Asma Barlas, Kecia Ali, and Juliane Hammer, have credited Wadud with influencing their work and starting an interpretive movement of Qur'anic feminism and gender justice. In 2012, Kecia Ali, Juliane Hammer, and Laury Silvers published an online (e-book) festschrift entitled *A Jihad for Justice: Honoring the Work and Life of Amina Wadud*. In it, 33 contributors from around the world wrote essays about Wadud's scholarship and activism.

13 For a detailed account of Wadud's experience in South Africa, see Wadud (2006, pp. 163–186).

14 While Wadud's prayer service in NYC had achieved considerable success, with about 80–100 worshippers in attendance, it is reported that three mosques and an art gallery had been dissuaded from hosting the event by a series of bomb threats (presumably delivered by American Muslim detractors) before it was finally held at the Synod House of the Cathedral of St. John the Divine in New York City (Wing, 2005).

15 To learn more about "why Amina Wadud led a mixed-gender Muslim prayer" service, watch or listen to Wadud's 2011 talk at the Chautauqua Institution: https://www.youtube.com/watch?v=E_flQbtI1U4

16 For more details about the aftermath of the Wadud Prayer, see Juliane Hammer (2012) and Elewa & Silvers (2011).

17 Wadud's activism for gender justice has come with grave personal consequences, such as: Wadud's teaching contract with the department of Islamic Revealed Knowledge at the International Islamic University was not renewed as a result of her activism with Sisters in Islam in Malaysia; following the March 2005 prayer, some members of the Muslim community in Virginia threatened to have Wadud fired from her position as professor of Islamic Studies at Virginia Commonwealth University; and, also as a result of the March 2005 prayer, there have been some Muslims who want to strip her of her title as a "Muslim" (Sharify-Funk, 2008, p. 55).

18 Elewa & Silvers (2011) describe and analyze a collection of fatwas and legal opinions on the issue of women-led prayers by internationally esteemed Islamic scholars (including al-Qaradawi and the former Grand Mufti of Egypt Ali Guma'a). This collection was in response to the Wadud Prayer. For more analysis of the exegetical processes and legal deliberations regarding women as leaders of prayer, see Simonetta Calderini's *Women as Imams* (2021).

19 It is important to note that there were highly publicized women prayer events outside of North America such as in United Kingdom, Sweden, and Germany. There is a dire need for more comparative scholarship about these events and the new gendered sacred spaces created because of them.

20 Nomani, a former journalist for *The Wall Street Journal*, was born in India to a Muslim family and raised in Morgantown, West Virginia. Nomani's work in promoting women-led prayer is heavily informed by the impact of religious conservatism and extremism which, in the American context, Nomani attributes to the growing presence of "Wahhabi"-influenced immigrants from the Arab world (Nomani, 2006, pp. 205, 231). She also raised awareness for and participated in the PBS documentary, *The Mosque in Morgantown* (2009) in which she challenged the sub-standard conditions offered to women at a newly opened Islamic Centre of Morgantown. For more information on *The Mosque in Morgantown*, see PBS film series *America at The Crossroads*, https://www.pbs.org/weta/crossroads/about/show_mosque.html

21 Silvers is a writer in Toronto, Ontario, Canada, describes herself as "a North American Muslim of the Sufi variety and a retired academic and activist". She also has written on Sufism in the formative period of Islamic thought, Muslim women's religious authority, and Muslim women's encounters with the Qur'an (HuffPost News, 2020a).

22 Other gender-inclusive mosques and communities include Masjid an-Nur al-Islah (Light of Reform Mosque) in Washington, D.C.; Haven: The Inclusive Muslim Union in Philadelphia; and Noor: LGBTQIA Muslims of Seattle.

23 The gender barrier debates in North American mosques have been one of the most prominent issues in traditional North American mosques. For more about these debates see Zarqa Nawaz's documentary *Me and the Mosque* (2005).

24 For more about why the Women's Mosque of Canada was established, and responses to criticism about it, refer to the interview with Farheen Khan (Let the Quran Speak, 2019).

25 For a detailed examination of the Women's Mosque of America and trends in Muslim women's religious authority, refer to Tazeen M. Ali's doctoral dissertation (2019).

26 Keeble, a convert to Islam, received her master's degree in religious leadership and social justice from Starr King School for the Ministry, a graduate theological school and seminary affiliated with the University of California, Berkeley, which donated space for the mosque (Escobar, 2017; Fernandez, 2017). Keeble is also an activist "who works on issues of homelessness, affordable housing, FGM, and protection of refugees" (American Friends of Combatants for Peace, n.d.).

References

Abdul-Ghafur, S. (Ed.). (2005). *Living Islam out loud: American Muslim women speak.* Beacon Press.

Ahmed, L. (1992). *Women and gender in Islam: Historical roots of a modern debate.* Yale University Press.

Ahmed, L. (2011). *A quiet revolution: The veil's resurgence from the Middle East to America.* Yale University Press.

Al Qaradawi, Y. (2005, March 16). Woman acting as imam in prayer. *Islam Online.* http://www.islamonline.net/servlet/Satellite?cid=1119503549588&pagename=Islamo nline-English-Ask_Scholar/FatwaE/FatwaEAskTheScholar

Ali, K., Hammer, J., & Silvers, L. (Eds.). (2012). *A jihad for justice: Honoring the work and life of Amina Wadud.* http://www.bu.edu/religion/files/2010/03/A-Jihad-for-Justice-for-Amina-Wadud-2012-1.pdf

Ali, T. M. (2019). *Rethinking interpretative authority: Gender, race, and scripture at the Women's Mosque of America* [Unpublished doctoral dissertation]. Boston University. https://hdl.handle.net/2144/37057

American Friends of Combatants for Peace. (n.d.). Rabi'a Keeble. https://afcfp.org/our_team/rabia-keeble/

Badran, M. (2009). *Feminism in Islam: Secular and religious convergences.* Oneworld Publications.

Calderini, S. (2021). *Women as Imams: Classical Islamic sources and modern debates on leading prayer.* I.B. Tauris.

DeLong-Bas, N. J. (2020). Women, Islam, and the twenty-first century. *Oxford Islamic Studies Online.* http://www.oxfordislamicstudies.com/Public/focus/essay1107_women.html

Dewji, S. (2018). "Beyond Muslim xenophobia and contemporary parochialism: Aga Khan IV, the Ismāʿīlīs, and the making of a cosmopolitan ethic," PhD. Thesis, Wilfrid Laurier University.

Elewa, A., & Silvers, L. (2011). 'I am one of the people': A survey and analysis of legal arguments on woman-led prayer in Islam. *Journal of Law and Religion, 26*(1), 141–171.

Elghawaby, A. (2019, May 20). Backlash over the Women's Mosque of Canada is predictable – and misplaced. *The Globe and Mail.* https://www.theglobeandmail.com/opinion/article-backlash-over-the-womens-mosque-of-canada-is-predictable-and/

El-Hibri, A. (1997). Islam, law, and custom: Redefining Muslim women's rights. *American University International Law Review, 12*(1), 1–44.

El-Hibri, A. (Ed.). (1982). *Women and Islam.* Pergamon Press.

El-Tawhid Juma Circle Unity Mosques. (n.d.). *Juma Circle.* http://www.jumacircle.com/

Escobar, A. (2017, April 17). Women-led mosque opens to build place where 'everybody is welcome.' *NBC News.* https://www.nbcnews.com/news/asian-america/women-led-mosque-opens-build-place-where-everybody-welcome-n746791

Fawcett, R. (2013, April 8). Female imams in America. *The Islamic Monthly.* https://www.theislamicmonthly.com/female-imams-in-america/

Fernandez, L. (2017, April 18). California mosque led by women opens doors to all. *Reuters.* https://ca.reuters.com/article/idUSKBN17G1L7

Goldman, K. (2021, June 23). Reform Judaism in the United States. *Jewish Women's Archive.* http://jwa.org/encyclopedia/article/reform-judaism-in-united-states

Haddad, Y. (2009, June 8). The global Islamic feminist movement. *The Mosque in Morgantown.* http://www.themosqueinmorgantown.com/forum/2009/06/08/haddad/

Hammer, J. (2009). Performing gender justice: The 2005 woman-led prayer in New York. *Contemporary Islam, 4*(1), 91–116.

Hammer, J. (2012). *American Muslim women, religious authority, and activism: More than a prayer.* University of Texas Press.

Hammer, J. (2015). A (Friday) prayer of their own: American Muslim women, religious space, and equal rights. *American Academy of Religion Religious Studies News.* https://rsn.aarweb.org/articles/friday-prayer-their-own

Hammer, J. (2020). Muslim women and gender justice: An introduction. In D. El Omari, J. Hammer, & M. Khorchide (Eds.), *Muslim women and gender justice: Concepts, sources, and histories* (pp. 1–14). Routledge Publishers.

Hidayatullah, A. (2014). *Feminist edges of the Qur'an.* Oxford University Press.

Huckabee, B. (Director). (2009). *The mosque in Morgantown* [Film]. Version One Productions, in association with WGBH.

HuffPost News. (2020a). *Contributor: Laury Silvers.* https://www.huffpost.com/author/laury-silvers

HuffPost News. (2020b). *Contributor: M. Hasna Maznavi.* https://www.huffpost.com/author/mhasnam-769

Husain, N. (2019, August 3). With female and LGBTQ prayer leaders, Chicago mosque works to broaden norms in Muslim spaces. *Chicago Tribune.* https://www.chicagotribune.com/news/ct-south-loop-mosque-female-prayer-leader-20190803-56axwv37arfm3i3gajgc4umgb4-story.html

ISNA. (2013). *Report number 3 from the US Mosque Study 2011, The American Mosque 2011: Women and the American Mosque.* http://www.hartfordinstitute.org/The-American-Mosque-Report-3.pdf

Karam, A. (1998). *Women, Islamisms and the state: Contemporary feminisms in Egypt.* St. Martin's Press, Inc.

Khan, F. (2019, April 24). First Women's Mosque of Canada opens in Toronto. *NOW Magazine.* https://nowtoronto.com/news/womens-mosque-canada-islamophobia/

Khan, S. (2015, February 5). The Women's Mosque evolves North American Islam. *The Globe and Mail.* https://www.theglobeandmail.com/opinion/the-womens-mosque-evolves-north-american-islam/article22793877/

Let the Quran Speak. (2019, May 20). *Women's Only Mosque: Farheen Khan.* https://www.youtube.com/watch?v=D3Ky19jTUyk

Ligier, L. L. J. (1978, March 2). The question of admitting women to the ministerial priesthood. *L'Osservatore Romano - Weekly Edition in English.* http://www.ewtn.com/library/Theology/ORDWOMEN.HTM

Mattson, I. (2005, June 5). Can a woman be an imam? Debating form and function in Muslim women leadership. https://ingridmattson.org/article/can-a-woman-be-an-imam/

Maznavi, M. H. (2015, May 20). 9 things you should know about the Women's Mosque of America – and Muslim women in general. *HuffPost Religion.* https://www.huffpost.com/entry/9-things-you-should-know-about-the-womens_b_7339582

Mernissi, F. (1991). *The veil and the male elite: A feminist interpretation of women's rights in Islam.* Trans. by Mary Jo Lakeland Reading. Addison-Wesley Publishing Company, Inc.

Mernissi, F. (1993). *The forgotten queens of Islam.* Trans. by Mary Jo Lakeland, University of Minnesota Press.

Mernissi, F. (1996). *Women's rebellion and Islamic memory.* Zed Books, Ltd.

Moghadam, V. (2005). *Globalizing women: Transnational feminist networks.* Johns Hopkins University Press.

Mubarak, H. (2009, June 1). Real indicators of female empowerment: Women's space and status in American mosques. *The Mosque in Morgantown.* http://www.themosqueinmorgantown.com/forum/2009/06/01/mubarak

Nomani, A. Q. (2006). *Standing alone: An American woman's struggle for the soul of Islam.* HarperSanFrancisco.

Qal'bu Maryam Women's Justice Center. (n.d.). *Education.* https://qalbumaryam.weebly.com/education.html

Ravani, S. (2017, April 13). Empowering women: Female-run mosque to open in Berkeley. *San Francisco Chronicle.* https://www.sfchronicle.com/bayarea/article/Empowering-women-Female-run-mosque-to-open-in-11072445.php#photo-12717680

Rhodes, J. T. (2020). Feminist exegesis and beyond: Trajectories in *Muslima* theology. In D. El Omari, J. Hammer, & M. Khorchide (Eds.), *Muslim women and gender justice: Concepts, sources, and histories* (pp. 17–32). Routledge Publishers.

Scrivener, L. (2004, November 13). Woman's sermon break tradition at local mosque—student, 20, to join with Imam—Not everyone has an open mind. *Toronto Star.*

Shakir, Z. (2008, April 22). Female prayer leadership (revisited). *New Islamic Directions.* https://www.newislamicdirections.com/new_nid/article/female_prayer_leadership_revisited

Sharify-Funk, M. (2008). *Encountering the transnational: Women, Islam and the politics of interpretation.* Ashgate Publishers, Ltd.

Sharify-Funk, M., Dickson, W. R., & Xavier, M. S. (2018). *Contemporary Sufism: Piety, politics, and popular culture.* Routledge Publishers.

Sharify-Funk, M., & Haddad, M. K. (2012). Where do women 'stand' in Islam? Negotiating contemporary Muslim prayer leadership in North America. *Feminist Review, 102*(1), 41–61. https://doi.org/10.1057/fr.2012.10.

Silverstein, B. (2013, September 6). Have female rabbis hit the proverbial 'stained glass ceiling'? *Toronto Star.* https://www.thestar.com/life/2013/09/06/have_female_rabbis_ hit_the_proverbial_stained_glass_ceiling.html

Stackman, M. (2006, October 20). A voice for 'new understanding' of Islam. *The New York Times.* http://www.nytimes.com/2006/10/20/world/africa/20iht-profile. 3237674.html?pagewanted=1&_r=1

Tan, A. (2015, February 4). Why Muslim woman started 1st all-female mosque in the US. *ABC News.* https://abcnews.go.com/US/1st-female-mosque-opens-us/ story?id=28725435

Taylor, J. (2010, June 10). First woman to lead Friday prayer in UK. *The Independent.* https://www.independent.co.uk/news/uk/home-news/first-woman-to-lead-friday-p prayers-in-uk-1996228.html

The Women's Mosque of America. (2020). *About.* https://womensmosque.com/about-2/

Wadud, A. (1999). *Qur'an and woman: Rereading the sacred text from a woman's perspective.* Oxford University Press.

Wadud, A. (2000). Alternative Qur'anic interpretation and the status of Muslim women. In G. Webb (Ed.), *Windows of faith: Muslim women scholar-activists in North America* (pp. 3–21). Syracuse University Press.

Wadud, A. (2002). A'ishah's legacy. *New Internationalist Magazine, 345.* http://www. newint.org/features/2002/05/01/aishahs-legacy/

Wadud, A. (2006). *Inside the gender jihad: Women's reform in Islam.* Oneworld Publications.

Wadud, A. (2008). Engaging Tawhid in Islam and feminisms. *International Feminist Journal of Politics, 10*(4). http://www.informaworld.com

Wadud, A. (2010). Back to basics: Feminism 101. *Religion Dispatches Magazine.* http://www.religiondispatches.org/dispatches/guest_bloggers/3413/back_to_ basics%3A_feminism_101/

Wadud, A. (2019, March 27). The first American woman imam explains the rise of Islamic feminism. *VICE.* https://www.vice.com/en/article/wjm3kn/amina-wadud-islamic-feminism-muslim

Wadud, A. (2020). Islamic feminism by any other name. In D. El Omari, J. Hammer, & M. Khorchide (Eds.), *Muslim women and gender justice: Concepts, sources, and histories* (pp. 33–45). Routledge Publishers.

Wing, M. (2005). The woman-led prayer that catalyzed controversy. *The Pluralism Project.* https://hwpi.harvard.edu/pluralismarchive/amina-wadud-2005

Women's Mosque of Canada. (2019a). *About us.* https://www.womensmosque.ca/ womensmosque

Women's Mosque of Canada. (2019b). *FAQs.* https://www.womensmosque.ca/faqs

Women's Mosque of Canada. (2019c). *Our herstory.* https://www.womensmosque.ca/ herstory

Yusuf, H. (2010). Women-leading prayer and Ibn Taymiyyah. https://www.youtube. com/watch?v=x45ysEfSuX0

Chapter 6

Veil Controversies
The Dynamics of Inclusion and Exclusion

With the emergence of North American gender-inclusive mosques which have become "safe" sacred places for diverse Muslims to express their authentic identities, one also witnesses in these spaces an openness to different understandings of veiling traditions. Significantly, such mosque settings for communal gathering are distinguished by a new openness to the full diversity of women's stances on these traditions, potentially including women who wear *hijab, niqab, burqa, dupatta, chador,* etc. as well as women who do not.[1] Although such intentionally inclusive spaces are unlikely to become prevalent in the near future, their presence has the potential to spark new debates and conversations within Muslim communities, of a variety similar to those that followed the advent of women prayer leaders, as discussed in the previous chapter.

While controversies and conversations over women prayer leaders and inclusive mosque settings are a primarily intra-Muslim phenomenon, the subject of Muslim veiling traditions evokes much broader contention that is not confined internally within North American Muslim communities. The competing and contradictory interpretations of veiling in Islam play out in the broader public sphere in relation to government policies as well as rules governing comportment in workplaces and even sports, through media coverage, court proceedings, and rhetoric in political campaigns. Thus, the Muslim veil is among the most controversial issues shaping the experiences of North American Muslim women in 21st century.

The heightened visibility – or what Sadaf Ahmed refers to as the "hypervisibility" – of Muslim veiling reinforces negative stereotypes, clichés, and, ultimately, conflict (2021).[2] Even as the Muslim veil moves incrementally toward normalization in some areas of North American culture, it remains a visible manifestation of what many consider to be essential cultural differences between Western and Islamic values – differences that are invested with meaning not just by those who regard the veil as "foreign" but also by Muslim revivalists and traditionalists. Although the "binary" patterns of conversation created by competing essentialisms often predominate

DOI: 10.4324/9780429341151-7

in controversies that become the subject of media and political attention, the actual positions present among Muslim women and interlocutors in real-life cases are frequently much more nuanced than controversies suggest. As Reina Lewis states, "the veil is a garment whose meaning cannot be contained" (2003, p. 10).

> [The veil] is a garment fought over by adherents and opponents, many of whom claim that their understanding of the veil's significance is the one and true meaning. But... the veil reveals one thing, it is that it cannot be contained within a single truth, experience or understanding. Instead, the veil emerges as a form of clothing that is rooted in specific historical moments and locations; its depiction is similarly contingent and its adaptation and rejection is always itself relational.
>
> (ibid)

Popular debates notwithstanding, there is no one way to look like or be a "real Muslim"; however, every Muslim woman negotiates the meaning of being both Muslim and a woman by engaging with ideas that associate dress with notions of identity and with values such as modesty.

This chapter explores a variety of controversies in America and Canada surrounding the *hijab* and its more uncommon and conservative cousin, the face veil or *niqab*. From *hijab* sports controversies, in which women and girls have been barred from athletic competitions to legislation campaigns seeking to deny public services to veil wearers, this chapter demonstrates the extent to which anxiety about Muslim veiling practices can shape popular opinions and political agendas while reinforcing defensive reactions. To begin, the chapter examines the competing and contradictory symbolisms, meanings, and motivations connected to the Muslim veil. In particular, distinct binaries are explained between many outside the visible Muslim community who promote all forms of veiling signifying entrenched gender inequality and outdated attitudes toward relationships between men and women to that of the majority view within most Muslim communities regarding the veil as an essential symbol of religious identity and values — a symbol that does not necessarily impede (and, in the view of religious authorities, facilitates and renders acceptable) integration within the larger society. These different perspectives on veiling are linked to further differences concerning the meaning of terms such as "liberation" and "secularism" as well as issues connected to safety and security. The chapter ends on the attempts to define cultural limits and religious boundaries with respect to veiling practices within the context of Quebec in Canada. An argument of the formation of a "slippery slope" is made by offering a brief timeline and trajectory of particular controversial issues and events within this context.

Competing and contradictory interpretations of Muslim veiling

Due to the complexity of meanings and contexts, a Muslim woman's decision to veil or not to veil is connected to multiple reasons and motivations in which questions of the sacred, power, and authenticity are often found. Because the Muslim veil carries a heavy symbolic load that is inescapably laden with "either-or" contradictions, the binary choice of either wearing or not wearing a veil confines the Muslim woman to an existence of navigating extreme oppositions wherein she becomes a banner for whatever cause is associated with her external appearance. The Muslim woman's encounter with the veil is a constant negotiation of personal, cultural, social, and political contexts as well as community gender and religious systems. As Lewis states, "Standing as a beacon of tradition or emblem of progressive modernity, the veiled or unveiled, de-veiled or re-veiled woman has been a feature of divergent struggles over decolonization, nationalism, revolution, Westernization and anti-Westernization" (2003, p. 10). Ironically, studying contention surrounding the Muslim veil uncovers a variety of contexts with which this symbolic item of clothing can be connected. Homa Hoodfar further complexifies this multilayered meaning of clothing in pointing out that:

> Clothing is probably the most silent of expressions used by human societies to demarcate social boundaries and to distinguish "self" from "other" at both the collective and individual levels...Clothing indicates that the wearer shares certain cultural values with others similarly attired,...Thus clothing is a means of visually creating community, while simultaneously delineating individual features of the wearer such as gender, geographical origin, religion, ethnicity, profession, class orientation and life cycle.
>
> (2003, pp. 3–4)

For some Muslim women, wearing the veil allows them to express their commitment to traditional Islam and carry sacred space into public realms. This spiritual aspect of covering as a means to constantly remember the Divine can be empowering for these women – and is particularly helpful in secular societies – as it provides a deep source of strength in facing everyday challenges while also enabling an outer life that is congruent with inward piety. For many, wearing the veil establishes identity, connection to community, and continuity with sacred traditions. In contrast, for some Muslim women who do not wear the veil, there is the argument that limiting remembrance of the sacred and the performance of one's religious duty to wearing a piece of clothing is profoundly reductive – especially if one's dress results in greater self-consciousness and even anxiety. In addition, they point out that if the intent behind veiling is to minimize attention drawn to oneself, in non-Muslim societies it can actually serve the opposite function; it draws attention to women instead of diverting the gaze. Rather than serving a protective function, it may provoke attack because the woman is visibly an "Other." Both of these understandings reveal that the decision to veil or not veil need not be construed as a simple choice between religion and secularity. Both positions can be embraced on spiritual grounds and understood as a means of protection or as a basis of living out the value of modesty.

In Islamic teachings, the value of modesty is incumbent on men and women alike, and is closely associated with remembrance of God.[3] Among proponents of veiling, a garment such as the *hijab* is both a means to protect oneself from undesirable forms of attention, and also the basis for forming an identity which prioritizes the inward over the outward and reinforces the notion of modesty. Among those who do not regard veiling as obligatory, however, there is a critique of developing too strong a linkage between modesty and a particular style of women's dress. As articulated by Amina Wadud (who was introduced in the previous chapter), this position maintains that just because the Muslim veil is "one of the ways in which this modesty has manifest itself does not mean that modesty is equal to the Muslim veil. The veil has no hierarchy over the concept of modesty" (2002). Wadud continues by stating:

> The head covering as a form of oppression comes to the end of whether or not a person or a collective of people in one cultural context has the right to choose. And when it is taken as a manifestation of correct Islamic modesty, there is no choice that you can have. You cannot be Islamic and modest unless you wear this form. And so it will be enforced, not only from outside, but also enforced from within. People will assume, women will assume, that they have to dress this way in order to be Islamic. And from the outside, governments and/or social groups will enforce it as a manifestation of Islam: this is the way to present yourself as Islamic.
>
> If we understand modesty as something that is not fixed in time, but is the primary principle that is being promoted within the Quran, for example, then we will recognize that there are many ways to symbolize this. And that the choice, to be able to adopt this particular one, or to reject this particular one, is in fact of equal merit. But the idea of attaining to the reality of modesty cannot be fixed in any one particular item. That's very hard for Muslims to grapple with, because again, the whole idea of identity reformation is being contested; not only from within Islam but from without as well.
>
> (2002)

For Wadud, the choice to wear or not to wear a Muslim veil is connected not just to an individual's views on matters pertaining to religious values, but also to human collectivities (from the family to the larger religious and cultural community) which generate norms associating particular forms of expression with deeper values.

Though convictions about the veil differ, ideas of modesty in Islam, and of the veil's potential functions, are closely associated with considerations related to sexuality, the objectification of women, and "the male gaze." For some Muslim women, the veil can be a direct challenge to the "panoptical power of the male patriarchal gaze" (Nye, 2003, p. 81) that controls women's appearances in terms of their bodies, movements, and dress. Thus, it serves as a counterbalance to the dictates of the (typically but not exclusively Western and corporate) fashion world, which encourages women to expose rather than cover their flesh (Tarlo, 2010). In this way, the Muslim veil is a direct challenge to Western-style patriarchal norms which serve to objectify women.

Paradoxically, some Muslim women adhere to a dissenting view, in which wearing the Muslim veil actually reinforces hegemonic patriarchal practices toward women and sexuality, especially but not exclusively within traditional Muslim societies. In Yousra Y. Fazli's view, the idea that Muslim women must wear the veil in order to not be seen in a sexual manner is problematic because sexuality is innately human; furthermore, Islam confirms that sexuality is a part of being human and a gift from God. The idea of mandatory veiling also contributes to an aversion toward sexuality among Muslims in general, leaving them unprepared to develop healthy norms in relation to it (Fazili, 2005, p. 77). This argument proposes that wearing the Muslim veil in order to be unalluring to men places responsibility on women to avoid arousing men rather than encouraging men to practice self-control and "lower their gaze" as a Quranic verse (24:31) instructs them to do. Consequently, wearing the Muslim veil plays into the expectation that it is first and foremost women who bear responsibility for upholding decency, Islamic values and morals in society – an expectation that is continually gaining more currency in the face of the challenge of Western secular and cultural influences. From this perspective, wearing "proper" Islamic dress indicates women's compliance with a double standard that relieves men of their duties to uphold morality alongside women, and that unfairly places society's burdens on the shoulders of women.

In the 21st century, due to the rise of Islamophobia, some Muslim women living in North America choose to wear the Muslim veil to serve as a rejection of Western cultural images of womanhood and as a promotion of Islamic norms. From this standpoint, the Muslim veil becomes a symbol not just of modesty but also of resistance to Western cultural hegemony (Ahmed, 2011; Beyer & Ramji, 2013; Haddad, 2012; Heath, 2008). Wearing the Muslim veil in America and Canada thus allows women to express Muslim pride and to challenge negative media and Orientalist depictions of veiled Muslim women, such as Margaret Wente's commentary for *The Globe and Mail* stating, "I feel sorry for the veiled women I see taking their kids to school.

Nobody can convince me that they are treated equally by their husbands, or that they are about to assimilate into Canadian life" (2009, p. A17). For critics of Islamophobia and populist journalism, such a characterization of Muslim family and gender norms in a national "newspaper of record," even if not representative of all coverage, is profoundly damaging and reflects broader stereotypical assumptions (Jiwani, 2007; McDonough, 2003, pp. 125–126).

Interestingly, Muslim aspirations toward authenticity are reinforced by Western stereotyping, in ways that increase bonds of sisterhood amongst visibly Muslim women who have experienced discrimination or prejudice in North American contexts. Some scholars even argue that solidarity amongst veiled Muslim women vs. unveiled Muslim women is stronger in countries where Muslims are a minority. Popular examples of such transnational solidarity are the World Hijab Day (WHD) and My Stealthy Freedom (MSF).[4] In response to feelings of isolation and discrimination, Nazma Khan of New York City created and organized the first "World Hijab Day" in 2013. This annual event invites "women (including both non-*hijabi* Muslims and non-Muslims) to experience the *hijab* for one day" (worldhijabday.com).[5] Khan describes how it is one of the best ways to counteract Islamophobic tendencies and promote religious tolerance and understanding. Consequently, "Wear a *Hijab* Day" was introduced by Khadeeja Islamic Center in West Valley City in Utah in 2015 and in 2018 the "World Hijab Day Organization" was established.

While such events undeniably generate sympathy for the experiences of *hijab*-wearing women and serve to erode stereotypes concerning their identities and life choices, not all Muslim women appreciate the implied message that *hijab*-wearing is integral to an Islamic worldview. For some unveiled Muslim women in North America and Europe, the WHD annual event and organization serves to reinforce and promote the idea that a "real" or "authentic" Muslim woman is one who wears the veil. Such an opinion is reflected in Asra Q. Nomani and Hala Arafa's "Opinion" article in *The Washington Post*:

> To us, the "*hijab*" is a symbol of an interpretation of Islam we reject that believes that women are a sexual distraction to men, who are weak, and thus must not be tempted by the sight of our hair. We don't buy it. This ideology promotes a social attitude that absolves men of sexually harassing women and puts the onus on the victim to protect herself by covering up…Unfortunately, the idea of "*hijab*" as a mandatory headscarf is promulgated by naïve efforts such as "World Hijab Day."
>
> (2015)

For Nomani and Arafa, WHD runs counter to an interpretation of Islam in which the *hijab* is not obligatory, and makes it harder for non-Muslims to comprehend an "un-veiled" Islamic standpoint. They are not alone in this understanding as reflected in other online media campaigns such as

My Stealthy Freedom (MSF) which focuses on "the political aspects of the enforcement of the mandatory *hijab*" (Rahbari et al., 2021 p. 120). Although mostly focused on the Iranian context and law-enforced veiling, MSF has over a million followers on Facebook worldwide, many of which are based in America and Canada (p. 121).[6]

In underscoring non-alignment with pro- and anti-*hijab* positions, other voices stake out a position that emphasizes the importance of applying a precautionary principle that favors the expression of views by those whose religious and sartorial choices make them more visible and, as a minority group, more vulnerable. Natasha Bakht, a Canadian law professor, points out that "*hijab* and niqab debates" are laden with contradictory, stereotypical views in which "there is little evidence to suggest that either typecast is accurate or reflective of the lives of Muslim women" (2008, p. 112). However, she characterizes some anti-*hijab* and anti-*niqab* Muslim positions are "unhelpful" because "different women may adhere to different levels of religiosity" and differences of opinion among Muslims about religious requirements should be characterized as such rather than construed in ways that reinforce popular prejudices (p. 112). To the extent that visible Muslim women already experience themselves as members of a besieged and vulnerable minority group, emphasizing diversity, pluralism, and dialogue would be more strategic than aligning with a contrary normative position of "freedom from veils" – a position that more conservative Muslims experience as an attack on their identities and values.

Public safety and security policies: North American cases

Due to the fear and politics of difference in the 21st century there have been a plethora of controversial debates and cases concerning the Muslim veil. As mentioned in previous chapters, in the American and Canadian imaginaries, stereotypes of the imperiled Muslim woman who wears a veil and the civilized West are rampant and reinforced. Many cases revolve around the need to rescue veiled Muslim women from "the dangers of the headscarf" and what it symbolizes, and such attempts in "saving the Muslim woman" is connected to a larger project of civilizing. In such circumstances, Muslim veiling is ultimately a symbol of victimization and not freedom or equality.

"The dangers of the scarf" in sports

The trajectory of contemporary controversies in North America surrounding Muslim women and sports offers a window into the view that veiled Muslim women need protecting from the dangers of wearing a headscarf. Rhetoric from national and international sports governing bodies tends to rationalize bans on athletes wearing religious head coverings and other apparel during athletic events by claiming that such clothing items pose safety issues, such as potentially harming athletes and concealing athletes' injuries.

In February 2007, member of Ottawa soccer team the Nepean Hotspurs, Asmahan Mansour, was ejected from a soccer tournament in Laval, Quebec, because her *hijab* allegedly posed a safety risk, although she had played in Ontario and in two previous games in the same tournament without any instructions to remove her *hijab*. In response, her team along with four other teams quit the tournament in protest. Louis Maneiro, the Nepean Hotspurs Coach, stated, "This is basically telling the world that no Muslim girl is allowed to play the sport" (Lewis, 2007). Valmie Oullet, the technical coordinator of the Quebec Soccer Federation replied, "Sometimes when we make choices according to faith, it is possible that along the line we won't be able to do everything we want to do." (ibid). Though the veil in question was designed for sport use, Jean Charest (the former Premier of Quebec) condoned the expulsion. Controversy ensued as to whether the decision to eject Mansour from the tournament was the result of racial/religious profiling, or whether a safety threat was actually posed by the headscarf.[7] The issue was sent to the Canadian Soccer Association and FIFA (International Federation of Association Football) and a policy was created to ban head coverings in soccer globally due to the potential danger of injury and harm.[8] The two rules in the FIFA's rule book which reinforced the ban were: "*Advertising on Equipment*: Basic compulsory equipment must not have any political, religious, or personal statement and *Safety*: A player must not use equipment or wear anything that is dangerous to himself or another player" (Ayub, 2011, pp. 43–44).

Since Mansour's ejection and subsequent global controversies over whether the Muslim veil should be accommodated in sports,[9] the Muslim veil has arisen as a source of debate in the context of soccer many times across North America. For instance, in June 2011, Sarah Benkiran was informed that she could no longer referee for the Lac St. Louis Soccer Association because she wears the Muslim veil. Additionally, in June 2012, Nine-year-old Rayane Benatti was sidelined because she refused to remove her veil during a soccer tournament in Gatineau, Quebec. As a response to the various controversies and campaigns against FIFA's "*hijab* ban,"[10] in October 2012, Montreal designer Elham Seyed Javad, cofounder of ResportOn, was one of two designers whose Muslim veil design was approved by the International Football Association Board (IFAB) and FIFA, as it adhered to criteria set out by the board (Chung, 2009). However, it would take two more years for FIFA to finally lift its "*hijab* ban" in 2014.[11] This would influence a variety of multinational athletic sporting corporations, like Nike and Adidas, to promote sports as belonging to everyone and to create their own versions of "soccer *hijabs*".[12]

Ironically, in 2014 as FIFA's ban was being lifted, another major "*hijab* ban" in women's sports would be created by FIBA (The International Basketball

Federation). Similar to FIFA, the ban was to prevent any injuries associated with a headscarf, but it also was to promote a religiously neutral environment. As stated by FIBA's communications coordinator, Simon Wilkinson, "FIBA's rules and regulations apply on a global scale and make no distinction between the various religions" (Mathewson, 2018). The creation of this ban too had a trajectory of different events. For instance, in January 2011, a referee sidelines Maheen Haq during a basketball game due to safety concerns regarding her Muslim veil. Her parents then had to agree to sign a letter following the game to assume all responsibility if an injury occurred, issued by the mid-Maryland Girls Basketball League. Also, Bilqis Abdul-Qaadir, the first NCAA Division I athlete to wear the *hijab* (who still holds (as of 2022) the high school record of scoring in Massachusetts), was told in 2014 that she could not play in the WNBA due to FIBA's "*hijab* ban" (Mathewson, 2018).[13] In 2017, after three years of petitioning, Abdul-Qaadir and Indira Kaljo (former college point guard for Tulane University) helped to overturn the ban. Abdul-Qaadir would start the campaign *Muslim Girls Hoop Too*[14] and *Dribbling Down Barriers* which is a program that "facilitates play between Muslim and non-Muslim athletes to get people of different faiths to be comfortable with each other" (Mathewson, 2018). Kaljo became the president at Global Aktivine/Athletic & Athletics, a not-for-profit organization that aims to get women and girls active across the world, and she also in 2017 helped to establish Muslim Women in Sport Network (MWSN).[15]

Soccer and basketball are not the only sports affected by the politics of veiling, in April of 2007, five Muslim girls aged 10–14 were expelled from a Taekwondo meet in Southern Montreal because they wore the Muslim veil, which was claimed to be impermissible and dangerous. It was speculated that the move was a result of pressure in the context of province-wide debates on reasonable accommodation, as wearing the Muslim veil in Taekwondo had not previously been an issue. However, the World Taekwondo Federation approved the decision by not supporting any accommodation for Muslim veils whereas the International Taekwondo Federation stated it allowed women to cover. Canadian company ResportOn's sports *hijab* design (which was previously mentioned) is partially credited for influencing the International Taekwondo Federation to allow Muslim women to compete in recognized tournaments (Al-Saied & Creedon, 2021, p. 76).

In the sport of weightlifting, after years of conflict, in July 2011, Kulsoom Abdullah was allowed to be able to wear the Muslim veil and cover her legs and arms, after the International Weightlifting Federation approved the new guidelines. She was supported by the U.S. Olympic Committee, which urged the IWF to make the changes.[16] In 2015, at the age of 39, with three children, Jeri Villarreal was one of the first *hijab*-wearing triathletes to compete in the Chicago triathlon.[17] Also, a 2016 Olympic medalist in fencing, Ibtihaj Muhammad is widely known for being the first American Muslim woman to wear *hijab* while competing at the Olympic Games.[18] In 2019, the restrictions in boxing prior to the changing of the rules affected many Muslim women boxers, including then 15-year-old American boxer Amaiya Zafar, who became the first athlete to wear a *hijab* during an American boxing match. Zafar was inspired by German *hijab*-wearing boxer Zeina Nassar (from the famous and controversial Nike advertising campaign in 2018).[19]

Additionally, in 2019, Noor Alexandria Abukaram at age 16, in the middle of her seventh high school cross country race of the season (the previous six having been run with no objections to her *hijab*) was disqualified by the Ohio High School Athletic Association. This was after beating her personal record for a 5K. Besides her coach failing to apply for a waiver for her to run with *hijab*, Abukaram launched the #LetNoorRun campaign to fight prejudice in sports. Throughout the campaign Abukaram invited athletes to speak up on discriminatory issues in sports and she was able to help introduce and advocate a piece of legislation (Senate Bill 288) in Ohio, which protects religious expression in extracurricular activities in the state of Ohio. This bill officially passed in October 2021.[20]

The various *hijab* bans across different sports have affected thousands of Muslim women. All the bans were ostensibly related to issues of safety for the player, while some also stipulated the need for all players to comply with a norm of religious neutrality while playing a particular sport. Many scholars, however, have perceived a deeper agenda, infused with implicit biases and even the notion that putatively "neutral" norms would help Muslim women by asserting a "civilizing" standard. Carolyn Prouse, for example, has framed such anti-*hijab* regulations as perpetuating a "Western colonial and racist" agenda which reinforces the idea of an essentialized Muslim woman who needs protection and must be regulated (2013). For Prouse the actions of supporting such bans by national and international sporting bodies cannot be separated from the questions of race, gender, and coloniality. In other words, the *hijab* bans are not isolated cases, and need to "be situated in a long genealogy of colonizing racial grammars that bestow meanings upon, and grant legitimacy to, the regulation of *hijab*-wearing women" (Prouse, 2013, p. 32). Even the lifting of a *hijab* ban, Prouse suggests, can be tainted by insistence on "benevolent" regulations that maintain a certain paternalistic power relationship:

> That many people celebrated the lifting of FIFA's *hijab* ban – which is perhaps more accurately understood as the allowance of only FIFA-sanctioned 'safe' headscarves – nods to the insidiousness of these regulations: they reinscribe the authority of FIFA and IFAB to regulate an object that has never injured a player, reproducing an authority that is made increasingly common sensical through discourses about 'protecting Muslim women'…. In an ironic yet unsurprising twist, FIFA's regulation of the *hijab* as a safety concern strangles Muslim women's voices in a continuing coloniality of racialized and gendered power.
>
> (Prouse, 2013, p. 32)

Chris Knoester and Carter Rockhill agree with Prouse in stating that both sport bans and their subsequent replacement by specific regulations can be means "to obscure racist and anti-Muslim sentiments," while also noting that most of the bans occurred in the shadow of 9/11 and at a time of growing Islamophobia (2021, p. 4). Given this polarized and politicized context, national and international sporting bodies needed to be more aware that bans would reinforce discriminatory stereotypes and harmful power dynamics. The necessity of these critiques is even more relevant since female Muslim athletes are wearing head coverings now more than ever before which instigates the opening of accommodation policies by sports authorities and federations (Harkness & Islam, 2011, p. 65).[21]

In light of the deleterious effects of *hijab* bans on individual players, what is particularly striking about these cases is the manner in which women were able to reclaim agency in challenging the right of sporting authorities to limit their capacity to play while remaining faithful to their religious identity. In the face of newly defined rules that often claimed to promote a culture of neutrality – in which sports like soccer and basketball were to be viewed as a secular reality devoid of any religious content – these women experienced a sporting reality that appeared to have been hastily redefined in an exclusionary manner. In insisting that these bans be overturned, *hijab*-wearing Muslim women challenged not just the gatekeeping rules that prevented their authentic participation, but also the stereotypical tropes they perceived to be lurking behind the official explanations.

Questions of national security and the Muslim face veil

Whereas cases over the acceptability of the conventional Muslim hair veil/ scarf (*hijab*) in sports have often invoked notions of safety for the *wearer*, controversies over the full Muslim face veil (especially the *niqab*) have been associated not just with concerns about religiously sanctioned repression, but also with claims about national security and the integrity of official processes. Whether refusing to issue a driver's license with a photo of a woman wearing a *niqab* or enforcing a demand that a woman remove the *niqab* while in court or at citizenship oath proceedings, the *niqab* has been interpreted as a basis for suspicion. Women who cover their faces have been challenged for undermining the dependable operation of a secular national system. At times, they have been viewed as harboring a potentially aggressive intent to harm the functioning of democracy. Distrust of the *niqab* and of a woman who might choose to wear one has increased in North America since September 2001, at times leading to new legislation or to a change in the application of existing rules.

One legal case that signaled increasing controversy surrounding the *niqab* occurred in January 2002, when the American Civil Liberties Union (ACLU) of Florida filed a lawsuit on behalf of Sultaana Freeman, a *niqab*-wearing

Muslim woman, against the state of Florida after the state's Department of Highway Safety and Motor Vehicle (DHSMV) revoked her driver's license. Faced with a change in requirements which required her to show her entire face for her driver's license photo, Freeman refused to replace a license issued in February 2001, at which time she had been allowed to wear a *niqab* for the photo. In the ensuing case (Sultaana Lakiana Myke Freeman v. State of Florida), Freeman claimed that replacing her past photo with one that displayed her face would violate her religious beliefs.

In May 2003, the ACLU of Florida argued the case before Ninth Judicial Circuit Court Judge Janet C. Thorpe to reinstate Freeman's driving privileges. ACLU of Florida cooperating attorney Howard Marks stated, "Rather than respecting this woman's religious values, the state is using her as a scapegoat in this so-called war against terror" (ACLU, 2003). According to its press release, the ACLU argued "the state's actions violate the Florida Constitution's free exercise clause, which limits governmental restrictions on religious exercise" (ACLU, 2003). In June 2003, Judge Thorpe refused to allow Freeman to obtain a driver's license without removing her *niqab* for the identification photo, ruling that if full-face veils were allowed in driver's license photos, it would set a precedent that could be exploited by people who "ascribe to religious beliefs in order to carry out activities that would threaten lives" (Dahlburg & Virtue, 2003). In July 2003, Freeman filed with the Fifth District Court of Appeal, arguing that Florida law does not prevent her from wearing a veil over her face in her driver's license photo. In February 2006, the court affirmed the orders entered by the trial court, "finding no violation of Freeman's constitutional rights" (District Court of Appeal of Florida, Fifth District, 2006). In sum, the court found that the state's "compelling interest in promoting public safety and combating crime [especially in a post 9/11 America] outweighed Freeman's religious rights" (Currier, 2004, p. 934).

Writing in the *Catholic University Law Review*, Patrick Currier has argued that this case offers an example of how changing perceptions of national security can undermine the principle of respecting religious rights, without the need to present proof that a genuine threat to public safety existed:

> The Freeman court argued that threats of domestic terrorism justified Florida's photo-identification requirement. This contention lacks merit because an appropriate analysis of the facts would have determined that Freeman posed no such threat. Additionally, granting an exemption based on her religious beliefs would have caused only minor administrative burdens to the State. Yet, the court performed no such analysis. Rather, it applied the facts in a post-September 11th vacuum, allowing current fears to weaken the strict scrutiny standard, thereby permitting the State to satisfy its burden under the guise of national security.
>
> Furthermore, the court failed to address the fact that Florida issued Freeman a valid driver's license while wearing her veil in February

of 2001, only to have it revoked after September 11th. In fact, Florida also denied at least two other Muslim women driver's licenses after September 11th because they refused to remove their religious coverings. These examples suggest a prejudicial targeting of Muslims by the Florida DHSMV, and yet the court ignores the issue. The court's failure to question the State's open act of discrimination suggests that the court intended to provide the State more deference in order to ease its burden under the strict scrutiny standard. A finding against Freeman acts as an affirmation of the State's actions, potentially leading to further targeting of Muslims and more encroachment on religious liberties.

(Currier, 2004, pp. 938–939)

As Currier notes, changing interpretations of what is required for public security appear to have been central to the shifting response Freeman experienced when seeking a renewal of her driver's license, without there having been any significant legislative changes or a systematic gathering of data to demonstrate the existence of a threat.

In the Canadian context, new threat perceptions associated with the *niqab* have driven federal as well as provincial attempts at legislative change, creating an impetus for legal challenges and further debates about the meaning of religious rights and the extent to which accommodations can be provided. An attempted change at the federal level occurred in 2007, when Prime Minister Stephen Harper's Conservative government introduced Bill C-6 as a piece of legislation to amend the *Canada Elections Act* regarding visual identification of voters. Even though there was a long-standing tradition to permit "non-photo" identification under the *Canada Elections Act*, for in-person voting as well as voting by mail, the proposed amendment required a voter to have their face uncovered so that election officials could visually identify them while voting in person (Bakht, 2020, p. 125). The declared reasoning for the implementation of this Bill was "to counter the problem of the multiple-voting veiled Muslim woman" – a problem which had not been demonstrated to exist – and to thereby remedy a threat to voting integrity (p. 125). The Bill was not approved (despite a variety of criticism); however, as pointed out by Natasha Bakht in her book, *In Your Face: Law, Justice, and Niqab-Wearing Women in Canada* (2020), it did reveal a deliberate absence of dialogue with *niqab*-wearing Canadian women. "Instead there was a monologue of the dominant society about their prejudices and its fears of Islam, the meanings of secularism, identity and the limits of tolerance" (p. 125).

Another controversial niqabi case in Canada was *Ishaq v. Canada (Citizenship and Immigration), [2015] 4 FCR 297, FC 156*. In this case, the issue was connected to the Canadian citizenship oath proceedings and how an applicant was asked to take off her *niqab* before she took the oath of allegiance. The applicant, Zunera Ishaq,[22] had been a permanent resident of Canada since October 2008; her application for citizenship was approved on December 30, 2013.

Ishaq was granted citizenship three days later pursuant to subsection 5(1) of the *Citizenship Act*, RSC 1985, c C-29 [*Act*]. However, to be considered a citizen under paragraph 3(1)(c) of the *Act*, she was obligated to take an oath of citizenship. Ishaq stated that she had no problem with the content of the oath, but she objected to the ban on wearing face coverings while taking it (Ishaq v. Canada, 2015 FC 156, pp. 1-2). Had she been offered citizenship a few years earlier she would not have faced this requirement, but Immigration Minister Jason Kenney had announced a change in government policy two years earlier, in 2011. According to this change, anyone taking the oath of citizenship had to *be seen* taking the oath – meaning one's mouth needed to be seen moving (Bakht, 2020, p. 126). Ishaq filed for a judicial review of this new expectation in January 2014, arguing that the amendment violated her rights as outlined in the *Canadian Charter of Rights and Freedoms* (Ishaq v. Canada, 2015 FC 156, pp. 9-10). Prior to her scheduled ceremony, Ishaq had taken her citizenship test on November 22, 2013, which she had removed her *niqab* for purposes of identification in accordance with section 13.2 of CIC's policy manual, CP 15: Guide to Citizenship Ceremonies (as amended to 21 December 2011) [the Manual].[23]

During Ishaq's challenge to the visible-face oath requirement, government practice was defended on the grounds that requiring Ishaq to uncover her face did not constitute a serious limitation on her religious freedom, especially considering that she had shown her face to a government official quite recently for identity and security purposes. It was also added that "wearing the *niqab* is just a personal choice, not a basic sacrament" (Ishaq v. Canada, 2015 FC 156, p. 16). Other criticisms were made "that it is unclear why a citizenship ceremony, which happens once in a lifetime, is not one of those rare instances where it is absolutely necessary for [Ishaq] to remove her *niqab*" (p. 21). Similar to the defense of *hijab* bans in sports, there was a projected interpretation concerning the significance of the religious dress in question, potentially raising questions about how far a religiously neutral authority structure ought to go in weighing the content of the beliefs professed by religious individuals.

The Federal Court of Canada decision (February 6, 2015) held that Ishaq could wear a *niqab* when she took the oath of Canadian citizenship at a public ceremony, as "the portions of the Policy and Manual that require citizenship candidates to remove face coverings or be observed taking the oath are unlawful" (Ishaq v. Canada, 2015 FC 156, p. 31). The Court declared that the policy was inconsistent with the regulations of the *Citizenship Act* because Section 17(I)(b) of the regulations of the Act requires a judge to "administer the oath of citizenship with dignity and solemnity, allowing the *greatest possible freedom* in the religious solemnization or the solemn affirmation thereof" (Bakht, 2020, p. 126). One of the Justices found that religious solemnization referred to permitting candidates to swear the oath on a holy book (or no book) but held that it could also refer to how the oath is administered and the circumstances under which candidates are required to take it (p. 127). Thus, the new policy was invalid as it infringed on the *Citizenship Act* and its regulations (p. 127).

As a result of this case, a new act, Bill C-75 was created in June 2015 to amend the *Citizenship Act*. The language within it was more nuanced:

> The bill requires those who take the oath of citizenship to do so aloud, with the face uncovered, during the citizenship ceremony. It also authorizes the Minister of Citizenship and Immigration ("the Minister") to make regulations specifying the time, manner, justification and evidence needed to support a request to waive these requirements, and authorizes the Minister to treat an application for citizenship as abandoned if an applicant does not take the oath in accordance with the *Citizenship Act*.
>
> (Library of Parliament, 2015)

Although the new language still maintained the importance of a visible oath, in allowing a waiver it enabled citizenship candidates such as Ishaq to seek an accommodation. On October 5, 2015, Ishaq received citizenship in a private ceremony.

Another highly contested *niqab*-wearing case took place from 2009–2012 in Ontario, and was ultimately resolved by the Supreme Court of Canada. This case, R. v. N.S., involved a woman accusing a relative of sexual assault against her while she was a minor.[24] The proceedings began to draw broad attention when, in October 2009, Ontario Court Justice Norris Weisman ruled during the preliminary hearing that N.S. had to remove her *niqab*, and, having seen evidence that N.S. had removed her *niqab* for a driver's license photograph, stated that her veil was more of a source of comfort for her than a religious belief. In March 2011, N.S. took the case to the Supreme Court of Canada, arguing that she should have been allowed to wear the *niqab* at the hearing and during any trial that followed, and that it was protected under the *Canadian Charter of Rights and Freedoms*. The Supreme Court of Canada agreed to hear the case. In December 2012, in a 4-3 decision, it was determined that, although many different factors related to religious freedom and trial fairness needed to be weighed in cases of this nature, greater harm would more often come from a rigid requirement to show one's face than from allowing a sexual assault complainant to make her case while wearing a face covering (Supreme Court of Canada, 2012).

As the above examples illustrate, Muslim women who cover their faces have faced increasing legal, administrative, and legislative challenges, but have also had recourse to legal systems that can potentially rule in their favor. As Bakht rightfully observes, although challenges to *niqab*-wearing are often justified on the grounds of national security and the integrity of state functions, they are underpinned by a deep and persistent assumption that covering one's face is "an affront to national values" (Bakht, 2020, p. 116). According to this logic, *niqab*-wearing is regarded as an offence against values of openness, transparency, and equality rather than as a choice an individual might legitimately make and pursue on the grounds of religious human rights.

To a significantly greater extent than the *hijab*, the *niqab* has evoked debates over basic questions about identity, rights, and belonging. On one side of the debate, many have argued that governments have a right to impose certain common expectations regarding women's public deportment – especially when interfacing with state administrative and legal processes – for the sake of advancing norms of equality and neutrality, and to prevent conceivable abuses that might not occur without the visibility of a face. When tested in a political context, this position has resonated with influential political constituencies and has also held a certain appeal among employers who wish to maintain standardized internal practices or to protect a particular public image.[25] On the other side, however, critics point out that basic rights and freedoms are at stake, and have noted that the politicization of the *niqab* does little to reduce its appeal to the small minority of Muslim women who wear it. These critics are also (and quite legitimately) concerned that preoccupation with the *niqab* reflects a deeper discomfort with Muslim immigration and distinctiveness, and an effort to draw symbolic boundaries. As pointed out by Katherine Bullock, the global COVID-19 pandemic has proven how "Coronavirus face masks reveal [the] hypocrisy of face covering bans" (2020). If society can function well enough in pandemic mode with most of its members face masks, Bullock asks, is it really necessary to single out religiously justified face veils as a unique barrier to communication or to the forming of social bonds? For Bullock as well as for other critics of face veil bans, denying a religious right to present oneself to society definitely creates a potential "slippery slope" situation in which greater scope is given for real underlying motivations that may involve mistrust of Muslims. They have feared that curtailing the rights of the most conservative Muslim women might soon lead to additional measures against more mainstream, publicly and professionally engaged women who chose to wear a veil.

"The slippery slope" and the politics of veiling within the context of Quebec

Within the 21st century of North America, the most heightened policy-talk on Muslim veiling can be found within the Quebec context. Some scholars have described the controversial cases connected to Muslim women in Quebec as a "slippery slope" (Emon, 2010; Zine, 2009). Each case within this province adds to a growing sense of public concern and debate, making subsequent controversies more likely. Cumulatively, these cases – a strong majority of which center around the politics of Muslim veiling – contribute to a growing atmosphere of Islamophobia in which visible symbols of Islamic identity induce public anxiety.

As already mentioned there have been sports controversies connected to the Muslim veil in Quebec but the tipping point in the politics of veiling was reached on January 25, 2007, when public discourse articulating anxiety about Islam reached a new level in the town council of Hérouxville, Quebec (a small Quebec town of 1,300 persons). This council adopted a "code of conduct" addressed to any new immigrants who might consider making the town their home. In this "Life Standards" Charter prospective new immigrants were officially declared unwelcome if they exhibited an inclination toward any of the following practices: Publicly stoning women, burning women alive, throwing acid on the faces of women, female circumcision, covering the face, school prayer, and wearing a symbolic weapon to school. The charter also informed such potential immigrants that they must reaffirm certain fundamental rights, such as a woman's right to drive a vehicle, vote, sign cheques, dance, and "decide for herself" (Bruemmer & Dougherty, 2007).

The offensive nature of the code, articulated in the wake of a series of highly publicized incidents surrounding the cultural accommodation of ethnic and religious minority groups in Quebec,[26] prompted the former Premier of Quebec, Jean Charest, to create the "Consultation Commission on Accommodation Practices Related to Cultural Differences" (later known simply as the Bouchard-Taylor Commission) in February 2007. This Commission was headed by sociologist Gerard Bouchard and philosopher Charles Taylor, with a mandate to conduct a public inquiry into the scope and limits of "reasonable accommodation." Through a series of public hearings and additional investigations, popular attitudes were aired and the concerns of recent immigrant communities were heard.[27]

Although the Commission was set up to investigate the management of cultural differences, the overwhelming majority of cases raised in debate have to do with *religious* and not merely cultural diversity. In their Consultation Document, Bouchard and Taylor stated: "In a word, it is, in particular, the management of diversity, especially religious diversity that appears above all to pose a problem" (Bouchard & Taylor, 2007, p. 3). Religious groups and religious practices and symbols, then, often became the center of public debate, with concerns about Muslims particularly prominent.

In the wake of the tragic events of September 11, 2001, in America and the resulting suspicion of Muslims worldwide, Quebec's relatively small community of Muslims received great attention. Particular Muslim practices – most notably the *hijab* and requests for prayer rooms – drove much of this attention, leading many Muslim groups to publicly explain their traditions in an effort to correct misconceptions and defend the place of Muslims in a pluralist Quebec. Acknowledging the salience of cases involving Muslim women in their report, Bouchard and Taylor noted that it was often Muslim women's attempts to integrate that made them more visible and therefore vulnerable to Islamophobia. They argued that "the way to overcome Islamophobia is to draw closer to Muslims, not to shun them. In this field, as in others, mistrust engenders mistrust. As is true of fear, it ends us [sic] feeding on itself" (Bouchard & Taylor, 2007, p. 235).

After accepting submissions from various groups and holding public consultations, Bouchard and Taylor produced a lengthy report and series of recommendations for the province in May 2008, rooted in a vision of "open secularism." Their recommendations included demands to better define terms such as "interculturalism" and "secularism"; to more effectively promote employment opportunities for immigrants; to increase representation of underrepresented groups in government and public services; to combat anti-Semitism, Islamophobia, and racism; and to make government spaces religiously neutral. To this end, Bouchard and Taylor recommended that the crucifix be removed from the National Assembly, and that certain public servants in positions of authority, such as judges, not be allowed to wear symbols of religious expression. This last recommendation would have horrible consequences for veiled Muslim women in Quebec.

Although the Bouchard-Taylor Commission served to dampen debate about minority communities for a time, subsequent events reignited and perpetuated the debate in largely unchanged terms. In November 2009, there was the story of Naema Ahmed, an Egyptian immigrant who was asked to leave her French class in Montreal when she refused to remove her *niqab*, and who was later expelled a second time after enrolling in another school (Quebec to Address Issue, 2010). This event and others ignited a polarizing debate about head coverings; Chantal Hébert, a journalist for the *Toronto Star*, argued that Quebec's French media played a decisive role in shaping and fuelling this debate (2015, p. A6). The prevalence of anti-*niqab* public sentiment provided a favorable environment for legislative action, and resulted in Bill 94 – the first piece of legislation on minority accommodation issues since the completion of the Bouchard-Taylor Commission's inquiry.

Minister of Justice Madame Kathleen Weil introduced Bill 94 to the National Assembly of Quebec on March 24, 2010, as a piece of legislation designed to "establish the conditions under which an accommodation may be made in favor of personnel members of the Administration or certain institutions or in favor of person to whom services are provided by the Administration or certain institutions" (National Assembly of Quebec, 2010, p. 2). The stated purpose of this Bill was to clarify standard practices associated with the provision of public services, to establish face veiling as a contravention of these general practices, and to stipulate the grounds on which requests for exemption from this ruling might be denied. The principled grounds for rejecting all forms of face covering was presented in section 4 of the Bill, which cited Quebec's Charter of Human Rights and Freedoms "as concerns the right to gender equality and the principle of religious neutrality of the State whereby the State shows neither favour nor disfavour towards any particular religion or belief" (p. 4). The pragmatic basis for the new ruling was provided in section 6, which contained both the clause stating that individuals must "show their face during the delivery of services" and the ruling that mandates a denial of accommodation requests when considerations of "security, communication or identification warrant it" (p. 5). If passed, Bill 94 would have required that all employees of the government and public services show their face at all times, and that all people making use of government or public services (including users of public and some private schools, health-care services, social services, and childcare services) would similarly be expected to have uncovered faces at the time of service delivery. Although the principal targets of the legislation are not mentioned in the text of the Bill, the legislation is generally understood to be aimed at Muslim women who wear the *niqab*, and would essentially prohibit *niqab*-wearing women from accessing public services.[28] At the time this bill provoked opposition not just in Quebec but also across Canada, through a diverse coalition that included a wide range of constituencies (i.e., feminist organizations, members of the Quebec Jewish congress, and LGTBQ+ advocacy groups) concerned not just about Muslim women's rights but also minority rights more generally. As a result, the bill was tabled rather than put into effect as legislation.

The tabling of Bill 94, however, did not end the impulse to enact legislation addressed to these issues. In November 2013, the Parti Quebecois introduced Bill 60, which was framed as a "Secular Charter of Values" in which values of religious neutrality, gender equality and state secularism were defined as the necessary "framework for accommodation requests." Following in the parameters of Bill 94, this piece of legislation specifically stated "in the exercise of their functions, personnel members of public bodies must not wear objects such as headgear, clothing, jewelry, or other adornments which, by their conspicuous nature, overtly indicate a religious affiliation" (National Assembly of Quebec, 2013, p. 1). This proposed legislation again ignited substantial debate, particularly insofar as it would prohibit individuals wearing religious headgear (including Jews and Sikhs as well as Muslim women) from working in such mainstream occupations as teachers, daycare professionals, nurses, or doctors, so long as their employer was publicly funded. Though initially popular, controversies surrounding Bill 60 ultimately stymied its implementation and contributed somewhat to Parti Quebecois' electoral defeat in 2014. However, assassinations perpetrated in Paris, France, in January 2015 against employees of the satirical magazine Charlie Hebdo sparked a new campaign to revive the secular charter (Gagnon, 2015, p. A13). Additionally, as Charles Taylor remarked in a CBC interview, the former Prime Minister Stephen Harper's comments about banning the *niqab* during Canadian citizenship ceremonies (previously mentioned in this chapter) played into the Parti Quebecois's implementation and influence of Bill 60 (Tasker, 2015).

With the buildup of all the previous proposed pieces of legislation, the Coalition Avenir Québec (CAQ) government introduced and passed in

2019 an even more restrictive bill – Bill 21(Loi sur la laïcité de l'État: An Act respecting the secularity of the State), otherwise known as Quebec's "secularism Bill." This bill prohibits public sector workers in positions of authority, which include teachers, elected officials, governmental lawyers, transit workers, physicians, police officers, and judges, from wearing visible religious symbols. Such symbols are defined as "any object, including clothing, a symbol, jewellery, an adornment, an accessory or headwear, that (1) is worn in connection with a religious conviction or belief; or (2) is reasonably considered as referring to a religious affiliation" while they are performing their civic duties (Legis Quebec, 2021). Ultimately, the bill exceeds previous related legislation in its scope and impact, both in terms of what types of symbols can be targeted and in terms of the types of positions that are subject to regulation.

In particular, this legislation impacts people from a wide range of backgrounds (e.g., orthodox Jews who wear the kippah and traditional Sikhs who don the turban or kirpan), but the weight of this impact is disproportionately felt by Muslim women who wear the Muslim veil, and who were previously able to apply for work in the public sector as regular government employees or as teachers in public schools. Due to its discriminatory impact on veiled Muslim women, the Canadian Civil Liberties Association (CCLA) and the National Council of Canadian Muslims (NCCM) have filed a constitutional challenge to suspend the law, which remains unresolved at the time of writing this book.[29]

Throughout these cases in Quebec there is *an insistence on defining limits to difference* in which relaxed norms and sensibilities concerning cultural and religious diversity are being challenged. While the *hijab* and *niqab* have not been the sole symbols of unacceptable difference – indeed, "oversized" crosses and Jewish kippahs have also figured into public debates – Muslim women's head coverings are at the heart of the ongoing controversies, and arouse the most consistent and vocal concern. The debates raise basic questions about the nature of secularism (understood more as freedom *from* religion than as a freedom *of* religion) and its relation to religious expression and practice.

In the Canadian context, it is widely recognized that identity-related sensitivities in Quebec stem not just from perceived insecurity of Quebecois French culture vis-à-vis new immigrant populations, but also from historical relations the country's traditionally dominant Anglophone culture and from the aftermath of the "Quiet Revolution" in which secularist attitudes displaced the traditional dominance of the Catholic Church. While it is critical for those who advocate for Muslim women in Quebec to understand the broader contexts and the deeper sociohistorical transformations that have shaped present attitudes, protagonists of a distinct majority culture in Quebec need to recognize that much of the proposed legislation intended to protect this culture reinforces divisions and undermines the stated goals of interculturalism, through which different cultures within the province influence one another and evolve together. From the banning of prospective *niqab*-wearing immigrants to Hérouxville, to the Bouchard-Taylor recommendation of banning all forms of the veil in specific public offices, to Bill 94's anti-*niqab* legislation which states that all employees of the government and public services show their face at all times, to Bill 60 (Secular Charter of Values)'s expectation that all people making use of government or public services (including users of public and some private schools, health-care services, social services, and childcare services) should have uncovered faces at the time of service delivery to the current active Bill 21, these pieces of legislation have sought for the prohibition of any type of Muslim veiling by employees at any place of public employment or service provision. In addition, by excluding women who wear a Muslim veil (and others who have a "visible" religious identity) from the public sector, these legislations reinforce an implicit hierarchy of identity and belonging within the province.

With such a trajectory of events, is there a way out of the impasse created by this clash of identities and attempt to define a more exclusive majority-culture? Can dialogue about a shared Quebecois identity extend beyond the official inquiry that was led by the Bouchard-Taylor Commission more than a decade ago? What can be done in response to the observations of those who have experienced a "slippery slope" inclining away from minority-culture accommodation, and toward the reassertion of majoritarian cultural norms that reinforce minority group marginalization? Is a vibrant Quebecois identity compatible with diversity, and with a more inclusive conversation about the substance of women's and human rights? Is there room in the public sphere for the voices of those who regard women's veiling as a valid cultural and religious choice that need not signal oppression and subordination? Where does religious diversity fit into the landscape of contemporary Quebec?

Conclusion

As much as the veil is fabric or an article of clothing, it also is a concept. It can be illusion, vanity, artifice, deception, liberation, imprisonment, euphemism, divination, concealment, hallucination, depression, eloquent silence, holiness, the ethers beyond consciousness, the hidden hundredth name of God, the final passage into death, even the biblical apocalypse, the lifting of God's veil, signaling so-called end times. When veiling is forced—then *enforced*—it is repression. Yet, as we see increasingly today, the veil is also a symbol of resistance—against ethnic and religious discrimination. When the veil is forcibly stripped from its wearer, that too is subjugation, not emancipation.

(Heath, 2008, p. 3)

Veiling is an inherently controversial topic, contested in multiple contexts and in relation to diverse values such as freedom, equality, and liberation. With respect to freedom, veil debates pit the freedom to express one's religious values and identity against freedom from religious conformity and social pressure. Should one of these freedoms prevail against the other, or are both legitimate constructions of value? As for equality, different questions arise. For example, if women face a greater burden to symbolically express a religious identity through clothing that is culturally traditional, are they equal? And yet if they are not allowed to participate fully in a Western society as a consequence of wearing clothing that signals a deeply felt identity, is that an equal or equitable outcome of restrictive legislation? And with respect to liberation, is it liberating to declare that women must be free of the traditions expressed by veils (and to simultaneously encourage an embrace the sartorial norms of a North American mainstream culture), or is the true meaning of liberation to be found in the expression of whatever one takes to be an integral part of one's identity and associated values?

In the face of the deep divisiveness surrounding these questions, clear answers are elusive. However, a number of observations are possible. First, Muslims do not agree, and the veil is not a matter for non-Muslims to decide. As noted at the beginning of this chapter, veils (both the widespread *hijab* and the much less common *niqab*) are and will remain a subject of debate among Muslims. While conservative (including traditionalist and revivalist) voices regard veiling as a normative sacred practice, more progressive and modernist interpreters of Islam assert contrary positions. While it is legitimate and indeed important for secular authority structures to acknowledge this dissensus, it is not the job of governments or international sporting associations to rule for or against veiling. Intervening in the debate is profoundly unhelpful, and detracts from the religious freedoms most Muslims find desirable in the North American context.

Second, although veils in general and *niqabs* in particular are often viewed as obstacles to integration, fixating on them is an unhealthy form of symbolic or "wedge" politics that deepens intergroup divisions and ultimately inhibits belonging. There may be good reasons why politicians choose to make the *hijab* or *niqab* a focus of political discourse, but these reasons generally have more to do with popular anxieties and potential political gains than with legitimate goals such as state security, efficiency, and due process. In a provocative op-ed, columnist Sheema Khan has made this connection between the politics of fear and the cultural politics of veils by speaking of a Canadian (and arguably broader North American) "fear of WMDs (women in Muslim dress)" (2009, p. 42). Although some issues, such as the question of whether courtroom testimony can be given while wearing a *niqab*, legitimately warrant careful scrutiny, much of the controversy around veils (e.g., bans in sports, rules for citizenship proceedings, prohibitions among public-sector employees) is linked to what Jenny Edkins calls "face politics" (2015) and to a variety of problematic assumptions: That veiled Muslim women are a sign of resistance to integration and assimilation, that veils hide malicious intentions and threaten national security, that head or face coverings signify the inherent oppression of women in Islam, and that there is an irreconcilable contradiction with secular norms and values. As cases in this chapter suggest, such assumptions encourage discrimination and can even reinforce cultural isolation. For a great many Muslim women in North America, the veil provides a means of participating in the broader society rather than a barrier to the pursuit of higher education or employment.

Third and finally, where dialogue is pursued, mutually workable forms of accommodation are often possible, as long as maximalist positions and unwarranted assumptions can be suspended. This availability of solutions was evident in various cases discussed in this chapter, such as the progress made beyond bans of veils in sports, or in procedures developed for verifying the personal identity or affirming the citizenship of a woman who wears a *niqab*. Despite the serious challenges present in contemporary Quebec and in other North American contexts where bureaucratic rigidity or political entrepreneurship results in negative outcomes, other cases suggest the possibility of "creat[ing] a new vision of society, one in which women's choice of clothing is respected and religious garb is viewed as either irrelevant or, at most, the source of respectful curiosity, opening a window of dialogue that increases mutual understanding" (Bakht, 2020, p. 13).

Notes

1 As stated by Emma Tarlo, "there is no such thing as a clear-cut category of Muslim dress. Muslims around the world wear a huge range of different garments, many of which relate more to local regional traditions than religious ideas" (2010, p. 5). Such diversity of Muslim dress can be found in North America and is reflected in the different Muslim head coverings such as the *hijab*, *niqab*, *burqa*, and *dupatta*.

The *hijab*, literally means veil, partition, separation, and screen. It refers to clothing that some Muslim women wear to fulfill their religious requirements of modest dress; namely long and loose-fitting garments. The term is popularly used to describe a scarf that covers the hair and neck, leaving the face exposed. During the period of the advent of Islam, it was connected to higher social status among Arabs, Assyrians, Palestinians, Indians, Greeks, Jews, and Syrians. The original *hijab*-like scarf in Arabia, called "*khimar*" draped loosely over the hair and back, leaving the breasts exposed. Islam modified this custom due to the Qur'anic revelation that requires that women "draw their veils over their bosoms" (Qur'an 24:31). The *hijab* became instituted into Islam in the mid-8th century and became widely adapted in the 10th century. It is worn in a wide variety of ways across the world and according to individual preference. For instance, decorative pins may be used to hold the scarf in place, or layers of bonnet caps may be worn underneath to add color. In Turkey, women tend to wear brightly colored polyester scarves folded into triangle shape, pinned underneath the neck with a bonnet cap worn underneath; in Iran, scarves made of light material tend to be worn loosely draped over the head, leaving the fringes exposed, and tied in a knot below the chin.

The *niqab* refers to a head veil that covers not only the hair, but also the face, save the eyes. During the early Islamic period, the *niqab* was worn only by the Prophet Muhammad's wives; the practice entered the mainstream Muslim world in the mid-8th century with Shafi'i and Hanbali schools of legalistic jurisprudence ruling that the entire female body, *including the face and hands*, be covered in front of men other than close kin. It is usually paired with the *abaya*: a long, one-piece, loose-fitting cloak-like garment. The *niqab* is most popular in the Arabian Peninsula but is worn by pockets of Muslim women across the globe.

The *burqa* is an Arabic term that most commonly refers to a garment that conceals the body from head-to-toe, in which vision is obtained only through a latticed panel of fabric over the eyes. It is popularly associated with the Taliban in Afghanistan, as Afghani women were forced to wear the *burqa* under their rule; however, it is also worn among women in Northwestern Pakistan, along the Afghani border. This garment is not mentioned in the Qur'an, nor is it aligned with the rulings of classical scholars in terms of Muslim women's dress. The term *"burqa"* is sometimes used synonymously with *"niqab,"* particularly in Pakistan, India, and Bangladesh.

The *dupatta/chunni* refers to the long, light scarf, which is part of South Asian traditional dress such as *shalwar khameez* (a long loose tunic paired with wide trousers). Muslim South-Asian women often drape it over the hair to fulfill religious requirements for modesty, but it traditionally may be worn around the neck, leaving the hair exposed. Wearing the *dupatta* over the hair is common practice among non-Muslim South Asian women as well, for varying reasons.

2 Ahmed argues that there needs to be a ban against using "the hijab as a lens" to access politics, especially within scholarship on Islam in North America. For more about Ahmed's thoughts on "hypervisibility," see "Time for a 'Hijab-Ban'? (2021).

3 See Soraya Hajjaji-Jarrah's chapter "Women's Modesty in Qur'anic Commentaries: The Founding Discourse" in S. Alvi et al.'s *The Muslim Veil in North America* (2003).

4 See Rahbari et al. (2021) for comparative case studies about these two online media campaigns with followers on Facebook, Instagram, and Twitter.

5 Launched by New York-based activist Nazma Khan in 2013, World Hijab Day (WHD) is an annual event that takes place every February 1st in 140 countries. It recognizes the "millions of Muslim women who choose to wear the hijab and live a life of modesty" (https://worldhijabday.com/our-story/) and aims to "foster religious tolerance and understanding by inviting women (non-Hijabi/non-Muslims) to experience the hijab for one day" (ibid.).

6 Launched by Iranian-born political journalist and activist Masih Alinejad as a Facebook page in 2014, My Stealthy Freedom is an online movement against compulsory hijab laws (https://www.mystealthyfreedom.org/our-story/). Since expanded across social media platforms with hundreds of thousands of followers, My Stealthy Freedom has created initiatives such as My Forbidden Voice, Men in Hijab, and My Camera is My Weapon (ibid.). As part of the movement, thousands of Iranian women have posted photos of themselves in public spaces without a hijab (https://www.wbur.org/hereandnow/2015/11/17/my-stealthy-freedom).

7 Several Muslim groups advocated for an official change in field attire rules and many Muslims expressed disappointment with Charest's support for the decision. The Canadian Council on American-Islamic Relations called the rule "arbitrary" and emphasized the importance of respect for religious difference. CEO of Ontario Soccer Association Guy Bradbury pointed out that it allows female Muslim players to wear the Muslim veil while playing the sport on the condition that it is securely tucked into their shirts (Ontario, 2007).

8 For more see Fadumo Olow's "The History of How Muslim Women Helped to Overturn Football's Hijab Ban" (2019): https://gal-dem.com/this-is-the-history-of-how-muslim-women-helped-to-overturn-the-fifa-football-hijab-ban/#:~:text=If%20FIFA%20wanted%20to%20promote,to%20be%20part%20of%20that.&text=So%20finally%2C%20after%20years%20of,2014%20they%20lifted%20the%20ban.

9 The most controversial issue around the FIFA hijab ban was in June 2011, when the entire Iranian Women Football Team was forced to forfeit a crucial Olympic qualifying match.

10 One major campaign against the FIFA "hijab ban" was a Canadian group called *Right2Wear* which through online advocacy was able to organize a trans-Canadian soccer tournament with the name "Red Card FIFA! Massive Solidarity Soccer". This event invited *hijab*-wearing and non-*hijab*-wearing women to participate and to speak out against the discriminatory hijab regulations in sports (Prouse, 2013, p. 31).

11 Prominent supporters against the FIFA *"hijab ban"* were Moya Dodd (Australian lawyer, sports administrator, and former vice-captain of the Australian football team), Assmaah Helal (Co-Founder of Global Muslim Women Sport Network and Operational Manager for Creating Chances which is a youth developmental agency), and Prince Ali bin al-Hussein of Jordan (President of the Jordanian Football Association and Vice President of FIFA) (Ahmed, 2018).

12 Nike came out with Pro Hijab in 2017, Under Armour designed their Sport Hijab with *hijab*-wearing and personal trainer Saman Munir in 2019, Sweaty Betty launched their performance *hijab* in 2021, and Adidas introduced Sport Hijab 2.0 in 2021. Nike's Pro Hijab design was nominated for a Beazley's Design of the Year in 2018 and the design process and marketing campaign was featured in a BBC Designed article by Emily Dawling (2018): https://www.bbc.com/culture/article/20180110-the-sports-hijab-dividing-opinions.

13 For more about Abdul-Qaadir's story, see the documentary *Life without Basketball* (2019).

14 Through these initiatives, Abdul-Qaadir has been able to not only offer a variety of opportunities for Muslim youth (e.g., Muslim Basketball League, tournaments and summer camps), she has also been able to address different barriers facing Muslim women's participation in sports, some being: accommodating facilities and environments, lack of supportive role models and teachers, and parental approval.

15 Khaljo is not the only North American executive committee member on Muslim Women in Sports Network (MWSN). It was established in 2017 by a group of Muslim women from around the world, and aims to "amplify the voices of Muslim women in sport and inspire Muslim women globally" (https://mwisn.org/about-us/). They facilitate an online platform for Muslim women across various sports industries to share their stories and raise awareness about Muslim women in sport (ibid).

16 For more on Abdullah, see her blog: http://www.liftingcovered.com/about-me/

17 For more on Villarreal, see https://www.runnersworld.com/runners-stories/a25320465/jeri-villarreal-hijab-triathlete/

18 Ibtihaj Muhammad, New Jersey-born athlete and 2016 Olympic bronze medalist in fencing, was featured in Nike's Spring 2018 marketing campaign for their *Pro Hijab* product: https://news.nike.com/news/nike-pro-hijab

   To learn more about Ibtihaj Muhammad, visit her website: https://www.ibtihajmuhammad.com

19 In November 2016, Minnesota-based teen boxer Amaiya Zafar was disqualified from a tournament for wearing *hijab* under her headgear. USA Boxing and the International Boxing Association claimed that the prohibition against the *hijab* in their uniform code was due to a safety issue, given that referees would not be able to see if boxers got injured during events. Following her disqualification, Zafar received national media attention for calling for the sports governing bodies to include the *hijab* in their dress code. In 2017, following advocacy by the Council on American-Islamic Relations, USA Boxing adopted a religious-exemption rule and lifted the ban on athletes wearing the *hijab* in boxing matches. See Townes, 2016; Lim, 2014; Jackson, 2017.

20 Noor Alexandria Abukaram's disqualification from a high school cross-country meet for wearing *hijab* prompted legislative change in Ohio. Senate Bill 288, written by Ohio State Senator Theresa Gavarone (R–Bowling Green), prohibits schools and interscholastic athletic programs from banning athletes who wear religious clothing, including head coverings, during sports and extracurricular events. To learn more about Noor Alexandria Abukaram, visit her website: https://letnoorrun.com

21 The argument supporting sports *hijab* bans, based on the contention that headscarves are "dangerous," has also been used in specific cases connected to veiled Muslim prison guards. During a 2007 training session at Montreal's Bordeaux Detention Centre, Sondos Abdelatif, who was enrolled to become a prison guard, was told to take off her Muslim veil (CTV News). Quebec's Public Safety Department supported the decision and how it was based on the understanding that Abdelatif's headscarf could be used against her as a strangulation device. Sarah Elgazzar, of the Canadian Council on American-Islamic Relations (CAIR-CAN), noted that there are especially designed veils used by women in the Canadian armed forces that could have been sought as an option for this aspiring prison guard. However, no alternative was sought. In December 2011, after years of deliberation, the Quebec Public Security Department called for an "accommodation rather than take the matter before the provincial human rights tribunal" (White, 2011). Similar cases can be found in America. For instance, in 2019, Jalanda Calhoun who worked at Rogers State Prison in Georgia was asked to remove her veil in "fears that she could use it to smuggle contraband" (Oppenheim, 2019). Georgia's Department of Corrections supported the decision. Additionally, in December 2019 at the Bedford Hills Correctional Facility in Westchester County, New York, a veiled corrections officer was asked to remove her veil.

22 Zunera Ishaq was a former high school teacher from Pakistan and a devout Sunni Muslim who voluntarily follows the Hanafi school of thought. She met all the preconditions for citizenship: age and residency, sufficient knowledge of one of Canada's official languages, no criminal prohibitions, and passed a test proving adequate knowledge of the country and the responsibilities and privileges of citizenship.

23 Section 13.2 stipulates:

> Candidates for citizenship wearing a full or partial face covering must be identified. When dealing with these female candidates it is the responsibility of a citizenship official to confirm the candidate's identity. This should be done in private, by a female citizenship official. The candidate must be asked to reveal her face to allow the CIC official to confirm the identity against the documents on file.
>
> The candidates must be advised at this time that, they will need to remove their face covering during the taking of the oath. Failure to do so will result in the candidates not receiving their Canadian citizenship on that day.

24 It was a sexual assault trial when N.S. accused her cousin and uncle for repeated sexual assault between the ages of 6 and 10.

25 From 2009–2012, there were a number of employment discrimination cases in North America involving employees/applicants who wore the *hijab*. Some that received the most media attention were lawsuits against American clothing retailer Abercrombie & Fitch and Disney's California Adventure Park.

26 A series of provincial and federal events have underscored and exacerbated deeper questions concerning the security of Quebecois identity, making this debate especially charged in the last decade. A 2002 Supreme Court ruling, for instance, to overturn a decision made by the council of commissioners of the Commission scolaire Marguerite-Bourgeoys and allow Gurbaj Singh Multani to wear his kirpan to school, was perceived by some Quebecers as a federal government attempt to impose multiculturalism on Quebec, and prompted increased media attention to the issue of reasonable accommodation (Bouchard & Taylor, 2008, pp. 33, 50). In 2005–2006, there was a dramatic increase in media coverage of reasonable accommodation issues: many citizens were concerned about the transition to frosted windows at a YMCA located in a Hasidic Jewish community, unsettled by sensationalistic and inaccurate coverage of Muslim ritual prayers at a sugarhouse, and provoked by various incidents in which *hijab*-wearing Muslim girls were barred from participating in sporting events. The controversies came to a head in January 2007 when the town council of a small, homogeneous village named Hérouxville announced a "Life Standards" act.

27 For more in-depth analysis of the Commission and its Final Report, see Sharify-Funk (2010).

28 For more information about the pro- and anti-sides of the Bill 94 debates, see Sharify-Funk (2011).

29 For more information on CCLA and a timeline of Bill 21, see https://ccla.org/major-cases-and-reports/bill-21/. Due to the Quebec Supreme Court's decision in April 2021 to uphold Bill 21, the case has gone before the Quebec Court of Appeal. Depending on the outcome (at the time of writing this book), the bill may have to go to the Supreme Court of Canada. In May 2022, Justice Minister David Lametti announced that "when [Bill 21] arrives at the Supreme Court of Canada, it is by definition a national issue, and we will be there" (Serebrin, 2022, p. B1). Additionally, Prime Minister Justin Trudeau stated, "We will be there to defend the fundamental rights of all Canadians that have been suspended by this law" (ibid).

References

ACLU. (2003, May 27). ACLU asks Florida court to reinstate suspended driver's license of Muslim woman forced to remove her face veil. https://www.aclu.org/press-releases/aclu-asks-florida-court-reinstate-suspended-drivers-license-muslim-woman-forced

Ahmed, L. (2011). *A quiet revolution: The veil's resurgence from the Middle East to America.* Yale University Press.

Ahmed, S. (2018, April 28). When women were forced to choose between faith and football. *The Guardian.* https://www.theguardian.com/football/blog/2018/apr/28/women-faith-football-hijab-fifa-ban

Ahmed, S. (2021). Time for a '*hijab* ban'? The hypervisibility of veiling in scholarship on Islam in North America. In A. Barras, J. Selby, & M. Adrian (Eds.), *Producing Islam(s) in Canada: On knowledge, positionality, and politics* (pp. 137–154). University of Toronto Press.

Al-Saied, N. & Creedon, P. (2021). Women's sports and fashion in Arab Gulf countries. In L. K. Fuller (Ed.), *Sportswomen's apparel around the world: Uniformly discussed* (pp. 69–82). Palgrave Macmillan.

Alvi, S., Hoodfar, H., & McDonough, S. (2003). *The Muslim veil in North America: Issues and debates*. Women's Press.

Ayub, A. (2011). A closer look at FIFA's *hijab* ban: What it means for Muslim players and lessons learned. *SAIS Review, XXXI*(1), 43–50.

Bakht, N. (2008). Victim or aggressor? Typecasting Muslim women for their attire. In N. Bakht (Ed.), *Belonging and banishment: Being Muslim in Canada* (pp. 105–113). TSAR Publications.

Bakht, N. (2020). *In your face: Law, justice, and niqab-wearing women in Canada*. Irwin Law Inc.

Beyer, P., & Ramji, R. (2013). *Growing up Canadian: Muslims, Hindus, Buddhists*. McGill-Queen's University Press.

Bouchard, G., & Taylor, C. (2007). *Seeking common ground: Quebecers speak out*. Bibliothèque et Archives nationales du Québec.

Bouchard, G., & Taylor, C. (2008). *Building the future: A time for reconciliation*. Bibliothèque et Archives nationales du Québec.

Bruemmer, R., & Dougherty, K. (2007, February 2). Herouxville: Cause celebre. *The Gazette*. http://www.canada.com/montrealgazette/news/story.html?id=8af3c4eb-5bc7-40bc-ba38-93f785c5646a

Bullock, K. (2020, April 27). We are all niqabis now: Coronavirus masks reveal hypocrisy of face covering bans. *The Conversation*. https://theconversation.com/we-are-all-niqabis-now-coronavirus-masks-reveal-hypocrisy-of-face-covering-bans-136030

Chung, A. (2009, November 12). Montreal designer creates sleek sports *hijab*. *Toronto Star*. https://www.thestar.com/news/canada/2009/11/12/montreal_designer_creates_sleek_sports_hijab.html

Currier, P. T. (2004). Freeman vs. state of Florida: Compelling state interests and the free exercise of religion in post-September 11th courts. *Catholic University Law Review, 53*(3), 913–942.

Dahlburg, J.-T., & Virtue, A. M. (2003, June 7). Veiled driver's photo disallowed. *The Los Angeles Times*. https://www.latimes.com/archives/la-xpm-2003-jun-07-na-veil7-story.html

Dawling, E. (2018, January 10). The sports hijab dividing opinions. *BBC Designed*.

District Court of Appeal of Florida, Fifth District. (2006, February 13). *Freeman v. Department of Highway Safety and Motor Vehicles*. FindLaw for Legal Professionals https://caselaw.findlaw.com/fl-district-court-of-appeal/1199365.html

Edkins, J. (2015). *Face politics*. Routledge Publishers.

Emon, A. (2010, May 5). NO to Quebec Provincial Bill 94. *Las Perlas del Mar*.

Fazili, Y. (2005). Fumbling toward ecstasy. In S. Abdul-Ghafur (Ed.), *Living Islam out loud: American Muslim women speak* (pp. 75–85). Beacon Press.

Gagnon, L. (2015, January 28). Quebec reopens a can of worms. *The Globe and Mail*, A13.

Haddad, Y. (2012). *Becoming American? The forging of Arab and Muslim identity in pluralist America*. Baylor University Press.

Harkness, G., & Islam, S. (2011). Muslim female athletes and the *hijab*. *Contexts, 10*(4), 64–65. http://www.jstor.org/stable/41960259

Heath, J. (2008). *The veil: Women writers on its history, lore, and politics*. University of California Press.

Hébert, C. (2015, February 28). Tories, Bloc risk inflaming Anti-Muslim bias. *Toronto Star*, A6.

Ishaq v. Canada, FC 156 2015. (2015). https://exhibits.library.utoronto.ca/items/show/2057

Jackson, A. (2017, April 26). Muslim teen boxer wins fight to box wearing *hijab*. *CNN News*. https://www.cnn.com/2017/04/25/us/amaiya-zafar-muslim-boxing-teen-trnd/index.html

Jiwani, Y. (2007). *Discourses of denial: Mediations of race, gender and violence*. University of British Columbia Press.

Khan, S. (2009). *Of hockey and hijab: Reflections of a Canadian Muslim woman*. TSAR Publications.

Khan, S. (2021, April 23). In Quebec, an act of injustice receives no accountability. *The Globe and Mail*. A15.

Knoester, C., & Rockhill, C. (2021). Multiculturalism and antiracism in sports? U.S. Public opinions about native American team names and mascots and the use of *hijabs* in sports. *Socius: Sociological Research for a Dynamic World, 7*, 1–16.

Legis Quebec. (2021, December 1). Act respecting the laicity of the state. https://www.legisquebec.gouv.qc.ca/en/document/cs/L-0.3

Lewis, K. (2007, February 26). Nepean team quits soccer event after girl told to take of *hijab*. *Ottawa Citizen*. https://www.pressreader.com/canada/ottawa-citizen/20070226/281509336723729

Lewis, R. (2003). Preface. In D. A. Bailey, & G. Tawadros (Eds.), *Veil: Veiling, representation and contemporary art* (pp. 10–14). The MIT Press.

Library of Parliament. 41st Parliament, 2nd Session. (2015). https://lop.parl.ca/sites/PublicWebsite/default/en_CA/ResearchPublications/LegislativeSummaries/412C75E

Lim, S. (2014, May 7). Muslim teen makes history as she competes in USA boxing match in *hijab*. *Global News*. https://globalnews.ca/news/3417299/muslim-teen-makes-history-as-she-competes-in-usa-boxing-match-wearing-hijab/

Mathewson, E. (2018, November 18). Bilqis Abdul-Qaadir endured the heartache of choosing faith over basketball. *Andscape*. https://andscape.com/features/bilqis-abdul-qaadir-had-to-choose-muslim-faith-over-fiba-basketball/

McDonough, S. (2003). Perceptions of the *hijab* in Canada. In S. Alvi, H. Hoodfar, & S. McDonough (Eds.), *The Muslim veil in North America* (pp. 121–142). Women's Press.

National Assembly of Quebec. (2010, March 24). Bill 94: An act to establish guidelines governing accommodation requests within administration and certain institutions. http://www.assnat.qc.ca/en/travaux-parlementaires/projets-loi/projets-loi-39-1.html

National Assembly of Quebec. (2013, November 7). Bill 60: Charter affirming the values of state secularism and religious neutrality and of equality between women and men, and providing a framework for accommodation requests. http://www.assnat.qc.ca/en/travaux-parlementaires/projets-loi/projet-loi-60-40-1.html

Nomani, A. Q., & Arafa, H. (2015, December 21). Opinion: As Muslim women, we actually ask you not to wear the *hijab* in the name of interfaith solidarity. *The Washington Post*. https://www.washingtonpost.com/news/acts-of-faith/wp/2015/12/21/as-muslim-women-we-actually-ask-you-not-to-wear-the-hijab-in-the-name-of-interfaith-solidarity/

Nye, M. (2003). *Religion: The basics*. Routledge Publishers.

Ontario, (2007, February 26). Quebec differ over soccer head scarf ban. *CBC News*. https://www.cbc.ca/news/canada/ottawa/ontario-quebec-differ-over-soccer-head-scarf-ban-1.632266

Oppenheim, M. (2019, May 16). Georgia prison guard says she was banned from wearing hijab at work over fears she could smuggle contraband. *Independent*. https://www.independent.co.uk/news/world/americas/georgia-prison-guard-hijab-jalanda-calhoun-a8917296.html

Prouse, C. (2013). Harnessing the *hijab*: The emergence of the Muslim female footballer through international sport governance. *Gender, Place, and Culture, 22*(1), 20–36.

Quebec to Address Issue. (2010, March 3). *CBC News*. https://www.cbc.ca/news/canada/montreal/quebec-to-address-niqab-issue-1.899729

Rahbari, L., Dierickx, S., Coene, G., & Longman, C. (2021). Transnational solidarity with which Muslim women? The case of the my stealthy freedom and world hijab day campaigns. *Politics and Gender, 17*, 112–135.

Serebrin, J. (2022). Ottawa would join challenge of Bill 21. *The Waterloo Region Record*. B1.

Sharify-Funk, M. (2010). Muslims and the politics of 'reasonable accommodation': Analyzing the Bouchard-Taylor report and its impact on the Canadian province of Quebec. *Journal of Muslim Minority Affairs, 30*(4), 535–553.

Sharify-Funk, M. (2011). Governing the face veil: Québec's bill 94 and the transnational politics of women's identity. *International Journal of Canadian Studies, 43*, 135–164.

Supreme Court of Canada. (2012, December 20). R. v. N.S., [2012] 3 SCR 726. https://scc-csc.lexum.com/scc-csc/scc-csc/en/item/12779/index.do

Tarlo, E. (2010). *Visibly Muslim: Fashion, politics, and faith*. Berg Publishers.

Tasker, J. P. (2015, March 27). Stephen Harper 'dumb' to say niqab is anti-women, Charles Taylor says. *CBC News*. http://www.cbc.ca/news/politics/stephen-harper-dumb-to-say-niqab-is-anti-women-charles-taylor-says-1.3013427

Townes, C. (2016, December 27). Harmless *hijab*s. *ESPN*. https://www.espn.com/espnw/voices/story/_/id/18361836/harmless-hijabs-boxer-amaiya-zafar-fights-right-outwardly-express-religion

Wadud, A. (2002). Interview: Amina Wadud. *Frontline*, PBS. https://www.pbs.org/wgbh/pages/frontline/shows/muslims/interviews/wadud.html

Wente, M. (2009, June 25). Ban the burka? No, but... *The Globe and Mail*. A17.

White, M. (2011, December 20). Quebec accused of caving over guard's hijab. *National Post*. https://nationalpost.com/news/canada/quebec-decision-to-allow-prison-guards-to-wear-islamic-hijabs-draws-oppositions-ire

World Hijab Day. (2022). *Our story*. https://worldhijabday.com/our-story/

Zine, J. (2009). Unsettling a nation: Gender, race, and Muslim cultural politics in Canada. *Studies in Ethnicity and Nationalism, 9*(1), 146–163.

Conclusion

~~The Muslim Woman~~

Zunera Ishaq, Pakistani-Sunni Muslim immigrant, defended her right of religious expression by wearing the *niqab* as she took the oath of citizenship in Ontario, Canada. Bilqis Abdul-Qaadir, daughter of African-American reverts to Islam and an award-winning as well as record-breaking collegiate basketball player, helped to overturn the FIBA *hijab* ban and fought for the right of *hijab*-wearing women to play all sports. Irshad Manji, Ugandan born Canadian journalist and advocate for reform of Islam, wrote a New York Times best-selling book on the trouble with Islam, in which she challenged barriers to progressive thinking. Mahdia Lynn, transgender woman and Shia Muslim convert, cofounded Masjid al-Rabia in Chicago, Illinois, which is the first trans-led, women-centered, and LGBTQ+ affirming mosque in North America. Ingrid Mattson, a *hijab*-wearing soccer mom, served from 2001–2010 as the vice president and president of Islamic Society of North America (ISNA), one of the largest Muslim advocacy organizations in North America, during which time she led efforts to foster greater inclusion for women through "women-friendly" mosque spaces.

As this book testifies there is no single narrative defining the Muslim woman in North America. There is no "Muslim woman." Rather there is a multitude of diverse Muslim women living and negotiating a variety of controversies and divisive issues. Perhaps we can glean from the German hermeneuticist and philosopher Martin Heidegger (d. 1976) and apply his idea of a Heideggerian erasure in which one draws a line through a word or phrase in order to imply that it has been erased and yet there will always be evidence that it was there. "~~The Muslim woman~~," "~~women and Islam~~," and "~~Islam and the West~~," are all deeply problematic categories whose erasure and dissolution would arguably advance understanding of contemporary Muslim identities in North America. Nonetheless, such terminology is likely to remain in the problematic labels of conventional as well as scholarly discourse.

This last chapter offers some concluding thoughts about contextualizing the cases analyzed in this volume within the broader setting of a global, diversified cultural experience that is replete with new opportunities as well as vexing challenges. After noting some underlying factors behind the

DOI: 10.4324/9780429341151-8

various cases and contradictory positions explored in the book, it concludes by underscoring the vital need for conversations that move beyond surface clichés and stereotypical representations, toward greater apprehension of the multiple realities of Muslim women in North America. The move from contradiction and cliché toward genuine conversation can only be achieved by cultivating greater capacity for dialogical engagement in modes that embrace diverse intersections of gender, religion, race, culture, and status, even while fostering new discoveries of common humanity.

The context of a global diversified culture

Embracing diversity is one of the most important challenges facing humanity in the 21st century. Despite populist and nativist reactions to international migration and to diversity more generally, there appears to be no possible or ethically desirable retreat from the diversified global culture which is now deeply woven into national cultures, within as well as beyond North America. Nonetheless, past assumptions about people's identities, interests, and values are still impeding genuine understanding of the "other," and of the many possible influences and ideas that inform contemporary cultural experiences. For example, "Eastern" luminaries such as Rabindranath Tagore and Jalal ad-Din Rumi have found a dedicated readership in the West, while major "Western" thinkers such as Hans Gadamer and Michel Foucault inform academic discourse in the East. Although powerful currents of global culture may reflect "modern Western" pop culture as well as preoccupations with maximizing technological innovation and economic productivity, even the materialist and consumerist emphases within the present global culture are no longer predominantly Western – if they ever were. Global culture as it exists today contains points of cross-cultural resonance as well as dissonance, and is textured by an assemblage of differences, contradictions, and power imbalances that impact human relationships and capacities for shared understanding.

Amid this interplay of similarity and difference, profound problems of perception and perspective reinforce the appeal and usage of misleading essentialisms. As the cases in this book repeatedly attest, the problem of essentializing the other – and sometimes even asserting an essentialized notion of the self – remains pervasive. From notions about "the victimized female Muslim" and "the male Muslim extremist" to convictions about a singular "truly Islamic" perspective that negates all others, stereotypical tropes have colonized the mental landscape in remarkably problematic ways. Popular English-language writings about Islam and Muslims in North American bookstores reflect this troublesome lack of diversity in representation. For example, as explored in Chapters 3 and 4, "clash literature" and female Muslim dissident writings have achieved impressive sales within the North American book market, and clearly resonate both with broader cultural assumptions and with the movements such as "#MeToo." Notably, the testimonials in most of these books, while inspired by genuine personal experiences, are frequently communicated in ways that reinforce broad essentializing comments about Islam and Muslim women. Many Muslim readers hear in these accounts an "echo of Orientalist stereotypes about an unchanging, monolithic religion that is unable to transcend medieval norms" (Shaikh, 2013, p. 22). Furthermore, popular works in this genre seldom recognize "the internal pluralism and myriad forms of lived contemporary Islam, as well as the rich internal contestations of gender ethics in the Muslim world" (pp. 22–23). As important as critical and reformist voices may be in contemporary Islamic thought, the marketing of "reforming Islam" for North American audiences frequently results in products that fail to provide readers with a nuanced comprehension of what is and is not happening within diverse Islamic communities.

Given the pervasiveness of essentialized notions (and often of defensive communal reactions to stereotypes held by a majority-culture), identity negotiations take place within a charged atmosphere in which the practice of dialogue itself has become contested. With which Muslims should a non-Muslim enter into dialogue? Who speaks for and represents Islam? Who has legitimacy as a "reformer" and who does not? What is often forgotten is that just as there are many Christianities and Judaisms, so too are there many formulations of Islamic piety and politics that contend for the attention of Muslims, and that represent themselves as the only "authentic" perspective. We face a fundamental paradox: Islam is one, and it is many. Its sacred meaning for believers transcends history, and yet the development of diverse Muslim standpoints and beliefs is an inevitable outcome of historic processes.

Better approaches to dialogue may emerge when Islamic identity is recognized as a work in progress, both in Muslim-majority lands and in countries where a larger proportion of the Muslim population has experienced immigration or conversion. In the latter contexts, "life in diaspora" creates special challenges and pressures, increasing the felt need of many Muslims – whether Sunni, Shia, or Sufi – to simultaneously prove that they are "Muslim enough" and also members of their new, chosen civic community. While there are inevitably those in Muslim minority communities who fully embrace or categorically reject the mores of North American culture, more complex and eclectic responses are more typical – for example, wearing a Muslim veil as well as high heels, or becoming a Muslim rap artist articulating Islamic as well as "quintessentially Western" themes. Beneath a surface-level agreement about symbolic reference points and essential values, there is impressive diversity in experiences and cultural syntheses.

As these examples in this book suggest, collective identities are also always works in progress, formulated, and reformulated through negotiations among contrasting and competing worldviews. For instance, contemporary American or Canadian identities differ profoundly from American or Canadian identities in the late 19th century, and despite the existence of generally agreed reference points (freedoms, rights, multiculturalism, cultural accommodation, integration, liberal values), their overall meanings are subject to contestation. American and Canadian identities continue to change and evolve through dialogue and debates about what is "genuinely American or Canadian." In some formulations of American or Canadian identity, the most authentic understanding of identity is one that manifests an attitude of genuine inclusiveness toward newcomers and minority cultural experiences, whereas in other understandings of authentic identity there is an exclusivist response toward those who are perceived to embody insufficient "Americanness" or "Canadian-ness." Collective Islamic experiences manifest a similar proliferation of rival viewpoints on themes such as authenticity and the boundaries of inclusiveness, and negotiations among these viewpoints transpire in national, minority-culture, and transnational contexts.

For contemporary North American Muslims, the realities of communal existence within a transnational and profoundly heterogeneous diaspora bring special complexities to the negotiation of identity and meaning. Insofar as life in diaspora brings new awareness of the *particularity* and historical contingency inherent in an inherited religious culture and experience, so too can it inspire new efforts toward a religious identity that somehow transcends and corrects perceived limitations of the inherited culture as well as those of a majority-culture that may practice discrimination. For some Muslims, part of the solution is to be found in aspiring toward what Oliver Roy calls a "deterritorialized identity" (2006). Such an identity can be fostered through participation in a transnational conversation that seeks universality by delinking itself from any specific culture. In Roy's view, such a deterritorialized identity is ultimately rootless, even while itself being a response to rootlessness in which an ideological "universal religious or cultural identity" fills an existential void.

At the other end of the continuum of migration experiences, and distinct from more common experiences of integration into a national culture that do not require negation of an Islamic identity or heritage, are those who brand themselves as "ex-Muslims." Where the transnational Islamic ideology of the deterritorialized extremist associates the essence of Islam with negation of anything deemed Western or inauthentic, ex-Muslims simultaneously identify this definition of Islam as correct (i.e., the "real" Islam) and reject it as an offense to the sensibilities and values of their newly "liberated" identity. Ironically, both ex-Muslims and deterritorialized extremists share in common the rejection of an inherited religious culture, while existing symbiotically through their interdependent negations of "wrong beliefs." Each manifests an allergy to all things associated with the "other" – that is, to all things Western or to all things Islamic. The manner in which these polarizing ideological discourses feed each other is worthy of further research.

Discomfort with simply accepting the diversity of Muslim experiences is in no small part a consequence of the reality that Islam has become a symbolically charged topic, with Muslim identities increasingly polarized between would-be "Westernizers" and defenders of various formulations of cultural authenticity and religious authority. In a context in which criticism of Muslims easily slides into essentialized representations and deeper nega- tions, and in which rival definitions of Islamic authenticity contend with one another, "community gatekeeping" becomes a salient phenomenon. Many of the cases discussed in this book reflect not just identity politics between Muslims and representatives of a majority-culture, but also an inter- nal Muslim identity politics connected to issues of authenticity and authority. For example, in Chapter 5 controversies over Muslim female prayer leader- ship and gendered sacred spaces involve competing claims over who has the right to define the role of women and the meaning of gender inclusivity. Although some of the voices in these debates are more influential than others, the growing diversification of practices represents a significant opportunity for new ethnographic research and for scholarship that takes the diversity of Muslim communities in North America seriously. There is a need for com- parative analysis of "women-friendly mosques" and "women-only mosques" as well as "gender-inclusive mosques," and an opportunity to engage with diverse voices on matters of marginalization and inclusion among North American Muslims.

The experiences of Muslim minority communities in Canada and the United States are not identical, yet dynamics associated with diversity, essen- tialism, identity negotiation, and diaspora exhibit manifold similarities and manifest in cases on both sides of the border. Additional research is warranted to develop cross-national comparisons further, in a manner that probes both similarities and differences. With respect to the latter, it is clear that the pres- ence of a Francophone experience within Canada is one notable distinction. Vigorous debates within Quebec – and a "slippery slope" leading to greater exclusion of women who wear Muslim veils (as explored in Chapter 6) – demonstrate the existence of different ways of defining secularism, and of parameters for accommodating difference that diverge from those that prevail in the rest of Canada and in the United States. Thus, specific dynamics in Quebec merit further investigation and monitoring. Is Quebec a bellwether or an anomaly? Will current dynamics be reversed, or will they provide endur- ing? Another theme that might be explored in greater depth is securitization. Securitization of identity issues clearly impacts Muslim minority experiences in both countries; comparative scholarship could reveal more about simi- larities and differences in these experiences. Finally, it is worth noting that Canadians and Americans are not equally aware of cases and events on both sides of the border. Even at the level of the scholarly community, there tends to be greater awareness of the U.S. experience in Canada than vice versa. Paying attention to both contexts is important, both for the sake of compari- sons and for the sake of a well-informed understanding of shared movements, of the influence of prominent personalities, and of different issues that may become salient in each setting. From female prayer leaders to sports *hijab* bans and the influence of mainstream as well as dissident Muslim writers, trends in both national contexts are profoundly interconnected.

Rethinking contradictions

In focusing on controversies, clichés, and conversations, this book has been structured as an exploration of a series of conflict cases involved significant contradictions between rival views. Parting thoughts on the nature of contradictions are therefore warranted, starting with the etymological reflections. Derived from the Latin *contra-* (against) + *diction* (speak), the term "contradiction" denotes "an assertion of the direct opposite of what has been said or affirmed" (Online Etymology Dictionary). A contradiction is an instance of difference, contrariness, and polarizing oppositions, in which two qualities or principles are presumed to be opposite. Although contradictions are at the heart of all conflicts, not all conflicts are of equal depth, nor are all perceived contradictions deeply rooted. Yet the perception of intense contradiction is central to all the major cases of conflict investigated in this volume – some of which have evolved through advocacy and gradual transformation, and some of which have evaded attempts at resolution and even progressed into deeper polarization. Although broad conclusions about the diverse cases explored are not warranted, what is clear is that these conflict scenarios are not static and are often responsive to influence strategies. At the same time, working to address these contradictions constructively can be a difficult task, because conflicts involving strong convictions about norms, worldviews, and values as well as implicit biases and unspoken interests do not automatically progress from thesis and antithesis to synthesis through some inevitable historical logic of opposition.

Contradictions within and between moral traditions

The contradictions discussed here are not just about how to apply a given set of norms to a particular case. Although sometimes the opposing positions have been articulated almost entirely *within* a singular moral and ethical framework – for example, opposition over how to apply Western liberal norms involving individual rights, defined over and against arbitrary or prejudice-informed efforts to undermine them, or to cite a different possibility, opposition between rival claims to principles of Islamic piety, involving different convictions on the nature and normative status of a past consensus and the extent to which it binds future generations. Other contradictions, however, which still involve internal conflicts within different camps, have also played out *between* ethical and moral traditions.

One key set of questions underlying these cases has to do with the extent to which Western liberalism and Islamic traditionalism ought to be compatible.

While the complexities inherent in deeper philosophical and religious world-views are beyond the scope of the book, it is important to at least name the moral and intellectual contexts in which contradictions emerge, and to acknowledge that beyond the presenting issues in each case (which often involve debate over how to most fairly and consistently apply Western liberal norms, or over whether or not Islamic norms can be reconciled with Western liberal principles) there are also different visions of "the good life" at stake. Significantly, spokespersons for both Western liberal and Islamic visions profess a desire to create conditions that facilitate "the good life" for women, and that are liberating in the sense of making life better for them. When these visions are perceived to be in conflict, each side claims to want to emancipate women, even while differing on how emancipation is to be defined, abstractly as well as in relation to specific circumstances. While it is important not to overstate differences between these traditions (both contain voices that argue for minimization rather than maximization of points on which they diverge), contemporary controversies suggest that women's emancipation is one of the more fundamental wedge issues between Islamic and Western cultures.

At issue here are two different understandings of freedom and human flourishing. Although Western liberalism is a broad and internally differentiated tradition of thinking, it is centered on the rights and choices of the individual within a context of personal freedom, rationality, and utility. Freedom *to do*, and *to choose*, are primary considerations. Islamic thought, also an internally differentiated and varied intellectual tradition, has traditionally been organized in ways that place the individual in a decidedly communal and transcendent context of significance. Existential freedom *to be*, along with personal responsibility to a greater whole, receives a stronger emphasis. Although it is a conviction of this author that stimulating and creative exchanges across these traditions are necessary, one need not be a hostile polemicist to ask if they can become healthier conversation partners than is currently the case.

We may use the notion of "conversation partners" as a basis for reframing and more deeply understanding major intellectual debates that have impacted world history. As a relational form of thinking about intellectual history, this approach reveals that a school of thought does not exist autonomously as a wholly formed and integrated corpus of ideas and texts; rather, the ideas that define an intellectual stance are formulated through conversations – sometimes civil, sometimes polemical – with other schools of thought. In pre-modern Islamic thought, for example, an epoch-defining debate between traditionalists and rationalists can be understood more profoundly when it is recognized that the opposing camps actually functioned as "primary conversation partners," each reading the other's works and staking out a position in contrast to the counterpart's stance. In the 21st century debates covered in this volume, it is arguable that Western liberalism has become a principal conversation partner for Islamic traditionalism (understood here broadly, to include both tradition-minded thinking within official institutions of Islamic thought and more diffuse conversations involving revivalist and reformist thinkers' ideas about how best to carry forward Islamic traditions and values). As the cases reveal, many but by no means all of these Western liberal-Islamic traditionalist conversations are convened on the subject of women and their rights in a society within which liberal traditions are predominant. Although the spokespersons for each camp do not always read one another's works in a sophisticated and penetrating manner – indeed, the contradictions might be mitigated if they did – they nonetheless function as conversation partners who are negotiating norms that impact Muslim women.

Revelation and reason

So what are the distinctive visions of these conversation partners, and what does each regard as the "good" it is seeking to advance? For Western liberalism, the "good" is pre-eminently a matter to be determined by the individual, yet society is to be organized in a rational manner that maximizes overall prosperity, security, and individual freedom of choice. Women's emancipation becomes a concern within this overall and presumably enabling context of a rationally organized state and marketplace that is expected to provide equal opportunities for all to personally choose a life trajectory in pursuit of the good as one sees it. This liberal perspective, although still valuing associational life and accommodating religious affiliations and pursuits, underscores that these associations and collective pursuits must be expressions of free individual choice, and do not otherwise exert claims on the individual. When referenced as a framework for resolving debates over a matter such as the wearing of a *hijab*, the essential criterion (in addition to any concerns raised about collective security and well-being) is that of personal choice. The manner in which this unfolded in the *hijab* ban cases examined in Chapter 6 follows this logic, according to efforts to proscribe *hijab*-wearing ultimately yielded to arguments couched in terms of individual rights, to be pursued within a revised set of regulations.

Where Western liberalism proposes a conversation about human reason without undue attention to metaphysical presuppositions (which presumably stand beyond empirical verification), for Islamic traditionalism the operation of reason is disciplined by preunderstandings about revealed truths. While much more has been debated within an Islamic intellectual context than a Western liberal bystander may suppose, Islamic traditions have long upheld a vision of the human condition that is teleological, in which freedom is to be experienced through adherence to an agreed upon moral and intellectual vision. Though the Islamic intellectual tradition is not monolithic with respect to women's rights and is in many respects undergoing a reformation on the subject, traditionalists have a different ontological starting point than Western liberals: Revelation as a basis for understanding reality, and as the proper point of departure for human reasoning, moral choice, and the organization of collective life. When a new understanding contradicts past consensus – as in the cases involving female prayer leaders – new debates are sparked within the community, including debates about the meaning of *sharia* and its authoritative norms about how to live in accordance with Qur'anic standards of justice and with the prophetic example of ethical life. Western liberal arguments about individual rights may have shaped the context in which open claims to female prayers leadership were made, yet they appear to have produced significantly less traction for resolving the matter than new investigations of traditional Islamic sources that reveal greater diversity of opinion on the subject than was previously thought to exist.

Can contradictions be complementary?

Both in the *hijab* ban cases and in the Muslim women prayer leader cases, the existence of a predominant ethical frame of reference does not change the fact that a broader conversation has been occurring. Islamic traditionalists uphold the value of the *hijab*, yet it is Muslim women who engage the wider (and presumably not-so-traditional) context of sports while retaining the *hijab* as a symbol of identity and meaning and arguing for freedom of choice on liberal grounds. Female *imamahs*, some of whom acknowledge inspiration by Western feminist examples in other religious traditions, nonetheless argued their cases in relation to Qur'anic sources, and ultimately sparked a richer set of conversations on the subject. In both cases, one can observe ways in which a seeming clash of worldviews has gradually given way to a somewhat broader and less solipsistic exchange of meaning.

This raises an interesting question: When, and under what conditions, can contradictions become "complementary," in the sense that the tension of seeming opposites yields to a less dualistic interplay of ideas and to the possibility of more flexible understandings. The idea of "complementary contradictions" (discussed in Chapter 2) is connected to the non-dualistic worldview of the 13th century Muslim philosopher Ibn al-'Arabi, yet it resonates provocatively with many current debates that can otherwise only be "resolved" through coercive efforts to impose one's truth upon the other party. To think in terms of "complementary contradictions" is not to smooth over real tensions, which will inevitably still exist. Yet it also allows a perception of genuine points of connection. Western liberalism and Islamic traditionalism, after all, propose social ontologies that have undeniable points of tension, and convey different ideas of human freedom. Both, however, purport to support the realization of a good, happy, and "emancipated" life, and convey truth claims as well as values that may in many instances constructively align.

Such observations do not change the fact that contradictions can be deeply painful, and harmful to those affected. *Hijab* bans, for example, were not only inconvenient but also very damaging to the sports careers of promising young athletes. Further scholarship on the subject would be valuable for revealing the human impact of such policies, while also foregrounding the narratives and agency of those who mobilized in response. Exploring the advocacy of women excluded by *hijab* bans could also reveal in greater detail the limits of a putatively "neutral" (but effectively exclusionary) secularism that many Muslims perceived to be driven by a hidden agenda to force change through the suppression of a symbolic garment. The activists were nonetheless able to demonstrate not just that the opposing positions were not irreconcilable, and that new rules might meet certain minimal expectations of both sides, but also that "feminist" and "traditional Muslim" are not necessarily opposing categories.

Dialogical opportunities

I have so many contradictions within myself, but I am still one. A part of myself goes on fighting with another part of myself and yet I am still one. When you are living a life and you are in an existential situation you have to live with contradictions as realities existing in your life.

(Manzooruddin Ahmad in Sharify-Funk, 2008, p. 82)

[Ibn al-'Arabi] acknowledges the validity of every mode of human knowing, and at the same time he recognizes the limitations of every mode. Thus, he considers every perspective, every school of thought, and every religion as both true and false. He does not offer a single, overall system that would take everything or most things into account, but he does present us with a way of looking at things that allows us to understand why things must be the way they are.[1]

(Chittick, 1994, p. 10)

It would be a mistake to presuppose, while examining social conflicts, controversies, and contradictions of worldviews, that the oppositions in question exist entirely within the neatly defined compartments of rival groups pursuing divergent objectives. Reflective and nuanced investigation of these contradictions can reveal a far more complex human and intellectual landscape, in which ideas with different genealogies and points of origin mix routinely within the minds of those involved in controversies, and in which certain axioms and convictions of "the other" are not in fact alien to the self.

When the dialogical occurs amid social controversies and is sustained long enough to reveal the deeper experiences and assumptions of opposing groups, the differences between self and other seldom collapse even as they begin to appear in more complex and relatable forms. It becomes possible to recognize elements of the other's experiences and ideas in oneself, and to see aspects of oneself in the other. There can be a growing willingness to accept moral and intellectual complexity, combined with the emergence of new ideas for bridging divides.

The dialogical is not a panacea for conflict, for Islamophobia, or for problems of injustice, exclusion, intolerance, and inequity. Yet a dialogical lens for interpreting reality, and for seeing the interwoven nature of lives as well as the interpenetration of ideas and ideologies, opens new possibilities for acknowledging a larger number of truths beyond those that are excluded by one side of a binary opposition or another. It allows for recognition that one's own truth is not a final truth that excludes the possibility of new learning.

Accepting the legitimacy of contradictions is the basis for dialogue, and for moving beyond the binary categories within which a conflict has been framed. In this respect, a desire to transcend conventional ways of framing conflicts in terms of dichotomies can be very helpful. Opposition such as "traditional vs. modern" as well as "Islamic vs. Western" serves to entrench conflict, and limits openness to ways of knowing and being that involve genuine encounter with rival claims.

Importantly, the dialogical does not preclude advocacy, protest against colonial harms, and vigorous reassertion of suppressed experiences. The dialogical is not a suppression of one's own lived truth. A predisposition toward dialogue does, however, invite active efforts to foster relationships within which new connections among people and experiences can be perceived, and within which harmful views and constructions can be challenged more effectively.

The dialogical does not remove differences, but it does challenge the reflexive dehumanization of the other in a confrontation over competing claims and realities. It asserts that no singular way of understanding or perceiving a situation can be entirely accurate and adequate, and that no experience is devoid of truth. Such an acknowledgment leaves room for discovery, and for conversations that produce mutual learning.

In addition to fostering intellectual humility, habits of the dialogical serve to undermine harmful dichotomies that fragment human experience, pitting social groups against one another in the service of misguided nativism, conspiratorial thinking, and claims to final truth. While such changes might appear to occur quite slowly, one conversation at a time, dialogical tendencies have the power to cut through clichés and enable a more interconnected perception of reality that inspires hope and new insight into ways in which self and other might together constitute a greater whole. Even amid controversy it remains possible to evoke visions of connection and mutual empathy, in which porous identities connect with one another through openness and hope.

One such vision of human connection was communicated in a Persian-language poem written by Sa'di of Shiraz (d. 1292) in his famous *Gulistan*.

This poem, entitled "Bani Adam," provides a fitting coda for this study, reminding us that within our great diversity of experiences, perceptions, and perspectives, we are still one.

> Human beings are members of a whole,
> In creation of one essence and soul.
> If hard times cause one member to feel pain,
> At ease and rest, the others cannot remain.
> If you have no sympathy for human pain,
> The name of human you shall not retain.

Note

1 For Ibn al-'Arabi every thought, claim, and concept was interdependent. Such thinking begged the question, "Can two parts which define each other ever be separated?" He regarded it as curious how humans have come to perceive oppositional qualities as separate modalities, effectively ignoring the relationship connecting the two opposites (each of which cannot be discerned without the other).

References

Chittick, W. C. (1994). *Imaginal worlds: Ibn al-'Arabi and the problem of religious diversity.* SUNY Press.

Roy, O. (2006). *Globalized Islam: The search for a new Ummah.* Columbia University Press.

Sharify-Funk, M. (2008). *Encountering the transnational: Women, Islam and the politics of interpretation.* Ashgate Publishing, Ltd.

Shaikh, S. (2013). Feminism, epistemology, and experience: Critically (en)gendering the study of Islam. *Journal for Islamic Studies, 33,* 14–47.

Index

For Product Safety Concerns and Information please contact our EU
representative GPSR@taylorandfrancis.com
Taylor & Francis Verlag GmbH, Kaufingerstraße 24, 80331 München, Germany